THE EARLY YEARS
- OF EVANGEL -

THE MESSAGE • THE MISSION • THE MIRACLES

MARY LEE MEARES

Christian Living Books, Inc.
Largo, MD

Christian Living Books, Inc.
P. O. Box 7584
Largo, MD 20792
christianlivingbooks.com
We bring your dreams to fruition.

ISBN Paperback 9781562293055

Unless otherwise marked, all Scripture quotations are taken from the King James Version of the Bible.

Printed in the United States of America.

Contents

Foreword

During the early years of the ministry, God was doing so much. There were many miracles of healing and so many people were being saved. And, we received so many letters telling us how they were being blessed. So, I thought it would be good to let the people know what was happening in our nation's capital. So, from 1959 to 1969 I wrote and published a little magazine called the *Fellowship News.* Over that time span, we mailed out 4,400 copies a month.

Not too long ago, I found a few old copies. As I was reading them, the Lord seemed to impress me to choose some of the articles and have them published. I am sure it will bring back a lot of memories to the charter members that are still with us, as well as giving present members a little history of the early days.

During a conference in 1969, a word of prophecy was said over me that was to change me and what God wanted me to do. Now, having helped my husband start three churches from scratch, I knew about most of the different things that you do. However, this prophecy said I was to teach. I really, really tried to dismiss it. However, the boys would say, "Mother, when are you going to start teaching?" I said, "I cannot take the time to study and gather articles for the *Fellowship News* both.

My first class consisted of 30 students. And for the next 45 years, my life was fulfilled in teaching. Over 3,000 have graduated from my class. Many people have told me that it gave them a foundation in the Word. Now, being 93 years old, I knew it was time to let my daughter-in-law, Jannie Meares, who had taught along with me for years, take over.

I found a local Christian publisher who would put this book together for me in under two months – in time for me to give away copies as Christmas presents. I had cut and pasted over 200 articles from the *Fellowship News* onto sheets of paper. I would have been fine with those pages being reproduced. However, the publisher graciously scanned the pages and reproduced the articles and clippings. Please forgive errors caused by the character recognition program. We did not have original copies or photos. These are copies of copies. At 93, when you want something done, you've got to go ahead and do it. Besides, I know people would appreciate the content, even when imperfect.

May you be blessed as you read about the early years of Evangel.

–Mary Lee Meares
Co-Founder and Elder

Chapter 1 – 1959

Editorial

—Mrs. John Meares

For sometime we have felt the need of having a monthly paper that would keep you better informed of what God is doing here in Washington, D.C. There are many testimonies that come into our office that we want to share with you, for we feel they will help you have a greater faith to believe for needs you have personally. Then we want to shore letters and news we receive from missionaries on the field, whom many of you help support. Because of this desire we ore publishing the first issue of the "Fellowship News". It is our desire for this paper to be a great blessing to you as you read it.

Perhaps during the Christmas season people show their love for one another more than any other time of the year. We send our cards, give our gifts to those that are close to us. I believe our heavenly Father is pleased with us showing our love toward others. Certainly He showed His love toward us when He gave His only Son to this earth to be born of a peasant maiden. Why did He leave His home in heaven, His position with the Father, and be born in a lowly manger? It wasn't just to be born in Bethlehem of Judeah, but that Jesus might be born in your heart and mine. Mary had to have faith in God to bring about the birth of the Christchild, and

First choir organized in 1956.

1

so must one today have faith in God for Jesus to be born in our hearts. Without Christ there is no Christmas. Many people will give gifts, and make merry this Christmas season and yet not know what it really means. At our house on Christmas morning, the first thing we do after gathering around the tree, is to sit down and read the Christmas story. We want our children to know that it is really His birthday, and that He above all others should be remembered. Just as Christ was born as a babe, but grew into manhood, so are we babes in Christ but also grow in the statue of the Lord Jesus Christ. We do not think of Him as only a babe in Bethlehem-but as our Saviour, our Healer and our eternal King.

May the fullness of His love be yours this Christmas season.

FELLOWSHIP NEWS
The monthly Voice of the Evangelistic Center

Vol. 1	December 1959	No. 1
John L. Meares		Editor
Mary L. Meares		Assistant Editor

First chair organized in 1956.

Article about Pastor Meares

Sylvia and Richie Meares did not realize as they looked into the eyes of their new-born babe that God would use him through the years as one of His chosen vessels. To these godly parents, John L. was born on January 21, 1923 near the little town of Largo, Florida. Some of the first memories of John's childhood were the times his father would call all of the six children around the table and read to them out of the family Bible. Then as they would kneel in prayer he would hear his mother speaking in a language of angels.

His father was a prosperous, hard working nurseryman who loved God and was an enthusiastic church worker. He taught his boys to follow in his footsteps. Three of the boys today are in the nursery business, but the fourth, John L., could not be a nurseryman. Even though he attended Cornell University in New York to study landscaping, he could not get away from the call of God which he felt upon his heart for the ministry. One day out in the orange groves, he surrendered his personal ambitions and said, "Yes, Lord, I will preach." Upon telling his father that he was called into the ministry, his reply was, "Well, son, if you must preach go ahead, but personally I don't think you will make much of a preacher." However, God knows what He is doing and certainly He has found a true and faithful witness in Brother Meares, the pastor of Evangel Temple here in Washington, D.C.

Even in his high school days, he proved to be an ambitious lad and worked many times all night long in a local print shop, going home just in time to prepare for school the next morning.

He attended a couple of Bible Schools in preparation for the ministry and during the summer months he spent his time preaching in the hills of Kentucky and Pennsylvania.

After his marriage in 1944, he and his wife evangelized a short while and then he entered the University of Tennessee where he received his B.A. degree. During these two years of college he pastored a small church on the outskirts of Knoxville, Tennessee. Immediately following graduation, he and his wife and three month old son, Vrigil, moved to Athens, Tennessee. Here in a cornfield a tent was pitched and three months later a church was built in which to worship.

After four years of pastorate in this little town, he felt an urge and compulsion to begin a church in a larger city, namely Memphis, Tennessee. Without knowing anyone, but believing God was a big God, he secured a $20,000 lot on one of the main thorough-fares and began having services. This time the services were conducted on just an open lot, as the city would not allow the erection of a tent. Much objection came from the surrounding neighbors and petitions were signed to try to keep a church from being built, but God helped remove the objections and members of a Pentecostal church across town came over at night and helped erect a church. It became known as "the church that was built at night." By the time cold weather had come, the church was far enough along to move into. Even though the congregation was small to begin with, a wonderful Presence and Spirit would fill the tabernacle as the people worshipped. God gave a mighty revival and the church grew and enjoyed four prosperous years under the leadership of Pastor Meares.

But God still had other plans for this young man's life. His spirit became restless and he knew that God was trying to teach him deeper truths and get him to launch out in even in a greater measure than he had heretofore. And so it was that one morning around 3 o'clock in the morning that he came into his bedroom, awakened his wife and said, "Honey, the Lord wants me to make a move; I don't know where, but He will make it clear." His wife didn't take it too seriously until a few months later he said, "Put the house up for sale." Then she knew he really was serious. God did make it plain unto him that Washington, D.C. was the field of labor that was His will for his life at this time.

It wasn't an easy task at first to just leave all behind and start out again on an unknown path. For in the natural there would have been no reason to leave. The church had overcome many an obstacle and was, so to speak, just now on a firm foundation. However, one cannot rest when God speaks to his heart, so again he, his wife and three children left Memphis for Washington.

Space will not permit the telling of what God has done through this yielded vessel here in this metropolitan city. Starting from exactly nothing, but a great faith in God, seven years later the results have been amazing. Through the preaching of the Word, many have been won to the Lord. He is a man with a steadfast faith and to him there are no impossibilities with God. God has raised up a mighty church through his leadership and as Pastor Meares would put it, our work in Washington has just begun."

~ ~ ~

Editorial   —Mrs. John Meares

It was in the winter of 1955 in Memphis, Tennessee that Brother Meares woke me up one morning around 3 o'clock and said, "Honey, the Lord wants me to make a move in my ministry." I thought to myself, perhaps a year or so and we might move so, I just said, "O.K." and went back to sleep. A month later my husband came in from a convention out west and said, "Put the house up for sale." I knew he was serious and meant NOW. For a day or two I went around in a daze. I was happy in Memphis. The Lord had helped us establish a good work there, and had given us a wonderful congregation of people to pastor. On the material side, we had a lovely home to live in, so I could think of no reason for leaving and going somewhere else. There was none—except that the Lord wanted us to work in another field of labor.

Brother Meares felt that the south had been blessed with gospel preaching more than the north, and that it was time to go north with the message of "Faith and Power." In July we tearfully—yet with an assurance of God's will, said goodbye to Memphis and moved to Washington, D.C. So it was that Brother Meares, our three children and I began our venture of faith. I say 'faith' for we knew no one in Washington nor had an invitation from anyone to come to Washington; yet we were sure that God would have an interdonominational church for all people of all races in the nation's capital.

The office staff in 1957.

It was not easy to find a building in which to have service—especially if one wanted to have service every night. Knowing that God's business is the greatest business in all the world, we
determined to keep the church doors open always, day and night.
Finally, for the sum of $2000.00 a month, we secured the Turner's
Arena which seated around 1500 people. This was not at all a desir-
able place to worship. On Wednesday and Saturday nights there were
boxing matches and dances respectively, so we always had to give up
these two nights of the week. However, the other five nights found
a great crowd worshipping the Lord in Spirit and Truth. Many sin-
sick souls found their way to the Saviour, while many, many more
found Christ as their Healer.

Just five months later we rented a large unused warehouse at
1331 'U' Street, N. W. Neither was this the building that we wanted;
but after a lot of cleaning and installing of seats, we moved in. At
least we could have service every night. We moved in Thanksgiving
week and had a Thanksgiving celebration. Everyone was happy to
be able to sit in a comfortable seat instead of the bleechers that the
arena had afforded.

Brother Meares engaged the best evangelists to come week after
week to preach and minister to the people. A remark often heard
was, "Where do so many good preachers come from?" For sixteen
months we leased this building, but then one day a notice came that
we must vacate. The government wanted to use it; and since they
would pay $70,000 a year for it, we decided there was no use for
us to make an offer. Once again we were faced with the problem of
a place to worship. Our people began to pray about a place of our
own—not just a place to rent. The Lord opened up (just in time)
the York Theater at 3641 Georgia Avenue. It was necessary to vacate
the 'U' Street building by the 18th of March. The last movie at the
York was shown on the 17th, and we had our first service in our
new home on the 18th. The down payment of $25,000 was raised
by the many fellowship members and friends of the Evangelistic
Center. The total cost of the building was $125,000 and it seats 800
people. We have painted; built a stage, and bought nice curtains for

it; carpeted the floors; and in general, given the place a new look. The doors are open to "Whosoever will", and people are coming and drinking at the fountain.

Oh no, we haven't made our last move. We anticipate a much larger building. At the present time we have our offices in another building, and also rent a building across the street where the teen-agers meet to worship. Larger facilities are needed to take care of the vision the Lord has given us. A burden for Washington has been placed in our hands. It may become heavy at times, but through God's help we shall not stumble. There are many, many others helping to carry the load. They too believe that "Christ is for Washington and Washington for Christ."

A nurse from Bridgeport, Connecticut telling of the condition of her patient who was brought by ambulance to Turner's Arena for Bro. Meares to pray for her. She had cancer of the spine, but after prayer she got up off her cot healed by the power of God.

Editorial   —Mary Lee Meares

So in the early summer of 1955, John Meares came to Washington, D.C. and rented the old Turner's Arena to begin a salvation, healing revival in this city that has continued since its inception.

National Evangelistic Center has become a spiritual "institution" in the Nation's Capital City. It is known of by congressmen, city officials, and those who make up the population of this metropolis.

There is hardly a taxi cab driver that cannot take you directly to it without your telling him the address. It is known across America by ministers and laymen who have heard of what God is doing here. Foreign lands have felt the influence of its ministry by the missionaries it has sponsored and by Brother Meares' own ministry in other countries.

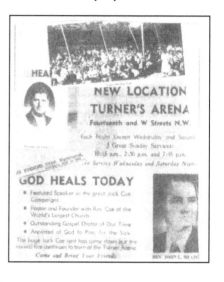

The multitude of men and women, boys and girls in this area who have been reached for God through the ministry of John L. Meares and the National Evangelistic Center, stand as a living monument of what God can do when He finds a man who will let Him move in his life—and produce a miracle!

Old York Theater, 3641 Georgia Avenue, NW, Washington, DC

We finally have our own building!!

Virgil, Mary Lee, Cynthia, John, Donnie Meares

Altar of Evangel Temple

After moving from the tent on Benning Road to Turner's Arena, then an old warehouse on U Street, we were able to purchase the old York Theater on Georgia Avenue N.W. for $125,000.00. This was home for the next 18 years. Immediately, Bro. Meares began drawing plans to remodel the stage. Then, he bought a huge bowl, painted it gold and had the people march up front and put in their tithes and offerings. After which, he would carry the bowl up to the altar, pray a prayer blessing the people for their giving. We were a happy congregation.

Reach the Children   —Johnnie Petrucelli

Because we want children today to know of His love, we have spent thousands of dollars and multiplied hours with great effort to reach them since our coming to Washington. Many, many children are not aware of His love, for the love of Christ can only be manifested to a child through a human being. Therefore, one of our greatest responsibilities is to let all children, everywhere, know that Jesus loves them. This is the most important discovery in the life of any human being. If we can get them to know this while their hearts are yet young and tender, how much more blessed it is. It is not only my responsibility to see that my own children are taught the ways of the Lord, but that other children whose parents may not care, and who know nothing of God's great love, that they remember their Creator in the days of their youth. The hippies and beatniks that roam our streets today are not teen-agers that were taught the love of God as a young child.

We must reach the children before they become a teen-ager. I have always felt that this is one of our most important outreaches here at Evangel Temple. The influence of church and the things of God are so very, very important in a young life. This is why we lease buses every Sunday morning and go out picking up children of all backgrounds and bring them to church to instill within them the love of God—that He is interested in them even as a child. We want them to know that the Lord wants to be their friend, Saviour and companion throughout their life.

Bible Adventure Kids

We were thrilled and excited as we watched the eager faces and expressions of hundreds of kids in our recent Children's Crusade. For one week, each morning, we gathered up children all over Washington and crowded them into buses and brought them to Evangel Temple. The churches of our land have several revivals each year trying to get grown-ups into the Church and to know the Lord. But do we try to shift the responsibility of helping just a child — not just save a soul, but to save a life? Most of our delinquency problems

Bible Adventureland on Georgia Avenue - Washington, DC.

would be solved if we would reach the children. It is sometimes too late when they become a teen-ager.

We have a wonderful, wonderful teen-age choir at Evangel Temple — one that we are proud for anyone to hear sing. They not only sing well, but they love God and love to come to church. We did not reach these young folk in their teens, but by far the majority starting coming to Evangel Temple as a child. As a pastor and as a church we cannot and will not shift our responsibility or our joy in reaching children. If a prayer is never said in the schools, or the Bible never read in the schools, or in the home, then where are they going to learn about the love of God? I believe in Missions. Our church believes in Missions. I believe in radio. Our church believes in radio. I believe in literature, and many other means of making God known. But one of my strongest beliefs is that we should put forth much effort in reaching a child at a tender age and teaching him the ways of the Lord. The Lord told Peter to feed His sheep, but He also told him to feed His lambs. This is our endeavor. We want to feed the young lambs the Word of God and train them in the way they should go, and we believe that when they are old they will not depart from it. Thank God for the opportunity He has placed before us in this great city, and by His help and guidance we will continue to reach out a hand and bring the young into the Fold.

The Spiritual Aspect of Camp Adventure Land —as reported by Harold Jackson

"Suffer the little children and forbid them not, to come unto me; for of such is the kingdom of heaven." Matt. 19:14

Harold Jackson

The spiritual results of the 1959 season of Camp Adventure Land was a glorious manifestation of this scripture. It seemed that at the slightest touch of the Holy Spirit upon their hearts, the children were submissive and yielding. As near as possible, records reveal that around 90 percent of the children who attended were saved. God alone knows what will happen to the "sown seed" in future years.

There were several factors which I feel attributed to the spiritual success of the camp. One was the unceasing prayers of the prayer band at the Center, joined with those of the camp staff. The young hearts were prepared by the Holy Spirit for the Word of God.

Two Bible classes held daily were instrumental in awakening a desire for spiritual blessings along with imparting a knowledge of the Word to the children. The night services, which were held by the lake side, were particularly blessed of the Lord as the boys and girls opened their hearts to receive Jesus Christ as their personal Saviour.

Daily devotions were conducted by the counselor in his or her cabin at bed time. Then too, the personal witness and untiring efforts of the counsellors and teachers in the individual cabins through private conversation with the campers, all added to the effectiveness of winning the children to Christ. The objective was to create a christ—conscious atmosphere throughout the camp. The words of one boy around eight years old was a witness that this objective was accomplished when he stated, "The thing I like the most about this camp is that every time I turn around, someone is talking about the Lord."

Plans are now under way for the 1960 camp season which will begin on June 20th. Last summer 960 boys and girls attended camp. We are expecting the enrollment for this coming season to be greatly increased over last year. Work is now under way at camp to prepare the buildings and grounds for opening date. I am believing God for another successful season, and that many boys and girls will find Jesus Christ as their personal Saviour.

A Bible School began under the direction of Rev. Harold Jackson.

Chapter 2 – 1960

Editorial

—Mrs. John Meares

Hitherto hath the Lord helped us, whereof we are glad. The year of 59 was a most glorious one. You stood by us with your prayers and finance in all of the needs that were presented to you. God was faithful—you were faithful. Many souls were saved, bodies healed, hearts lifted out of despair, and prayers answered. There were problems and obstacles, but the Lord gave the victory over them all.

The year of 1960 began with a great New Year's service at N.E.C. Every seat was taken and people stood around the walls. There was such a wonderful spirit prevalent and especially as we break bread and had communion together were our hearts knit in love and unity. We could not help but praise God for all He had done for us, and to consecrate anew our time, talent and our all for His service in the year of 1960.

Fourteen people followed the Lord in water baptism after the New Year was ushered in with prayer.

Reverend Morris Cerullo, a converted Jew, began a great meeting with us this night. Our eyes beheld great miracles for the next ten nights, and the greatest of all was the thrill of seeing people come forward for salvation. They left the altar a new creature in Christ Jesus. Three times there were cases where people were prayed for who had one leg several inches shorter than the other. In each case both legs became the same length immediately.

The Sunday night services were held at Capitol Arena because of the large crowds. As most of you remember, the Arena was the place of worship when we first moved to Washington to establish N.E.C. As we sat there in the dimly lit Arena, we could not help but thank God for giving us our present place of worship.

Neither you or I know what this year holds for us, but this one thing we are sure of and that is it shall be a year of service for the Master. Day by day our vision enlarges, our burden increases for the lost and needy. With Paul we say, "forgetting those things that are behind, we press toward the goal of the high calling in Christ Jesus." Instead of just turning over new leafs, we have turned over our life completely into His hands. We want it to be a year of service to others. May this also be your prayer and goal for this year of 1960.

FELLOWSHIP NEWS
The monthly Voice of the Evangelistic Center

Vol. 1	February 1960	No. 2
John L. Meares		Editor
Mary L. Meares		Assistant Editor

Published monthly by Herald of Deliverance, Inc., for the purpose of spreading the ministry of Bible deliverance. Receipts for contributions are tax deductible.

Oh That Men Would Praise The Lord
—John L. Meares

The Psalmist said, "Oh, that men would praise and confess to the Lord His goodness and loving kindness, and His wonderful works to the children of men!" Psalm 107:31, (Amp.) Praise is so very, very important. For when He is being glorified in praise, He turns the power of that praise to the good of His people. We learn more about God and can sing with the Psalmist, "Thou art holy, O Thou that inhabitest the praises of Israel." God does not change and so today he confirms praise by granting His power and a sense of His presence. God is always present when an individual or a congregation is praising Him.

Praise releases the power of God. It is an expression of our faith, and faith is our victory that overcomes the world. The devil hates to hear us praising God, for he knows this shows our love and trust in our heavenly Father.

You will remember Paul and Silas were in jail and at midnight they began singing psalms of praise. Even though they had been beaten with many stripes and their feet put in stocks, and they were now jailed in a Roman prison, they were free in their spirit. And what happened? Suddenly a miraculous earthquake opened the prison doors and unshackled all of the prisoners.

Jehoshphaphat, king of Judah, was facing battle against the combined forces of the Moabites, Ammonites and Edomites. What did he do? He appointed singers to sing to the Lord and to praise Him in their holy priestly garments, as they went out before the army, saying, "Give thanks to the Lord for His mercy and loving kindness endureth forever!" What do you do when the battles in your life arise? How do you face them? Do you have a song in your heart? Do you have faith that the Lord will fight your battles and bring you out victorious? It seems that all most people talk about in this day is the trouble our country is in, and the difficulties that beset us, etc. They seem to have forgotten that God is still on the throne and we are to "Bless the Lord."

Editorial   —Mrs. John Meares

Some people are like the poor fellow at the Pool of Bethesda, "Someone always gets in ahead of me." Others are like the elder brother, "You never gave me anything." God would have us be like the repenting prodigal son, "In my father's house there is plenty and enough to spare. I will arise and go to my father."

Some do not have more because they look to man rather than to God for their needs. Paul says that it is God who "shall supply all your need." Some lack because they do not have faith. Others never have enough, because they live for and think only of themselves. Jesus said, "It is more blessed to give than to receive." There is a reward promised for giving. There are so many ways you can give. Maybe it is just a kind word spoken at the right time, or some little act of kindness on your part, but it is said or done when the person needed it most. If you wish God to share with you, then remember to share with others.

When you begin to share, you will find that you have a surplus. Instead of having less because you have given, you will have more left than when you first gave. This is God's law in giving. I desire to have God share with me of His abundance, and I realize that all my blessings come from above and that I am wholly dependent upon Him.

I am not ashamed to call upon the Lord in good times or bad times. To feel my need of Him does not make me feel weak; rather, in my turning toward him, I feel strength and courage. Will you open your whole life and receive all the fullness of God in Spirit, soul and body? Then as you receive will you say, "Lord, lead me to someone that I may help in spirit, soul and body? This is the truly happy life.

FELLOWSHIP NEWS
The monthly Voice of the Evangelistic Center

Vol. 1	March 1960	No. 3
John L. Meares		Editor
Mary L. Meares		Assistant Editor

Published monthly by Herald of Deliverance, Inc., for the purpose of spreading the ministry of Bible deliverance. Receipts for contributions are tax deductible.

Address all correspondence to:
John L. Meares, Box 1922, Washington, D.C.

Trusting The Lord   —John L. Meares

Most of us take for granted that we trust God, however, in our daily pursuits, or on our jobs, we often have very little thought of the Lord Jesus Christ. Jesus said in His sermon on the mount, "Ye cannot serve God and mammon." One or the other will be the master. In the next verse the Lord exhorts that we take no thought for our life or livelihood: what we shall eat, drink, or what we shall wear. If our lives are so absorbed in the pursuits of our necessities that God cannot be related to every act of our life, then we displease Him. There are many very good people who are morally upright and indeed attend church, who we classify as "good providers," that Jesus would say to, "Ye cannot serve God and mammon." In the following verses of the sixth chapter of Matthew, the Lord speaks of the lily and its beauty, but yet it does not toil and labor to become so, and of the grass that is so lush one day and the next day is destroyed. And then God asks, "Why are ye of so little faith that you are so anxious about what you should eat, drink or be clothed with." He emphasizes that He is aware of our needs of all these things.

Only after assuring us that our heavenly Father knoweth that we have need of these things does the Lord command, "Seek ye first the kingdom of God and His righteousness and all these things shall be added unto you." This is a real lesson of trust and it teaches us that for our every day provisions, we are to look to God. Therefore, on our job, in our business, or by what means God uses to supply our needs, we must put Him first in these affairs. Thus, we manifest true trust in the Lord.

God has no need of the labor of our hands, nor of the material things that He blesses us with. But He has lovingly condescended to accept that which we offer unto Him, and to rejoice in it, and return to us a hundred fold.

To regularly give ten percent of our earnings as a tithe is an expression of trust in God manifested in our everyday lives. On our job, or business we acknowledge the Lord in the fruits of our labors by tithing. Not only do we acknowledge Him, but we express sincere trust. From the natural standpoint none of us would be able to take ten percent of our earning and lay aside, much less give it away. But because of our trust in the Lord, with joy we bring our tithes into His storehouse for we "Seek first the kingdom of God and His righteousness," knowing that "all these things shall be added unto us."

There are many people who will emphatically tell you that they have faith in God and that they trust the Lord, but if you question them concerning tithing, immediately they will give you many excuses why they are not able to carry out this command of the Lord. There is really only one reason — one simply does not trust the Lord. If in our everyday livelihood we cannot thus trust the Lord for our supply, how then can we trust the Lord for the healing of the body? for the salvation of our soul? for eternal life? If my trust in the Lord is not great enough to bring joy in the paying of my tithes, I do not believe I could dare to trust Him to preserve my soul, or to give eternal life. Tithing, therefore, expresses the simplest principle of trust and faith in God. To say that we have faith in God, or that we trust Him and fail in one of the first principles of trust is only to deceive ourselves.

The scriptures declare, "The tithe is *holy* unto the Lord." If the Lord then regards the tithe as *holy*, it is very wrong to take that which is the Lord's and use for our own needs. Now we can understand the question of Malachi, "Will a man rob God?" And immediately there is a protest, "But where have I robbed God?" And God's Word answers, "In tithes and offerings." The scriptures then go farther to say, "Ye are cursed with a curse: for ye have robbed me." The command then is, "Bring all the tithes into the storehouse — and prove me — saith the Lord of hosts, If I will not open you the

windows of heaven, and pour you out a blessing, that there shall not be room enough to receive it." Can you trust God? Can you trust Him with the returns of the labor of your hands: from the source of which you receive your needs? Are you seeking first the kingdom of God? It is impossible to expect the blessings that God would shower upon you if you fail, with joy, to bring your tithe into the house of the Lord.

Letters to the Pastor

Psalms 103:3

Pastor Meares took me in his arms not long ago and prayed for me for asthma. I had had asthma since birth. Then my Grandmother took me to the doctor to be checked, after examining me he said my lungs were completely clear, that I no longer had a sign of asthma. My grandmother said, "thank you, Jesus." The doctor said, "what did you say?" She repeated it and he looked at her as though she were crazy, and then she told him you prayed for me and God healed me. I am now six years old, and it is wonderful not to be bothered with asthma any longer.

Alicia Tyler
515 Que St.
Washington, D.C.

* * *

Greetings from the love of our Lord. I have received your letter and also your Fellowship News, and they both have been so inspiring to me. I have attended your services a couple of times, and how much my soul has been filled with a new faith. I am a foreigner, and I didn't know that when I came to live in Washington I could find a church like the one I grew up—one where you could praise the Lord with all your heart and soul and sing to Him the way your heart desired.

My husband is stationed at Andrews Air Force Base, and no doubt we will be going overseas soon again. I will appreciate receiving the paper until then, as I feel as if I am one of you already. May the Lord continue blessing you every hour of the day.

Teatesta Coward
Washington, D. C.

* * *

Dear Reverend Meares:

Your Fellowship News is a blessing to me. It even saved my life one time, as I was at the point of no return in a weak point in my life. I looked up to God for help, and there, no more than 3 feet from me was a Fellowship News. I read it, was encouraged, and the next day I sold my gun. I now believe in God again.

Name withheld by request

* * *

I am very sorry for the long delay in writing to you. I had a wonderful trip over the Atlantic Ocean to Morocco. I like it here and also my assignment at the Embassy. All the people are nice to me.

I received my first bulletin a few days ago. It was very much appreciated. I have found a protestant church here and enjoy it. However, I miss the "Inspiring Voices" and the choir director, Bro. Anderson. I have done a lot of gospel singing here. The Moroccans, Arabians and French like the gospel singing very much. I had a packed theater when I sang in Rabat and I am singing in Tangier, Morocco, tomorrow night. I also have another concert scheduled in Kenitra, Morocco, and one in Fez, Morocco. God is good to me and blessing me, and I will ever praise His name.

Thank you for the prayer the Sunday before I departed from Washington. It was kind of you to take the time with me. I have always enjoyed the services at Evangel Temple and also singing with the choir. Continue to pray for me, as there is no distance in prayer. Give my regards to all. Enclosed find a small donation for the church.

Miss Lois Gene Gore

Secretary to Agricultural Attache American Embassy Rabat, Morocco

* * *

Dear Sir:

I want to render my sincere thanks for the Temple's Fellowship News that have been coming into my hands from month to month without fail. The spiritual food they contain are food for my soul. If there are any other publications or if you have a spare Holy Bible, I would appreciate your forwarding them to me. Kindly give the believers my sincere greetings for the coming Season's Christmas and for a prosperous and happy New Year.

J. A. Amissah
Accra, Ghana

"I Am Alive Forevermore" — Mary Lee Meares

The words of Christ, "I am alive forevermore" have been quoted again and again. These words have brought comfort many many times to our hearts. But what really makes me happy is the fact that I, Mary Lee Meares, am alive forevermore. This body, 'tis true, is always dying in a process of decay, but I am an immortal being. Jesus Christ was just as immortal when He walked the dusty roads of Galilee or hung helplessly upon the cross as He was when He burst out of the tomb and shouted, "I am alive forevermore." The real Jesus was not slain. Christ is immortal.

Because I am a child of God I have immortality within me. "He that believeth in me hath eternal life already... he that liveth and believeth on me shall never die." My body may be put in a tomb, but the christian tomb is always empty. Perhaps I cannot prove this, and shall not try, but this I truly believe. Eternal life is a gift given to us at the time we accept Christ, not something to be received way out in the future. A few years ago I stood inside the empty tomb in Jerusalem. I had not gone to seek the living among the dead. My faith is in a resurrected Christ, and because of this faith, my Life is a resurrected one from a life of sin to a life of peace and joy. How can I ever find words to praise Him this glorious Easter for having resurrected me and given me eternal life.

FELLOWSHIP NEWS
The monthly Voice of the Evangelistic Center

Vol. 1	April 1960	No. 4
John L. Meares		Editor
Mary L. Meares		Assistant Editor

Published monthly by Herald of Deliverance, Inc., for the purpose of spreading the ministry of Bible deliverance. Receipts for contributions are tax deductible.

Address all correspondence to:
John L. Meares, Box 1922, Washington, D.C.

Lovest Thou Me More Than These?
—Mary Lee Meares

Recently as I was reading John 21:15 where Jesus asked Peter, "Simon, son of Jonas, lovest thou me more than these?" I stopped and put my name in the place of Peter's and searched my heart for an answer to this same question. This is a personal question the Lord asks each of His children. It is a question no one else can answer for us. I know it is easy to say, "Oh, yes I love God," but when our love is tested does it always prove true? Peter answered and said, "Lord, thou knowest I love thee." How could he say this so assuredly? Was it not still fresh in his mind how he had so miserably denied the Lord and failed Him in the time of greatest need? Did he not remember how he had said, "Lord, though all should be offended, I am ready to go with thee both in prison and to death." Had his love not been tried and failed? But I think when Peter saw the look of compassion and forgiveness in the eyes of Jesus as he was walking out of the court of the palace, after being tried by Pilate, he found a different love for His Master.

His prayer was one of repentance and remorse, and asking for forgiveness. His Master would prove His love by even death on the cross.

The account of Peter's denial, along with the other disciples, not only shows our human weaknesses, but it shows the Lord's great love for us in spite of the many times we disappoint and fail Him. What is more comforting than to come to God in our times of failure and for Him to reassure us of His love for us? He doesn't ask us why we failed Him, but He just says, "Do you love me?" But He wants to know if we love Him. He is not asking us how many talents we have, how much we can give, or what kind of gifts we possess. The question is "Lovest thou me more than these?" To what degree do you love Him? Are there certain things or people that hinder you in loving God with all your heart? Do you do some things only for man's approval rather than a real love for God? Do you ever stop and ask yourself how much you really love Him?

Peter said, "Lord, thou knowest I love thee." He said, Lord, thou knowest all things. The Lord previously had told Peter that he would deny him before the cock crew thrice. But now He said, Peter, you will even be hung on a cross because of your faith and love for me. One would not do this without a real love deep in their heart. Yes, the Lord knows just how much we love Him. Then after Peter said, "Lord, I love Thee," he was commanded to feed the lambs and the sheep. Not until a child of God has a genuine love for their Master are they ready to feed the flock. This is the first and only requirement to be of service to the kingdom of God. We do not have to know all of the Word of God and explain all the scriptures, but we do have to love God. And when we do, we cannot help but feed and bless the lambs. The love we have in our heart for Christ will be expressed through our lives. But without this love, we are only sounding brass christians.

I cannot help but love the Lord when I see how much He has done for me; when I see the faith He puts in me; when I see how I fail Him and yet He loves me. He longs for my love, for my companionship, to be in me and with me as a constant Friend and Companion. When you really believe this, your love will get bigger and bigger each day.

You will think about Him more; you will talk about Him more; you will commune with Him more. You will not only spend a few hours on Sunday in the house of God to express your love for Him, but every day you will express your love for Him in some way. Others will see our love for the Lord in the life that we live, and nothing can separate us from the love of Christ. It is so easy to love One that wants to bless me, direct and protect me. Never let the devil tell you the Lord doesn't love you because of your failures. But when the Lord asks, "Do you love me?" be sure your answer is, "Lord, thou knowest I love Thee."

Letters to the Editor

What a great joy and privilege has been mine to be with my very dear friends, Pastor and Mrs. John Meares, and their precious congregation at Evangel Temple. My opportunity to come to America is so seldom, but I would not have missed the wonderful blessings I received from preaching in this great church and worshiping with his people. And my how the choir blessed me with their singing. I have heard no better.

John McTernan
Rome, Italy

* * *

Always I have enjoyed your Fellowship News, but never as much as I did your May issue. I have read many articles on tithing, but never so much good material in one magazine. The editorial by your wife, your own inspired message, the illustrations, and the tithing testimonies all breathed life. The anointing of God was surely upon this issue. Thank you so much for sending it to me. I am sure it will do untold good.

God bless you and your people in the great work you are doing for the Lord.

Rev. Earl Cox Alexandria, Virginia

≈ ≈ ≈

Editorial   —Mary Lee Meares

Always in May we set aside a special day in which to honor our mothers. Remembrances of our mother are something we all cherish and love to talk about, for it was she who nourished and cared for us as a child, who gave us love, tenderness and affection as we grew into womanhood, and is one who is just as concerned about us even after marriage. I shall always be thankful for my mother's christian guidance in my life. One of my earliest recollections is when my mother would call me from my play for morning prayer. There is nothing, no greater career one can pursue than just being a godly mother. I always feel so inadequate in trying to show the love I feel for my mother, but if one can do nothing but just drop a line and let her know you still remember, still think of her, that you wonder how she is—these little things will make her happy. Why do I know? Because I am a mother and it is the little things that my children do that make my heart glad. These little things overshadow and outweigh the burdens that go along with motherhood. I am sure you that read this message agree with me that a godly mother, whether still with us or passed on, is someone God given and to be appreciated more than words can ever express.

> No painter's brush nor poet's pen
> In justice to her fame
> Has ever reached half high enough
> To write a mother's name.

FELLOWSHIP NEWS
The monthly Voice of the Evangelistic Center

Vol. 1	MAY 1960	No. 5
John L. Meares		Editor
Mary L. Meares		Assistant Editor

Published monthly by Herald of Deliverance, Inc., for the purpose of spreading the ministry of Bible deliverance. Receipts for contributions are tax deductible. Address all correspondence to:
John L. Meares, Box 1922, Washington, D.C.

Are You In Love With Jesus?
—Mary Lee Meares

Sometime ago I read an article in which the writer said, "I knew Christ a long time, or a good many years before I fell in love with Him." This struck a chord in my heart, and I asked myself the question, "Am I really in love with Jesus?" I know I say I love the Lord, but just how much do I love Him?

I know a lot of people by their faces; I know others by name; others I know a little about them, and yet I could not say I really love them for I don't actually know them. You cannot really love someone until you know them and that not just in a casual manner. You must know and be known for there to be a bond of love between you. This was what the person meant when he said he knew Christ a long time before really falling in love with Him. Some people meet Christ as their personal Saviour, but the friendship doesn't grow very much from day to day. There are those times that they feel they must have His help so they renew their acquaintance at these times, but for an every day companionship, it is yet not  a reality. He has not become that Friend that sticketh closer than a brother. He is not yet that person that gets up with them in the morning and goes with them to their job; they as yet only know Him as one to go to church to meet on Sunday morning. Until you learn to let Him abide in you and you in Him in all your ways, you will not have known what it is to really love Him. There is a difference! And the more we learn of Him, the more we will love Him. It is up to us just how much we love Him. So many Christians think if they are busy all the time working for the Lord in carrying out certain duties for the church, etc. that this proves their love for God. But this is not the case. I had rather my children or my husband would spend some time with me just talking with me and having fellowship than I would them spending all their time working for me. I believe it is this way with the Lord. He wants us to just simply commune with Him — take time to talk to Him and let Him talk to us; take time to meditate on His Word (his love letter to us). We can test our love by asking ourself how much we love to read what He has to say to us.

When two people are in love with each other, they want to be together, to be in each other's presence. They can not be together enough. There is a love that draws them to each other. And so it is when we really fall in love with our Lord. We will ponder the things He says in our heart, and we will have a desire to know Him better every day.

In Christ —Pastor Meares

"Blessed be the God and Father our Lord Jesus Christ, who hath blessed us with all spiritual blessings in heavenly places in *Christ*" Ephesians 1:3.

You ought to know that God is not only a Father, but He is a good Father. There is no greater phrase than "God is a good God." I hope that your relationship with God is such that your heart is continually crying out praises and blessings unto God. Some people are always complaining about their troubles, and asking God, "why?" I don't see God like that. I see Him as a tender-loving Father with outstretched arms and with hands full of blessings. I must shout, "Blessed be God." I want to bless God because the above scripture verse says, "who hath blessed us." You can't help but bless someone who blesses you. Even though a person has many faults and failures, if they have been good to you, you overlook their failures. But God has no faults, no failures, only blessings. I trust you have a praise and hallowedness in your heart. If you have been praying to God for something for a long time, just stop and thank

God for what He has already done for you and the prayers He has already answered for you. See how many good things He has done for you that you didn't even ask Him for. Then begin to bless God. The greatest part of real prayer is not asking, but thanking. We cannot repay God for all His blessings, but we can bless Him. David said, "Forget not all of thy benefits." Then again David asked, "What shall we render unto God (or give back) for His blessings unto us?" The answer was, "just accept more of what He has blessed us with and then praise Him." God does not run out of blessings.

The text reads, "Blessed be the God and the Father of our Lord Jesus Christ." God was the power, the deity that Jesus Christ respected here on earth. Jesus who was co-equal with God and became the Son of God, counted God as His God and His Jehovah. He did nothing apart from His Father. It is one thing to count God as God, and it is another thing to count that same God as our Father. Your earthly father may be respected and honored for his hard labor and his devotion toward his family. You may say, "I have a good father, the best that ever lived." But you could never think of worshipping him as a God. Never, because he is only a human being. He has his limitations. By the same token, our God who has all power in heaven and earth, is our Father as well as our God. You can hardly conceive of the great God of heaven becoming a Father, but he is just that. He is not only our God and our Father, but He is the "God and Father of our Lord." Inasmuch as Jesus Christ is our Lord, then His God is our God and His Father is our Father, and Jesus Christ is our Lord. Our Lord belongs to us because God gave us the Lord Jesus Christ. We are begotten of Him; He is our elder brother, therefore, the God of the Lord Jesus Christ is our God; the Father of the Lord Jesus Christ is our Father, and Jesus Christ is our Lord, "who hath blessed us with all spiritual blessings in heavenly places in Christ."

The secret and the key of this revelation are the words, "in Christ." We can only bless God as we are in Christ. There is no real worship outside the Lord Jesus toward our heavenly Father. We only have access to His throne when we pray through Jesus Christ. He has become the "new and the living way." He is the way unto God.

Outside of Christ there is no way, no glory, but it is "in Christ." God sees everyone in one way or the other—in Adam or in Christ. Adam was the first man whom God created and Adam represents our physical being, the body and person that we are. Adam is the Father of us all in a physical sense and in a spiritual sense that Adam had a soul. However, God desires to see you in His second creation which is in Christ. Jesus Christ was the second man God created. You are in one family or the other. Some people boast of their family while others boast of their race or nation they belong to. The Germans, under Hitler, claimed to be the super race. The Chinese, under communism, want to become the super race. The Russians are striving to become the super race. But thanks be to God, there are really only two races, the race of Adam or the race of the Son of the living God. You are in one or the other, God has proposed to have a family of people who are "in Christ." I want to be like Him. I want people to see Christ in my deeds and in my countenance. Outside of Christ, we are nothing. That is why He has brought about a family in Christ, so we can become like the Lord. You will find all of your blessings "in Christ."

His purpose then is to have this new family to become like Christ and then one day to be with Christ. I don't know where you plan to retire. I am providing very little for my retirement in Adam, but my hope is "in Christ." I am looking forward to a rest that I have already entered. I have not found the completion of that rest, but have already entered it. For one day, if I shall strive to be like Him, I am going to be with Him. Until I go to be with Him, He has come to be with me and take me by the hand to guide and direct me and lead me to where He is. He is with me here in the presence of the Holy Spirit, which is the Spirit of Christ.

Editorial

—Mary Lee Meares

Back in the days of sailing ships, a young, inexperienced seaman was sent aloft in a storm to disentangle a broken rigging from the mainmast. Despite the raging winds, the youngster climbed up swiftly and did the job. But as he started to descend he looked down and became dizzy and frightened when he saw the vessel tossing and rolling in the angry sea. He felt his grip weakening and cried to the first mate on the deck far below: "I'm falling!" "Don't look down, boy! Look up!", the mate shouted back. Following this advice he soon regained his calm and made his way safely back to the deck.

It is a human tendency to "look down" and see only the difficulties and discouragements within the narrow confines of one's life.

"By looking up" to God and out to the cause of all mankind, your own personal problems will seem incidental, and will be more easily solved. David said, "I will lift up mine eyes unto the hills from whence cometh my help. My help cometh from the Lord, which made heaven and earth." Psalms 121:1-2. Many are the times that I look up to God and realize that my help in personal problems must come from the Lord. What greater power could I ask for help? Nor until I "lift up mine eyes and behold the fields that are ready for harvest" will I be able to help anyone else. There must be a vision or people will perish. God help me if I ever cease to be moved by the needs of humanity as I look on the whitened fields. "Is it fair," I sometimes have asked myself (especially while in a foreign land) that I should be so blessed with a knowledge of the saving grace of God, with a Christian family, with all the necessities of life, while others go so neglected?" I must not close my eyes to the needs of others.

Then when Christ was speaking of some of the signs before the coming of the Lord, he said to "look up, and lift up our heads; for our redemption or deliverance draweth nigh." So in order to receive help and help others and be ready for His coming I must "LOOK UP."

FELLOWSHIP NEWS
The monthly Voice of the Evangelistic Center

Vol 1	September 1960	No. 8

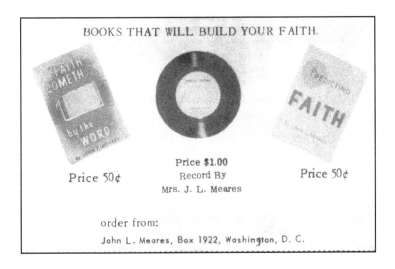

BOOKS THAT WILL BUILD YOUR FAITH.

Price 50¢

Price $1.00
Record By
Mrs. J. L. Meares

Price 50¢

order from:

John L. Meares, Box 1922, Washington, D. C.

Editorial   —Mrs. John Meares

In the little town of Plymouth, Massachusetts there is a famous rock where our Puritan fathers landed one cold, dreary day in December of 1620. The little village has been reconstructed to look just as it did when the Pilgrims lived there.

An interesting feature in each home was the large Bible box. It was the most important piece of furniture in the house.

Would this not be a different place to live, if we could say the same of our homes today? Our forefathers leaned upon the Word of God for their strength and guidance. They had come to a new country where they could worship God as they desired. The Bible gave them a comfort during their many times of trial and sorrow.

But today, in most of our schools, the Bible is not allowed to be read or prayer offered. Very few homes today have a time of praying together and thanking God for His bountiful supplies.

I remember, as a child, my mother would call me in from my playing in the yard, and say, "it is time for morning prayer," As a child I read my Bible through, but today it seems parents are too busy to take time out for gathering the children together and teaching them the worth of prayer to the Heavenly Father.

Let us not forget to thank God for the things that we often take for granted—for still the freedom to worship Him as we please. Soon after Brother Meares and I married we went to Old Mexico to a convention. One afternoon there was a memorial service for 50 of their ministers who had been killed that year for preaching the gospel of our Lord and Saviour. Yes, we can be thankful for freedom of religion—to worship God as we please.

Let us be thankful for the abundance God has given us and for His promise to never leave us or forsake us. I pray that I might show my gratitude by my life as well as by my lips.

The monthly Voice of the Evangelistic Center

Vol 1	October, 1960	No. 9
John L. Meares		Publisher and Founder
Mary L. Meares		Editor

Published monthly by Herald of Deliverance, Inc., for the purpose of spreading the ministry of Bible deliverance. Receipts for contributions are tax deductible.

Editorial   —Mary L. Meares

A year ago this December the first issue of the Fellowship News was published. It has been a joy to come into your homes each month by way of magazine. I am grateful for the letters and words of comment that have come in, and trust that the paper will continue to be a blessing to you.

Christmas is a wonderful time of the year—a time we especially show our love to others. I always have a kind of excited feeling as Christmas draws nigh. And, I think that is the way it should be. After all, the most important event of mankind was the birth of Jesus. It is something to be excited about. Already my children have put up the manger scene in our living room. This is always the most important part of our decorations, for it is Christ's birthday.

I began to think tonight as I read where there was no room for Him in the inn. I am not an innkeeper, but I am the keeper of my heart. You are the keeper of your heart, and you alone can find room for the Lord as He seeks entrance to be born into your heart. No one else can let Him in for you. Sometimes we become so busy that, without realizing it, we have turned the Lord away. This holiday season, of all times, let us not become so busy with the buying of gifts, the sending of cards, and the different preparations that we fail to find time to worship our Saviour whose birthday we celebrate.

Just as a star shone in the east and directed the wise men to where Jesus was, there can be a light shining in our life that will help others find Him. And when they find Him, they cannot help but worship Him. There might not be gold, frankincense, or myrrh to offer, but one can offer a heart of love, adoration and dedication. There could not be more acceptable gifts. Then after you leave your gifts, go, as did the shepherds, and make known abroad the wonderful news, and glorify God for the birth of His Son.

FELLOWSHIP NEWS
The monthly Voice of the Evangelistic Center

Vol. 2	December, 1960	No. 10
John L. Meares		Publisher and Founder
Mory L. Meares		Editor

Published monthly by Herald of Deliverance, Inc., for the purpose of spreading the ministry of Bible deliverance. Receipts for contributions are tax deductible. Address all correspondence to:
John L. Meares, Box 1922, Washington, D.C.

≈ ≈ ≈

Christmas is Love   —Mary Lee Meares

The greatest force in all the world is love; the only universal language in all the world is love. Even if you cannot understand what a person is saying, you can understand the love they project. To me, the simple meaning of Christmas is love. God so loved us that He gave the best He had. When someone gives you their very best, you know they love you. The love of God was beyond our understanding, so He said, "I will give my only Son that he might be born of flesh, and become one of them. I want them to understand how much I love them." So it was on that cold, December night in the city of David that the Christ Child was born. The angels came to the lowly shepherds and proclaimed, "Behold, I bring you good tidings of great joy, which shall be to all people. For unto you is born this day in the city of David a Saviour, which is Christ the Lord." Luke 2:10-11.

A babe was born just like you and I were born. He grew into adulthood just like we grew into adulthood. He had his joys and sorrows just as we have our joys and sorrows. He walked among people blessing them, healing them, speaking words of comfort and showing love toward them. He brought hope to the hopeless and salvation to all that would believe in Him. He was God's gift to a lost humanity. Love is expressed in giving. A mother loves her child so she gives of her time, her energy, and her all simply because she loves. A father loves his family so he works in order to be able to give them the necessities of life. A young boy falls in love and he expresses that love by giving gifts. The wise men came over a long, hazardous trail and when they finally reached the Christ child they gave Him gifts to express their love. However, I think their real love was expressed not in gifts, but in their deep desire to find their promised Messiah. This love was the thing that kept them searching and following the star. God gave His Son to us, and then Jesus gave His life for us. And if we love God, we will accept God's gift and receive the Lord into our heart, and then give our life back to Him. We can give back to God.

These tidings of great joy were and are for *all* people. Love brought us a Saviour. So Christmas to me is a most wonderful time of the year. It is a time when families and friends express their love by exchanging cards, greetings, gifts and times together. I believe God is pleased with this. If only every day of the year, and not only during the Christmas season, we would manifest love for one another. The girl that has lost her way needs love; the boy that says, "no one cares"; the mother that carries a heavy burden—they all need love. God is love and the greatest gift you can give in this day is the same good news that was given on the Judean hills. You can assure them that there has been a Saviour born that is ready to give them peace, joy and love.

The Christmas story still lives. When I think of the star that shone so brightly that glorious night some 2000 years ago, I think of the Bright and Morning Star that was born and lives even now in my heart. When I think of the angels singing of peace on earth, I think of the Prince of Peace that was born and brought peace into my life. When I read of the lowly shepherds whom the angels chose to announce this great advent, I think of the great Shepherd who watches over me day and night. As I think of there being no room in the inn for the Christ child to be born, I am made happy because I have found room in my own inn for Him. Just as the prophet Simeon rejoiced when he said "the Light" that would lighten the Gentiles and the Light that would be their salvation, so do I rejoice because that Light has shined upon my pathway and I no longer walk in darkness. The tidings of great joy are a reality to me. Christmas is a story of love.

Chapter 3 – 1961

Editorial

— Mrs. John Meares

No matter what has been accomplished with our lives in the past, God can still do more with them in the future, or we could say, all that God has done for us in the past, He will do more for us in the future. Luke 6:38 says "Give, and it shall be given unto you; good measure, pressed down, shaken together, and running over — So many times this verse is interpreted only in terms of money, but I believe it means also to give of our time to Christ; give of our love to others; share our blessings with our neighbor; offer words of praise and kindness to those we work with, etc. Any time we give of ourselves, we receive in return either through God or man. God does not always give back to us in the same form as we give Him. Health, happiness, peace, and prosperity are just a few of the many ways God gives back to us for giving of ourselves. He sees our deeds and they do not go unheeded.

For some people it is relatively easy for them to give of their finances to God's work, and yet they find it hard to take time out to spend alone with Him in prayer, or to sit down and to meditate upon the reading of His Word. When you love someone you don't just want what their money will buy you, but you want to spend time with them and talk with them. So it is with God — we are His children, and He loves us and desires to be alone with us. He wants more than just our money to spread the gospel. When we take time to commune with Him, we will receive blessings in measure that cannot be obtained in any other way.

There is also a time not to just be alone with Him, but to go out and witness to others. Great are the returns, and what we will witness ourselves from witnessing to others will cause our cup to run over. If there comes that time in the days ahead when you feel that others are receiving more from God than you, stop and see if you are giving all you have to Him. May 1961 bring you an increased understanding of God, His love and His blessings. To have a full life you must fully give.

Vol. 2	January, 1961	No. 11
John L. Meares		Publisher and Founder
Mary L. Meares		Editor

The Kingdom of Heaven   —John L. Meares

"The kingdom of Heaven is come to you." These words were proclaimed by John the Baptist, by Jesus Christ, His twelve, the appointed seventy and also Paul. This was their theme. Jesus teaching his disciples to pray said, pray "thy kingdom come, thy will be done on earth as it is in heaven." We know that God declared that all will be brought under subjection—every power and principality, and put under the feet of Jesus Christ. This is the consummation of God's great plan.

All about us we are aware of rebellion, stubbornness, disobedience of authority, and every other evil. The so-called church has long since lost its voice. It is very rare to find a home that is blessed with discipline and respect.—Youth everywhere is rebelling against governments. There is hardly any respect for law. The criminal seems to have more protection than the victim. From looking about us there seemingly is no evidence to be seen of the Kingdom of God. Notwithstanding, we are to proclaim, "the kingdom of heaven is at hand."

The disciples were confused, dejected, and scattered when Jesus would not fulfill their aspirations for him to drive out their Roman captors and enthrone himself upon David's throne, and set up a material kingdom. But they were to soon realize that He came to establish a kingdom far beyond any imagination they could have thought. For His was a spiritual kingdom. His kingdom was not to be legislated nor enforced with earthly weapons. But His kingdom was to come to pass by the will of men everywhere, to be completely subjected under His plan and purpose. By turning around and creating a new spirit by a new birth, we are to make men everywhere one in Christ, whose first aim in life is to do the will of God on earth as it is done in heaven.

The so-called church of today has little experienced this transforming power to subject the will and spirit of man to the will of God. Thus the "church" has missed its purpose and has become an institutionalized society to lift an objectional voice, weak and powerless, concerning some of the social ills it finds itself entangled with. The oneness of the believers in the Lord Jesus Christ for which Jesus prayed in John 17 is hardly distinguishable in our world of competition and compromise. The meaning of *one accord, unity* and *fellowship* as is many times used in the Epistles is *almost* completely unknown in the so-called church. There is a much greater bond of fellowship and unity in some of the man-made orders and fraternities than in most church congregations, denominations and inter-denominations.

The mystery which Paul spoke so much about, that was kept by God from the beginning of creation, was made known through Jesus Christ. Paul expressed in Ephesians 2:14-18 that God in a divine order has created the *new man* through Christ and there is a holy fellowship with God, and thus with man, that is not of this world. It fulfills the declaration of John, "By this shall all men know that ye are my disciples that ye have love one for another." Again, John asks, "How can you love God whom you have not seen if you love not your brother whom you have seen?" This making of one new man (the church of all nations and races) through Jesus Christ is the mystery hidden from the foundation of the world, that God in these last days has revealed to the saints. And this is the true church which is the body of Christ, who is the Head of the church. And this is the Kingdom of God that is at hand. This divine work of God in the hearts of men is expressed as being "born of the Spirit," translated out of the kingdom of darkness into the kingdom of light," "being made one in Him," "baptized into His body." This is the gospel of the kingdom — making all men one in Him, the Head of the church.

For this purpose in the council of His own will, God has raised up Evangel Temple and indeed every assembly of believers. Unfortunately, we have failed to understand the divine purposes and calling of God and have substituted programs of men and social functions; never coming to know the meaning of the gospel as it is said of the believers in Jerusalem, "They continued steadfastly in the apostles' doctrine and fellowship and in breaking of bread, and in prayers. And fear came upon every soul: and many wonders and signs were done by the apostles. And they continuing daily with one accord in the temple, and breaking bread from house to house, did eat their meat with gladness and singleness of heart, praising God, and having favour with all the people. And the Lord added to the church daily such as should be saved. Acts 2:42-47. This is the divine unity that brings reality to the Kingdom of God. Without this Charisma visible, we only have a *part* gospel, certainly not the *full* gospel.

The challenge that God through His Spirit is bringing to us at Evangel Temple is to make our calling and election sure. Do we dare to arise and accept that in a world of rioting, hatred, law breaking and strife, that God can make of us such a people — a light set upon a hill which cannot be hid and salt of the earth. This is our calling and God is faithful who has called us. If our spirit will be subjected to the Father of all Spirits and to His Word, we can become this people called by his name. We must become this people that God in His purpose has called us to be to His honor, glory and power forever, worlds without end.

Editorial   —Mrs. John L. Meares

Youth is something we cherish — something we like to look back upon. One enjoys saying, "when I was young, I had to do so and so." Or we seem to enjoy talking about what we didn't have, and how our children ought to appreciate what they have in this day. No one would say that times have not changed to what they were twenty-five or even ten years ago. It is quite different for a child growing up today. Some may say this is a better day, and some may think the old days the best, but to me the important factor in rearing the children is still the same. That is to instill into the hearts of every child the love of God and give them a faith that they can grow and live by. You say, "that is the parents job." True, but what if the parents have no knowledge of this faith, or of the love of God, or what if they just don't care? Can we let our youth be wasted and their lives ruined and destroyed without having tried to help them?

When we first began having services here in Washington I remember making the remark to Brother Meares, "Don't these people have any children?" I would look out over a vast audience of adults, but see very few little ones. I didn't know whether they had children or just didn't bring them with them. This disturbed me, for I had been use to seeing children in church, and had myself grown up in one.

So the staff had a meeting to discuss plans on how to get the children out to church. As we had no Sunday School rooms, only a large auditorium, we decided on a program that would interest all ages. We call this hour Bible Adventure Land. There were men that volunteered to drive the buses and others whom we call shepherds that began going out early every Sunday morning, gather the children together and ride with them on the bus to Bible Adventure Land.

FELLOWSHIP NEWS
The monthly Voice of the Evangelistic Center

Vol. 2	February, 1961	No. 12
John L. Meares		Publisher and Founder
Mary L. Meares		Editor

≈ ≈ ≈

Testimonies

I feel I must write this testimony. On August 11th I was suffering with a terrible crippling affliction that I have been bothered with for the last eight or nine years. This time I seemed to be getting worse. All day it had been on my mind to dial-a-prayer, but it seemed that every time I would get near the phone, I would fail to dial. Finally, though I had my son help me up, and I hobbled to the telephone and agreed with you in prayer as you prayed. My body was all one sided, crooked and in much pain. After the amen, I immediately straightened up which I had not been able to do all day. In a few minutes I was free and was shouting and praising God.

I also have been blessed since I began paying tithes. I was raised in a church where tithing was not stressed, but I gave more than a tenth of my income to the many clubs to which I belonged. After the death of my husband in 1957 I started working overtime and during the holidays and on Sundays also. I felt that I must work all I could in order to make ends meet. But then I joined a Pentecostal church and began to pay tithes. God began to bless me financially until it was no longer necessary for me to work on Sundays, holidays, etc. I praise God that I can serve Him and trust Him.

Jamie Pinckney

* * *

I have so much to praise the Lord for. I was saved and filled with the Holy Ghost at Evangel Temple in 1958. I never had a chance for a school education because of illness. So I was unable to read. I would carry my Bible with me but could not read a word in it. Then one night we had a prayer meeting at my house and after everyone had gone, I cried out to the Lord to teach me how to read. The next morning I opened my Bible and the words started coming to me. It was a glorious miracle. From then on I have been reading my Bible and going out and witnessing to other people.

Maggie Jackson
Washington, D.C.

* * *

I was in Washington last year and spent some time with my daughter. It was through your radio broadcast that I learned of you and your church. When I heard your message, I said, "that is where I want to go." I received the greatest blessing when I came to your church that I have received since being saved and filled with the Holy Ghost. I love all of God's people, but it seems something was in your services that I haven't found other places. I am enclosing a dollar for your broadcast and will try to send in a dollar every month. Also I enjoy the monthly church paper you send me.

Sarah Brown

God's Tenth   —Mary Lee Meares

One of the greatest ways the devil cheats us in receiving blessings from the Lord is to make us imagine and not only imagine, but convince us, as good christians, that it is all right if we do not pay our tithes. He will say to us, "God knows your circumstances and you need your money more than your church, so He will understand your keeping the ten percent or the tithe." Yes, many sincere christians have convinced themselves that they are not doing wrong by keeping the ten percent that God said is *holy* and belongs to Him. You say, "I give in offerings and the Lord knows that is all I can afford."

If you owed a friend a debt and you decided you were not able to pay it, but you would give him a gift, do you think he would consider the debt paid? No! Then why do we try to make ourself believe God will accept and bless our offering until we have first paid the tenth that He says we owe Him.

We believe literally the other commands and promises in God's Word, but for tithing, that is just one command that within our heart we say, "The Lord didn't mean that." It is though we just cut it out of the Bible. It could be no less wrong to say that God did not mean it when He said, "Ye must be born again." Who of us would believe that we could get to heaven without being born again? We don't dare try to deceive ourself. We don't dare to take the risk of waiting and seeing when we die if He meant that we must be born again in order to get to heaven. And yet, we take the chance of coming before Him and being pronounced a robber or a thief. No, you would not think of taking anything that belonged to your friend or your neighbor, but God? Oh, well, He understands! He does not understand, but this God knows — if you really had faith in His promise to bless you if you gave Him the tenth that He said belongs to Him, you would pay your tithe. You would not hold back His part if you believed He really meant He would bless the nine-tenths that you keep and make it go farther than if you kept it all.

Who of us would not give to someone if they told us that in turn they would give us something much better or much more than we had given them? Then why will we not believe God? Why do we make excuses for not paying our tithes? It is only because we do not believe God. How can we love Him if we do not believe Him? When one loves someone, it is not hard to give to them, even though it may seem to be a sacrifice.

We have heard testimonies again and again of God's blessings after one began to tithe, but the devil whispers in your ears, "that wouldn't happen to you." And you believed the devil and consequently are still struggling on the 100 percent. God will not force you to pay Him the tenth, just as He will not force you to live for Him, but you are the loser. You will never be a victorious christian; you will never be the example to others that you could be; you will never have overflowing joy; or you will never be blessed as God would like to bless you because of your disobedience to His command, until you once and for all say, "Lord, here is the tenth that belongs to you. Whether or not I have money left for my needs, I am first going to bring my tithe into the storehouse." Do you believe that God in all His goodness and love would let your needs go unmet if you came to Him in this attitude of faith? Never! There has never been a testimony as such and there never shall be. God's Word is true and the devil is a liar.

Praying and fasting alone will not make us a victorious and happy child of God. Giving of our tithes and offerings is a vital part of our christian life. "The Lord *loveth* a cheerful giver." I want God to love me, and I know I have not given an offering until I have first paid a tenth or that which belongs to Him. If you are having a battle in the paying of your tithes, be determined to win the victory. Tell the devil you need God's blessings and cannot afford *not* to pay your tithes. Tell the devil you are not paying to a man, but unto God. Tell the devil you love God and with joy you are going to trust Him for all your personal needs. Tell the devil he has cheated you from God's abundant goodness too long and from this time forth you have won the battle of tithing. If you will, your life will be changed and you will have a testimony of victory and no one will be able to tell you God will not bless those that will have faith enough to give Him the tenth that belongs to Him.

* * * *

I have a lot to be thankful for, a lot to say, but one is I have received the Holy Ghost since I joined the Temple. I also have been blessed more since I started tithing. I didn't know about tithes before. Now I love to pay them, and I have never wanted for anything since I started. The Lord has blessed me, and my cup is running over.

Julia Beckwith
Washington, D.C.

Excerpts of Praise   —John L. Meares

Thank you for the FELLOWSHIP NEWS. It has really been a blessing to me as I am unable to attend services regularly. I enjoyed the inspiring message in the February issue on Confession. God has blessed me in many ways through your prayers. Thank you and God bless you.

Ivy Weathers
1309 Quincy Street, N. W.
Washington, D. C.

* * *

Saturday night I was suffering with great pain in my body. About 3:00 a.m. I dialed the prayer phone number. After you prayed the prayer of faith, I went to sleep and slept until time to get up. I can't thank God enough. We listen to your broadcast each morning and it is such a blessing to us. Thank you for the FELLOWSHIP NEWS.

Mrs. Raymond Smith
24 Transverse Avenue
Baltimore, MD

* * *

I can't find the words to thank you for your interest in me, and for your prayers. Two of the head doctors talked to me and told me my T. B. test was negative. I left their room sobing with joy and gratitude to my God and creator.

Annie Stickler

* * *

Dear Brother Meares,

I received the wonderful letter and the spirit reviving "FELLOW-SHIP NEWS". It was heart warming to hear about the thousands who turned from Voodoo worship to the great God who has all power.

Rev. Meares, I am very interested in hearing from some of the young christians in your church. I am 20 years old and don't have a lot of christian friends. I feel that a young christian needs to be around other christians his age. If you have some christians in your church that would like to correspond with me, I would be so glad.

Pray for me.

God's heir,
A/2 C William Green
4083 Inst. Sqdn., Box 207
APO 23 N. Y., N. Y.

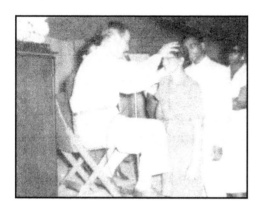

Brother Meares praying for Marie Herndon, who is a charter fellowship member.

With God   —John Meares

The whole theme of Christ may be summed up in the term, "With God".

When the Son of God was born in a manger, it was God living among men. The angels came to herald His birth and sing His glory as they announced to the lowly Judean shepherds the King of peace that had come. All of the heavens stood in wonderment when God came to live with men. Everywhere that Jesus went all of the people realized that they were in a presence that was strange and glorious. Although many refused to believe Him, yet they must join in with the words of the Roman soldier, "Never a man spake like this man".

When one stops to ponder it is easy to understand the wonderment of the angels of Heaven at the birth of God's Son in a world of human selfishness, greed, and hatred, but God wanted to be with us.

When the ministry of Christ was completed and an atonement was made by the blood of Christ, Jesus arose and returned to the right hand of His Father. However, this did not mean that our association with God was ended, but rather a door was opened that all of the generations to come could be with Him. I am completely overcome when I consider the challenge that is ours in our association with God. The Apostle Paul said, "We then, as workers together with Him, beseech you also that you receive not the grace of God in vain". The plan of the eternal ages hinges upon the birth of the Son of God by a virgin. But this was only the beginning of working out God's plan of the ages. Christ only opened the door and then we stand back and hear God say to us, "We are workers together". To realize that you and I are included in God's great plan, and that He works with us as we work for Him is a joy beyond human contemplation.

In this Christmas season as you see the many familiar scenes of the Christ child, and you hear the stirring pronouncements, "Peace on earth, good will toward men" I pray that your heart will be stirred within you to bring you to the realization that you have a part in God's eternal plan. For as Christ was born the Son of God, so you and I are born of the Spirit through Christ that we may share His anointing and proclaim to our fellowman that "The Kingdom of God is at hand". The sick are made whole, the sinner is cleansed from his evil ways, for Christ is manifested through the believers.

Letters to the Pastor

New Office Secretary

I came to Evangel Temple almost six years ago. I was saved at the time, but a little down in spirit. But as I walked into Evangel Temple, I felt the Spirit of God in such a way as I had never felt Him before. Right then I began to praise God within my heart for leading me to such a wonderful place.

Later I became very ill. The doctor had told me if I were troubled with this condition again I would have to be operated on. However, I had heard Brother Meares preach a sermon on healing, the like of which I had never heard before. It built my faith for healing.

I was so sick I could hardly get to church that night, but I knew that God would heal me, and sure enough He did. Pastor Meares laid hands on me and God wonderfully touched me. I have not been troubled with the condition since.

For the last few months I have been working as one of the secretaries of Evangel Temple, and enjoy my work very much, because I always am having an opportunity to encourage someone who is down in spirit or sick in body. I know what He did for me, and I know He will help others also.

I enjoy working with such a wonderful staff and all the wonderful people that we have at Evangel Temple.

Lena Patton
Washington, D.C.

* * *

I would be remiss if I did not take this opportunity to sit down and reflect on the beautiful message I heard over the radio this 14th day of September, 1961.

I was in my automobile on my way back to my office, after having spent a busy morning in a contested court case; and, needless to say, I was nearly exhausted. I turned on my radio and heard the beautiful song Mrs. Meares was singing, "Jesus Took My Burden," and later I heard your message.

Both Mrs. Meares' song and your message were a great source of comfort to me; and almost immediately my fatigue, the pressure of my office and the problems of my clients seemed to become inconsequential and I had a fresher outlook to carry me through the balance of my busy day.

I am very appreciative to God that such devoted people are working constantly, endeavoring to bring messages of this kind to a troubled world.

You may rest assured that I shall continue to pray that you may have the strength to continue with God's Word.

John R. Willett, Attorney at Law
Alexandria, VA.

God's Business —Mrs. John L. Meares

God's business is the greatest business in all the world. That is why the doors of Evangelistic Center are open 365 days a year. If the business house down town can stay open, why not God's house?

You ask, "What is God's business?" My answer is "winning souls for the kingdom of God." The Bible says, "He that winneth souls is wise." Proverbs 11:30. To me, winning souls is the most important mission one can have in this life. For, what does it profit a man if he gain the whole world, yet loses his soul. Jesus says, a soul is worth more than all the world! Can you even begin to imagine how much that would be?

Man is so created by God that he hungers for His Creator; his soul is restless until it finds rest in God. The pity is that the person in the world does not know what he is seeking. This is where you and I can help in God's business. We can tell them about Jesus and the peace He alone can give. Peace can only be found when one sheds the old habits like a worn-out garment and dons a new nature of godliness. Jesus said He gave a peace that the world could not give. The world—the individual is seeking peace. Let us be about our Father's business and tell them where the true source of peace comes from.

In colonial days, a much-respected villager was asked by a stranger: "What is your business?" "My business," the man replied, "is to serve the Lord. I make shoes to pay expenses." Let it be the same with us. No matter what we do to make a living, let us keep God's business paramount—that of winning souls.

(Note) Reverend Harold Jackson will be working with us (beginning the middle of May) during the summer months while Reverend A. A. Petrucelli is directing the program at Camp Adventure Land. I am sure Brother Jackson's many friends will be glad to learn of his coming.

FELLOWSHIP NEWS
The monthly Voice of the Evangelistic Center

Vol. 1	April, 1961	No. 14
John L. Meares		Publisher & Founder
Mary L. Meares		Editor

Published monthly by Herald of Deliverance, Inc., for the purpose of spreading the ministry of Bible deliverance. Receipts for contributions are tax deductible.

A battery of Dial-A-Prayer telephones are kept busy with thousands of calls per week from people who are in need of prayer. Testimonies come in each week from those who have received help after calling TAylor 9-9200.

A Look At The Cross   —Mary Lee Meares

There have been thousands of hymns written about the cross. Hundreds of sermons have been preached on the cross. Millions of people have knelt at the cross. For the last 2000 years, the story of the cross has not lost its power. What is it in the cross that holds such an attraction? Why do we single out one cross and always refer to it as "the cross"? Jesus was only one of thousands of people that have died upon a cross. In the days of the Roman Empire many people were burned and hanged on crosses. This was a way of punishment. The

Apostle Peter died on a cross. There were two other crosses by this cross—the cross that Jesus hanged upon. The difference was not in the cross, but the man that was hanging upon that cross. That is why one look at the cross and we will be a different person. Our lives will be changed if when we look, the scales fall from our eyes and we behold the only Begotten Son of God dying for our sins. Sad though it be, many people look at the cross in this day and see no more than some of the people that looked that day as Jesus hung upon the cross.

The Roman soldiers looked and only saw a man that was being hanged because a lot of people, especially religious leaders, wanted Him out of the way. The priests saw Him as an enemy to be destroyed. Many people passed by out of curiosity and looked at the cross, and laughed and said, "If you be the Son of God, come down from that cross." Perhaps, there was a leper standing by that Christ had healed, or the little woman who had had an issue of blood for twelve long years, and she said, "I touched that man's garment and I was made whole. Why would they do this to him?"

Among the crowd that day could have been the little boy who gave Jesus his lunch to feed the hungry multitudes who had come to hear Him preach. No doubt he was thinking, "why are they mistreating a man that was always doing good and said to love your enemies, do good to those that treat you wrong and forgive them." This little boy would never forget the miracle as long as he lived. How he wished he could have offered help in some way at this time.

One of the malefactors hanging on a cross beside the Lord saw only another criminal, like himself, being crucified. The other thief looked as he hung upon a cross and saw hope for himself. He said, "Lord, remember me when thou comest into thy Kingdom." The longer the centurion looked the more he became convinced, "Surely this man was the Son of God."

Standing as close by as the soldiers would allow was the mother of Jesus. Through tear dimmed eyes, she looked and saw her son with a crown of thorns upon his brow. He was bleeding, suffering and dying unjustly, and she, who loved him so, was unable to help

Him. "Why did my son's life have to end on a cross?" Next to her was Mary Magdalene trying to comfort her. "I never knew what it was to be happy and know real joy until I met your Son. He freed me from the miserable life I was living. I can't understand why they would do this to Him."

John, the beloved, stood there with a heavy heart and as he looked he saw his best friend dying. Jesus had tried to tell him that this would happen but he couldn't believe it. Even though the other disciples had fled, John still had faith in Him and knew his life had been transformed since having met this man.

I am sure Mary and Martha were there, bewildered. "Why would a man that had power to raise our brother who had been dead for four days not show His power now and come down from that cross?"

As Joseph of Arimathea looked, there was a desire burning within his bosom to go and ask Pilate for this body, so he could lay it in his new hewn out tomb. This was the least he could do for Him.

Pilate did not want to look. He did not go out to Golgotha to see this man hanging on the cross he had condemned Him to die upon. He was glad it was over, and he had now washed his hands of the whole thing.

No doubt, the angels looked and said, "Why don't you let us come down there and take you down from the cross. You don't have to die."

And even though those standing by did not understand, God knew this was the only way of redemption. Here was His only Begotten Son giving His life as a sacrifice for a lost and dying people — people that were at that moment passing by making fun; soldiers who were gambling over His Son's garment. God could not even look at the cross, for the sins of the whole world were hanging upon it. God had to forsake His Son in his darkest hour.

When you look at the cross what do you see? What do you feel? I came and bowed at this cross when only a child. At that time it meant only that Jesus died on the cross for me, a sinner, and if I would believe on Him I would be saved. That alone would have been most wonderful, but through the years, as I have kept looking, the cross has meant more and more to me.

"Culpepper Star Exponent" Article

Washington Religious Group Opens Camp For Underprivileged Near Richardsville

By Bill Ashworth

A youth camp with very big plans for the future has quietly opened ten miles east of Richardsville on the edge of Culpeper County.

One week old, the camp is described by its director as "interracial, interdenominational — in short—a camp for everyone."

Speaking of his new-born Bible Camp Adventureland, Director Robert Streblow said, "With our camp, first privilege goes to the underprivileged".

Camp Adventureland is run exclusively for the underprivileged children of Washington and its environs by the National Evangelical Center in Washington. Streblow describes the center as a "pleasant place for persons of all faiths to meet and to worship, regardless of color." Streblow is the youth director of the center completely staffed by whites, which has a predominately colored membership. A majority of the campers belong to the center's Sunday School.

The Rev. John L. Meers, of the National Evangelical Center, conceived the idea of a fresh air camp for the underprivileged of Washington, to be built somewhere in Virginia and, after some consideration, decided to locate in the Richardsville area. Construction began in May.

At present, the camp is a group of unfinished buildings, four tents, and over a hundred campers located in a sea of mud. Recent rains and heavy machinery have combined to riddle Camp Adventureland with water-filled ruts. In addition, piles of brush are scattered about as mute testimony to the tremendous amount of energy spent in making the site livable.

The main building, the dining hall, is about half finished. The roof is almost on and the kitchen is walled in but the rest is exposed to the elements.

Most of the campers sleep in the four wall tents scattered about the camping area. Each contains approximately 12 bunks.

in double rows. Some of the 117 campers sleep in the dining hall in double-decker bunks.

All indoor recreational activity is by necessity, held in the central dining hall, as it is the only permanent building near completion. Meal meals are served in the building and, despite the large number of beds found in the dining hall, ample room is

(See Camp, Page 7)

BIBLE CAMP ADVENTURELAND dining hall is now nearing completion. This will be the first completed building, to be followed by the bath house. Campers sleep in tents and this building at present. Cabins will be ready next year.
(Star-Exponent Photo)

1958 opens the first session of Camp Adventure Land. Almost 1,000 children attended last summer. Many facilities have been added since its opening--one being the big lake below.

The "Why" of Camp Adventure Land

Pastor Meares speaks about Camp Adventure Land

One of the great opportunities we have for the Lord and for His kingdom is among the children. It was through this conviction that Camp Adventure Land became a reality. In 1958 we began our first camp with very inadequate facilities, but since then the camp has been improved so that it will compare with any camp in this area. The beautiful woodland which surrounds the camp; the lovely lake that abounds with fish; the cabins; dining hall; all of these things are the physical requirements for any child to have a delightful time during the summer months. There is a program to give the proper physical exercises and activities that the child should have, but this is certainly not the main purpose of Camp Adventure Land.

The very first session of camp confirmed our faith that God would meet with us in this effort. There was such an overshadowing of the presence of God in the midst of these children that even though most of them came from homes that lacked any real knowledge of the Lord, they came to understand His nearness and reality.

JESUS LOVES CHILDREN

When I was a lad, to be a Christian meant that children could not live normal active lives, but were expected to be grown up adults while still a child. But at Camp Adventure Land it is proven that God loves the children. He delights in their times of joy, and God shows interest in being near and making Himself known to the child. While there is this overshadowing of God's presence at Camp Adventure Land, you will also see a gleam in the eye of everyone of these boys and girls running, playing, filled with jubilation and having the time of their lives. Certainly the invitation of the Lord Jesus Christ, "Suffer the little children to come unto me and forbid them not..." is an invitation as sincere and real as any the Lord ever set forth. It is in this invitation that the presence of the Lord is so very near.

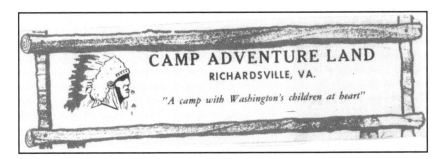

CAMP ADVENTURE LAND
RICHARDSVILLE, VA.
"A camp with Washington's children at heart"

5TH ANNIVERSARY OF C.A.L.

This summer will be the fifth session that camp has convened. Each year we have increased in both attendance and blessings. We believe God is going to meet with us this summer in a greater measure than in any previous camping session. There has been several thousand dollars spent in improving camp facilities, but more than this there has been far the greatest preparation made for the spiritual activities for this session. We will be having the best prepared counselors and workers that we have ever had. Each of these counselors are not only dedicated in their efforts toward the Lord, but are qualified to fulfill their place of responsibility in the many different activities of camp such as swimming, horseback riding, etc. We will have a spiritual qualified staff to instruct the children in the simple truths in the Word of God. Each counselor will be looking for the opportunity to reach the heart and soul of the individual throughout the activities of the day by giving personal witness of the grace of God.

C.A.L.-AN OPEN DOOR

Heretofore, approximately 90% of the children that were in camp were from homes that have no real knowledge of salvation. It would be impossible for us to reach these children in any other way. Therefore, this has given us an open door into hundreds of homes. Many have been the glowing accounts of 8 to 10 year old children who have come to know a warm, personal relationship of the Lord Jesus Christ and went home to tell their fathers and mothers about salvation. The scriptures declare that "a little child shall lead them" and Camp Adventure Land is doing its part to see this fulfilled.

Testimonies

God is so good, and I praise Him for His goodness and mercy toward me. I am grateful for His leading me to Evangel Temple. It has been almost nine years since I first entered the doors of the church, and when I did, I knew that this was the place that God wanted me to do service for Him. I am most grateful for the saints and the fellowship we have shared and it has become most precious to me. Being a part of Evangel Temple and being able to minister through music has been wonderful. It is a joy to render service unto the Lord and to know that He has seen fit to choose me to be one of the members in the Body of Christ in the unity of the Spirit. I pray that as I minister in music and songs that I will do it unto God and for His glory and honor and with the anointing of the Holy Spirit. For without His anointing all my efforts would be in vain.

Dorothy James
Washington, D C.

Note: Sis. James is the organist for the church, pianist for the choir, and part-time secretary in the church office. (Editor)

* * *

Carrie White

When Reverend Meares came to Washington six years ago I began to attend his services. Up to this time I thought I was saved, but after hearing the gospel preached in simplicity I found that I was not even saved. I gave my heart to the Lord down at Turner's Arena where the services were first held. I received the Holy Ghost when we worshiped at U Street. In the past six years I have missed one week of attending services because I was sick. The Lord made it possible for me to move just four doors from the church where I can go every night. I am 74 years old and love the Lord better every day I live.

Pastor Meares, I must tell you that it has been wonderful having you for the last eleven years as my pastor. And even though you have been firm, you have been so humble and full of love as you have preached nothing but the Word, which we all need. I am praying for you that you will be blessed with all that your heart so desires.

Carrie White
Washington, D.C.

≈ ≈ ≈

Giving Praise on Thanksgiving

—John L. Meares

Praise ye the Lord. Praise God in his sanctuary: praise him in the firmament of his power. Praise him for his mighty acts: praise him according to his excellent greatness. Praise him with the sound of the trumpet: praise him with the psaltery and harp. Praise him with the timbrel and dance: praise him with stringed instruments and organs. Praise him upon the loud cymbals: praise him upon the high sounding cymbals. Let every thing that hath breath praise the Lord. Praise ye the Lord. Psalm 150

The highest form of worship is praise and thanksgiving. There is a great deal concerning this in the Word of God. It is not the form or ritual—for many times this is lip service rather than true praise, but it is sincere thanksgiving that God finds delight in receiving from his children. Many people endeavor to live a good life, to give to the work of the Lord, and yet have never learned the true worship of praise and thanksgiving.

Through praise our hearts burst forth in gladness for God shares with us his joy as we delight ourselves in Him. Through praise, blessings of God are made available to us that cannot be ours in any other way. With praise we express faith and trust in God that cannot be expressed by any other manifestation. In fact praise makes it possible for God to work in our lives in a manner that He could not otherwise work. "Whoso offereth praise florifieth Me, and maketh a way whereby I can work." Psalm 50:23.

During this Thanksgiving season I trust yours will not be just another holiday, or the mere entertaining friends with a lovely meal, but you will find in your hearts a true gratitude toward God, and if to God then toward your fellowman. It is only through this manner of praise from our innermost being that our hearts and lives are enlarged and the Spirit of God can make entrance to direct us in the path that He would have us to follow.

The Prince of Peace   —John L. Meares

As Christmas approaches we find mankind gripped with a fear for what might come at any time. Our nation wants peace, yet it seems the harder we seek to find it, the farther we are from it. We desire to live peaceably with other nations, but our desire finds no answer and we know not what move to make next in order for the peoples of this world to live together in peace.

Almost two thousand years ago the Prince of Peace was born into a world that was also gripped with fear. The Jews feared the strong rule of the Romans and the power that they exercised. They were looking for their Messiah, and yet when He came they did not recognize Him. How could a baby born in such a lowly place as a cow stall be a Prince of Peace and one who could free them? Only a few shepherds out on the Judean hills realized that the Christ child was the Promised One. Also the wise men from the east knew within their hearts that He was the One born to be their Saviour—One worthy of their best gifts. But the world at large would not accept Him, and neither does the world today sincerely within their heart accept the Saviour. They do not understand that He is the only answer to lasting peace. He who is the Prince of Peace is the only one who can give peace to either a nation or that lost, perturbed individual who knows not which way to turn. People are too busy living, trying within themselves and their own power to solve their problems, to recognize the Prince of Peace.

There will never be a day here on this earth that every nation will choose to serve Christ and let Him be their leader. Thus, we can never expect to live peaceably with all nations. But whether or not a nation so chooses, you and I can choose the Prince of Peace to rule our lives and receive a peace within our hearts. We can say,

"Lord, there is room for you always in my life." He gives a peace that passeth all understanding—a peace that the world cannot give.

When you possess this peace, then you are able to help others. No doubt some of you will not be able to give gifts of great monetary value this Christmas, but me thinks there is something greater you can give. Have you thought about giving a smile to a tired store clerk, or a "thank you" to the stranger? What about the person who is alone this Christmas. Could you drop by and say "hello" or perhaps read the Christmas story to them? Can we not give without always expecting a gift in return? We can honor the Christ child by giving out His love, His peace, and His understanding to others. During these special days of the year, give the Prince of Peace to the people who surround you. You will have a happier and a more"meaningful Christmas if you will. Your peace will increase as you share it with others.

≈ ≈ ≈

Letters to the Pastor

For twenty years I have been drinking and because of this habit I have lost many opportunities for good steady employment. Each day I would tell myself that I would stop the next day, but I found myself so bound I couldn't stop.

I began attending services at Evangel Temple about two years ago and asked Rev. Meares and the congregation to pray that I might be delivered from this habit that had me so bound. But I was constantly back at the old habit. Finally I became so ashamed of myself until I couldn't ask for prayer anymore. I just had no will power to refuse a drink, and I thought my case hopeless.

One afternoon after drinking heavily for two days, I sat down and observed some of my friend's conversation and actions. As I watched I became so disgusted with it all until I really became depressed. Then I thought again about Evangel Temple and something seemed to compel me to get up and catch a bus and go to church. Although

I was" intoxicated, it seemed as if some strange force was carrying me there.

It is hard to explain in words the exact feeling I had when I entered the church. It seemed as if my prayers, the minister's and congregation's prayers were all combined into one big prayer. When I came to myself, I felt as if someone had lifted a ton of steel off me. I was so happy and contented. Now I know I will never take another drink again for the desire is all gone. This will be my best Christmas in many years for I will not be drunk on wine wherein is excess, but drunk on the Spirit of God. The days since my deliverance have been the best days I can recall for so very long. For this may God be praised!

Charles Stroman
Washington, D.C.

* * *

Some months past, I went to Brother Meares on a Sunday night for prayer. I was suffering from a chronic case of hemorrhoids which I had had for more than 30 years. When he touched my forehead, I felt the power go all through me. He said, "That's enough power to heal anything." I staggered away and the ushers helped me back to my seat. I came home still suffering and all the next day I was no better. By the time I came home from work, I was seemingly worse than ever. I was hurting worse all the time, and I just couldn't help from crying. Finally when I felt I couldn't stand anymore pain, I just laid down and soon fell asleep. When I awoke the next morning I was perfectly well-all swelling and pain was gone. The Lord had completely healed me and for these many months I have had no more attacks. It is wonderful to know I am well this Christmas.

Annie Deaton
Washington, D.C.

≈ ≈ ≈

Earthen Vessel   —Mary L. Meares

II Cor. 4:6-7 "For God, who commanded the light to shine out of darkness, hath shined in our hearts, to give the light of the knowledge of the glory of God in the face of Jesus Christ. But we have this treasure in earthen vessels, that the excellency of the power may be of God, and not of us."

An earthen vessel today is a thing rarely used, for we have plastic bags, cardboard cartons, bottles, etc. to take care of things we need to store. However, back in your mother's time an old earthen crock was a useful vessel. There was not a great deal of value attached to it for it was made out of clay—clay that could be gathered right out of the hills somewhere. But when it was molded and properly tempered the crock became a vessel of service. Perhaps, some of you can remember how the butter was put in an earthen crock and put down in the spring. It was never used particularly for a thing of ornament or a thing of beauty. Generally it was just a dull ivory or maybe a brown color.

In Biblical days the earthen vessel was not of monetary value but was a vessel of service. However, if it had a crack in it, it could not be used and was of no value whatsoever. It was of no service unless something could be put in it. It was made to hold things; made to put things in, not to be empty. And what was put in it determined the value of the earthen vessel.

Second Corinthians says the treasure (the gospel) is put in these mere earthen vessels of ours. Can you see the contrast of this glorious, wondrous, and excellent treasure being put into our worthless vessels? Our vessels are useless until this treasure is placed within. But when God comes and cleanses us and places this glorious gospel within our hearts then we become valuable—we can render service. As long as we are empty vessels we can be of no service to anyone.

Does not the scriptures say we are made of the dust of the earth and to the dust we shall return? Our earthly vessels are just clay, weak, mortal flesh, but when we will let God take us and mold us into a vessel of service for His kingdom, then and only then, can the light of the glorious gospel shine through us and be a blessing to others.

Do not be an empty vessel, but let God fill your life with the things of God. Let your life be filled with joy, peace, and love and you cannot help but be of great value to the one that made you.

A New Experience   —Willie Mae Castle

I was at Turner's Arena the Sunday morning that Pastor Meares opened or began the Washington Revival Center in 1955. The service was wonderful. I had never seen anything like it before. I was a Baptist and well contented, so I thought. I was not in the habit of visiting other churches, but somehow I did this Sunday. And something got hold of my heart. I even stayed for the Sunday afternoon service and then the service that night. I knew nothing of Pentecost or the Holy Spirit. It was all strange to me. The next day and the entire week found me at Turner's Arena. The Lord blessed in such a wonderful way, and besides people being saved in every service, there were miracles and wonderful healings. I was thrilled beyond words at the moving of God's Spirit.

One night Pastor Meares called for those who had habits and wanted to be delivered to stand up. I was smoking two packages of cigarettes a day and was a nervous wreck. He prayed for me and I was delivered immediately and completely. I have never wanted a cigarette from that time until now. I knew now that what I had seen and felt was real. God continued to deal with my heart and a few nights later when the altar call was given I went forward. I didn't go to receive the Holy Ghost, but before I left that night I had this wonderful experience. I was beside myself. All through the night, in my sleep, at work, everywhere I went, I was speaking in tongues. I could not speak unless it was in tongues. During all this time, I kept thinking I must go back to my church, but a whole year passed by and I had not gone back. Then I was ashamed to go back, and perhaps I would not feel comfortable there anyway so I just stayed at the Center. God was leading me, but I did not realize it. But I did know I was happy as I could be. My cares all left me and I felt so free inside. Then the services were moved to You Street and God made Himself even more real to me. I was healed of a heart condition.

I do thank God for sending Pastor Meares to Washington. Since his coming my life has been completely changed. I have learned what it means to have love for my neighbor, even those that don't love me. I attended Rev. Harold Jackson's Bible classes which were so very helpful. I learned to study the Word and learn about God's laws.

(Note): Willie Mae is a faithful usher at church and one that can be depended upon at all times.

Chapter 4—1962

That I May Love God — Mary Lee Meares

Have you ever looked at a person and his face shone so until you thought, "My, that person must really love the Lord"? And that was exactly right. He just really loved God. There is something about loving God that will cause our countenance to glow and people will see Jesus through us.

Many people-made new year resolutions, both Christian and sinner alike. The sinner perhaps resolved to live a better life, and the Christian no doubt determined to be a better Christian, and said, "I want to pray more, read my Bible more, and be a better witness for the Lord." This is good, but you know what my resolution is for '62—just love Jesus more. Sometimes I wonder if we love God as much as we think and say we do? Does He really have first place in our heart? Is He really our first love? When one stops and thinks of all God does for him, it shouldn't be hard to love God more than anyone or anything else on earth, but does God really believe us when we tell Him we love Him above all others? When we let the pressing duties of the day, no matter how necessary and legitimate they may be, crowd out our communion and making love to God—when we let even the church duties crowd out that intimate closeness that comes only when one takes time out just to love Jesus, does Jesus believe we really enjoy His presence and His fellowship?

Oft times my children say, "Mother, come play this game with us, or do this or that with me," and many times I'd say, "Oh, I am too busy right now, later I will." Usually later never comes. I do not feel bad in that I do not neglect my children's needs in the way of clothing and feeding them, etc., but sometimes I do feel bad in that I do not show them my love by taking out time to just be with them and share with them their joys, sorrows, and secrets. You remember how Martha was so busy working when the Master came to visit their home, but Mary only wanted to sit at the feet of Jesus and talk to Him and learn more about Him. Jesus said, "Mary hath chosen the good part." Both Mary and Martha loved Jesus, but Mary's way was more acceptable. Like Mary I just want to learn more about Jesus.

The Resurrection   —Mary Lee Meares

The dominant note of Easter is hope. It is a festival of rejoicing as Good Friday is a day of sadness and sorrow. Earth's saddest and gladdest days are only a day apart. For the followers of Jesus, and especially His disciples, it seemed that the death of Jesus brought the end to all their hopes. They had expected to see their Master ascend a throne, relieve them from the Roman rule and bondage, but instead they saw Him nailed to a cross. They watched from afar the horrors of the crucifixion. From all appearances there was not even a gleam of hope. This looked like the end. Evil had proven stronger than good; hate had defeated love; wrong had vanquished right. One of the twelve had hanged himself; Peter had cursed and denied that he had ever known the Lord. They had all forsaken Him in His last crucial moments and fled for fear. With the huge stone against the mouth of the sepulcher, it seemed to forever seal not only their Master within, but the hope of His kingdom being established. The spiritual truths that Christ had tried to teach them in the three short years seemed to fade into oblivion, and they could only think in terms of the natural.

Fellowship News

Vol. 3	April 1962	No. 4

However, their despondent and hopeless situation soon changed from despair to one of great joy-the greatest they had ever known. Early one morning, before daybreak, a group of devoted women who came to the tomb to show their love for their Lord, found the tomb empty! An angel of the Lord greeted them with the words, "The Lord is risen from the dead!" The news spread like wildfire throughout all Jerusalem. The Crucified had become the Victor, their Friend on earth was now the sovereign Lord of Heaven. A living Flame had burst from the tomb.

It is said that on Easter Eve a strange event occurs at the Church of the Holy Sepulchre in Jerusalem. Hundreds of people sleep on Good Friday night in the church, and thousands more mill for hours in the neighboring streets. They wait for fire to break from the tomb of Christ. They have been told that the fire is symbolic, but they believe it comes from heaven. When the flame leaps, and the priests light their torches, the crowd presses forward to light their candles from the sacred flame — to light a lamp at the fire of Christ's triumph.

When Christ appeared to His disciples, He said, "Peace be with you." They had heard their Master speak these words before, but now they held a new meaning to them. Their doubts as to His really being their Messiah had vanished. Peter no longer would try to lie his way out of danger. The resurrection of Jesus Christ had so resurrected their faith until they were now ready to go forth and tell the world of their living Saviour. They would count it a joy to be worthy to suffer for Him who gave His life for them.

As Jesus left His disciples the next time, He did not leave a group of fearful and despondent people with no hope for the future. They believed His words, *"Because I live, ye shall live also."* John 14:19.

To the child of God, the Resurrection is more than a hope — it is an assurance. With the Apostle Paul we can say, "In this life Christ lives with me; after death I live with Him. I am not afraid either to live or to die."

SCHEDULE OF SERVICES EASTER SUNDAY

SUNRISE PLAY 7:00 A.M.

DARKNESS BEFORE DAWN

MARCH 26—7:00 A.M.

(1-Hour Play in Three Acts)

You will not want to miss this heart warming play portraying the resurrection of Jesus. Peter could not forgive himself for denying his Lord, but Jesus forgave him. And as the title suggests, darkness always comes before dawn.

CHARACTERS

PETER .... ROBERT MATTHEWS
JOHN .... CARL GAYMON
ANDREW .... BEN NORTHINGTON
JUDAS .... JOHN GRAY
MARY .... DOROTHY JAMES
MARY MAGDALENE .... LENA PATTON
ANTHONY (ROMAN SOLDIER) .... NATHANIEL JAMES
MARCUS (ROMAN SOLDIER) .... DENNIS FITCH
ANGEL .... JAMES DOLFORD

BIBLE ADVENTURE LAND—10:00 A.M.—A gift for each child present. Last year there were over 1000 children.

MORNING WORSHIP   11:30 A.M.   EASTER MESSAGE,
                                                                   PASTOR MEARES

AFTERNOON SERVICE   3:30 P. M.

EVENING SERVICE   8:00 P. M.

∼ ∼ ∼

Letters to the Pastor

Greetings in the name of our Lord. I have received some good reports about the services, and am always glad to hear how the Lord is moving by His Spirit. I really do miss the services there. I have wished many times that I could be back and be in just one service.

I am getting along fine so far. The Lord has been by my side all the way and really helped me in everything I have done. I have joined the chapel choir and it has been a blessing to me. The singing we do is nothing compared to the choir there.

Lorraine and I are getting married on July 30, during my leave, and would like very much for you to perform the ceremony.

Enclosed are my tithes. Give the church my love and have them pray for me.

Willie Perrin
Fort Jackson, S. C.

* * *

(Note): Brother Perrin is one of the fine young men of Evangel Temple that is now serving in the army in Fort Jackson, S. C. He has been a faithful member for a number of years and lets his light for the Lord shine whever he might be.

God has blessed me beyond measure for which I am most grateful. Before I began to tithe I was in so much debt, I was afraid to look at people. It seemed I owed everybody. For a whole year I could not even pay a little bill of seven dollars. Since I started tithing seven years ago, I have paid every bill (on time). I have made good money, and now after working for forty-three years I am retiring next month. I thank God that I don't owe anyone and God has blessed me abundantly.

Henry Kelley

* * *

Thirty-eight years ago I was hospitalized and learned that I had diabetes. At the time, I was not saved, but attended a church that did not teach divine healing so I knew nothing of the power of God to heal. As others in my family had diabetes, I too, calmly accepted it. For three years I kept this illness under control by following a very strenuous diet. However my condition finally grew worse, and the doctor kept me on insulin for eighteen years.

By this time God had saved me. Later I began attending Evangel Temple, and here I found just what my soul was crying out for as I listened to Reverend Meares preach. After attending services for several weeks, I decided to have Pastor Meares pray for me. He prayed a simple prayer and God healed me. This happened ten years ago, and I have not had any trace of diabetes since. *Sender Unknown*

Recently my eight year old son, while on the school grounds, was hit with a stone. He was semi-conscious and they brought him home almost covered with blood. I did not take him to the doctor until two days later and the doctor told me that in my waiting to bring him, I had played with fire. The injury was so close to the brain until the child could have died. The eye was closed and swollen and he was suffering great pain. Then shortly before we went to the eye specialist the next day, I called Pastor Meares and he prayed for my son's healing. He said, "the work is done." The specialist confirmed it when he examined his eye. He said, "there is nothing wrong with this child's eye, where did you take him?" He was able to go to school the next day, and suffered no pain or discomfort. *Sender Unknown*

God Moved In South Africa —John Meares

Several miracles of travel were wrought before we reached South Africa, both in relationship to our flights, which would have delayed our having made our speaking appointments, and another miracle that would have prevented us from being granted entrance into the country of South Africa. We left without visas, with orders to pick them up in Paris. However, the South African chancery in Parish had not heard anything about them. Although they advised us not to fly to South Africa unless we had our visas in hand. However, we took the next flight to South Africa and believed God for the results, in spite of the fact that we had made a determined effort for more than two months to secure the visas. Arriving in Johannesburg, we were the last in line at customs. When our turn came, we simply stated that we had arrived without visas and wanted entrance to the country. The officer went and talked to the superior custom officer and came back smiling, saying, "Everything is all right."

We were in the great con-vention that Rev. Bhengu holds annually in East Lon-don on the east coast of Africa which is 750 miles from Johannesburg. The church is one of the largest of the many churches which has been raised up through the ministry of Rev. Bhengu. It seats over 3000 people. However, during  the convention it was packed with 4000 or more. This church is built on what is called "The Location." Here the native people are designated living quarters by the government. There were those who had come by truck and bus from many other churches in South Africa. Each delegation had a trained choir. Their singing was most unusual, and an experience never to be forgotten. The choirs would sing in two or three languages, including English. There was not a musical instrument in the church, but it was never missed. They sang in perfect harmony. There was not even the clapping of hands until Bro. Petrucelli taught them the chorus, "Jesus is the Light." The singing would rise as a great volume of praise unto God. I am certain that the angelic choir became silent and listened to these melodies of praise.

There were three services a day. The anointing of the Lord was greatly on this convention. Bro. Petrucelli and I preached in two of the services a day. The enthusiasm and spiritual hunger of the people was contagious. After the convention was over, Bro. Bhengu said that many school teachers and professional people came to him with tears in their eyes and said they wanted to quit their professions and go out and preach the gospel to lost souls. He said it was the greatest convention they had ever had. There are many well qualified, educated, and spiritual workers who are ready to work for God in South Africa. However, because of many conditions some means of support is essential. To begin with, as they go into the cities and villages that have not yet been evangelized. Nevertheless, their burden, with Bro. Bhengu, is to reach not only South Africa, but the whole of Africa with the gospel of Jesus Christ. No longer is the burden to evangelize Africa in the hearts of only a few western missionaries, but in the hearts of these native Christians. Had they the tools and the finances available to them as is to us, they would complete the evangelism of that great continent.

From the convention, we traveled back to Johannesburg where Rev. Bhengu had set up a large gospel tent that seated between 1500 to 2000 people. This was on a native location of about 500,000 people. The very first night the tent was filled and each night thereafter it was packed to capacity with people standing around the outside. During these services I became tremendously aware that the "gospel is the power of God unto salvation." Each night we preached a most simple message from the Word and the Holy Spirit brought conviction in great power. When the people were asked to express their desire for Christ, two-thirds of the people responded. Rev. Bhengu had about 100 of his workers in each of the services. It was utterly impossible to deal with each one. Nevertheless, the Holy Spirit did a perfect work and multitudes were saved. Here at Evangel Temple we had asked God for at least 1000 Converts. It was reported to me that in the afternoon convert classes conducted by Rev. Bhengu and his ministers that 1800 came to receive further teaching. For this we greatly thank God.

Miracles of healing were wrought in a most unusual way in every way. There were no prayer lines formed—only a mass prayer for all who wanted healing. Many cripples were brought to the services.

Some were bed-ridden and completely unable to walk. God raised them up. Paralytics began to walk and run. Blind people received their sight and many deaf and dumb were healed. When the people received their healing out in the audience, they came to the platform to give their testimony of God's healing power. In no service were we able to hear all of the testimonies of the greatness of God's healing power. "The gospel is the power of God unto salvation."

Editorial   —Mary Lee Meares

"Remember now thy Creator (the Lord) in the days of thy youth." This is the best advice that could possibly be given any child or teen-ager. Our character is formed in our youth; our goals are often set and ambitions and desires are created within us.

How many of us have been guilty, when we saw a child coming to the altar for salvation, say in our heart, "Oh, they are just a child." God forgive us. Just the other day my mother wrote me a letter and was telling me how she used to watch my sister and me play church as little girls. And that desire that was created in my heart for the things of God as a child has followed me up to this present time. The influence of church and the things of God are so very, very important in a young life.

I feel that one of our most important outreaches at Evangel Temple are the children. Why do we lease 8 city busses each Sunday morning and crowd them with children? Because we know the time to reach them for the Lord is while they are yet children. Why do we burden ourselves with the extra load of a summer camp and take on the responsibility of hundreds of children? Because we feel it is indeed a duty of ours to let these boys and girls know that the Lord loves them and wants to be their friend and companion throughout life.

This will be the sixth summer for Camp Adventure Land, and we are looking forward to the best and most profitable season of camp yet. These 200 acres of ground were dedicated to God in the very beginning and we know God is pleased with the time and effort and money that we use to help the children in this our day. It is not only my responsibility to see that my own children are taught the ways of the Lord, but that other children, whose parents may not care, might also know and remember their Creator in the days of their youth.

Camp Time

In just a few more days, the breakfast bell at Camp Adventure Land will be ringing and hundreds of boys and girls will be rushing to the dining hall for a hearty breakfast and then a day of fun, relaxation and learning about the Lord. This will mark our sixth season and the emphasis this summer will be the spiritual need of each individual.

How God has blessed me since 1958 when Dave Wilkerson first introduced me to Jesus Christ. Since then I have traveled around the world speaking in high school assemblies, churches, city auditoriums and the like. We have a Center established to house boys in trouble from off the streets in Los Angeles. Now God is making it possible to purchase a school near Fresno, California for the further training of the boys that come through our center.

NICKY CRUZ

Former Leader of the Violent Mau Maus,

A New York City Gang,

Which Indulged in Sex, Dope, and Brutality,

Will Be The

GUEST SPEAKER

FEB. 18 at EVANGEL TEMPLE

He will be speaking at 3:30 in the afternoon and also at the 8 o'clock evening service.

He is well qualified to speak with authority about today's dissatisfied. lawless young people who are experimenting with disaster.

REMEMBER — FEBRUARY 18th

≈ ≈ ≈

A Sacrifice of Praise — Mary Lee Meares

The other day I was reading Hebrews 13:15 which reads: "By him therefore let us offer the sacrifice of praise to God continually, that is the fruit of our lips giving thanks to his name." As I read, my eyes fastened on the word *sacrifice*. Just what did a sacrifice of praise mean?

It is a daily custom in my life to praise God for the abundant blessings He has bestowed upon me and my family. It is easy and natural for me to raise my hands during a service just because I love and praise my God. I do not think of sitting down and eating a good meal without first giving thanks to God for having supplied it and given it to me to enjoy. When I stop and begin to think of the many, many times God has answered my prayers, I utter a thanks in my heart. I have found a worship in my praising God, and it is easy to praise God for He has been good to me as long as I can remember. As the scripture says, "God inhabits the praise of His children."

But when I read the scripture admonishing us to offer the sacrifice of praise, I said, "Is praise a sacrifice?" Is something easy to do a sacrifice? Or are there times in our lives when praise is a sacrifice? Certainly, it is an easy thing to praise God when everything is going right for us and we feel God's presence with us, and we see His bountiful hand bestowing blessings upon us. But what about the times when we seemingly can't feel God's presence—when a praise isn't on the end of our tongue, when it would be easier to complain than to praise God. You can, no doubt, think of times when Satan has come and planted distasteful thoughts in your mind. You have had times when it seemed there was no answer to your problems.

Even though we are Christians, we are not exempt from the trials and heartaches that come to every human being in this life. Are we to give praise to God in these times? The scripture says to offer a praise continually, which means always, which would include the bad as well as the good things of life. So it dawned upon me when one could look up in adverse circumstances and praise God in spite of these situations, that was a *sacrifice* of praise. You hear people say, "The Lord will bless you for giving a sacrificial offering." We understand this to be an offering that we really don't have to give, but we give it anyway. We give it because we love God and want to give it. We always receive a greater blessing when we have sacrificed to give of our means, or of our time to God. So could not this sacrifice of praise just as well mean to give thanks to God when in the natural it is hard to do—when you actually don't feel like it. Yes, anyone can praise God when everything is going good, but can you praise Him when things are going just opposite from what you would like them to do, and when there seems to be no hope?

No, it does not mean that you are thankful for the trials or your circumstances you are in, but you are thankful that God has not left you in your hour of need. He has given you precious promises to stand upon in your time of trouble. Amidst all of these things, you can still have a peace within—a peace that the world does not understand how we can have. No matter what comes, you can still praise God that your sins are under the blood and you are a child of God. You can still praise God that eternal life is yours. You can still praise Him that He will not allow you to be tempted above that you are able to stand, but with the temptation make a way of escape. On and on we could go with things to praise God for, no matter what the situation for the moment might be.

And so it is as we praise Him in times like these, there comes a joy and peace from our *sacrifice* of praise that we could not know otherwise. We don't wait until the victory is won to offer praise, but before it is won. I believe this is when God is well pleased as the 16th verse of Hebrews says. If a praise is to come from our lips continually, it will have to include the obstacles as well as the blessings of life. May we as children of God learn more about offering the sacrifice of praise to our heavenly Father.

The Ungodly Are Not So   —John L. Meares

The ungodly are not so; but are like the chaff which the wind driveth away. Psalms 1:4. This verse of scripture refers to those who sin openly and wilfully, and to those who are scornful. But also the ungodly are those who do not include God in all of their thoughts, acts and deeds. For as a godly man considers God in all that he does, the ungodly man leaves God out of certain areas of his life. This is the great failing of so-called Christianity today. Many have divided their life up and religiously given God a portion, but the truly godly person includes God in all of his life. Therefore, there are many who attend church regularly and who may even be involved in church activities, but are ungodly from the standpoint that God is not given their complete life—their work, recreation, and even their rest. A godly person is one who meditates in the law of the Lord day and night. Even his sleep may be filled with the songs of the night that the Lord giveth. So according to the psalmist, one's whole life must center around the Lord Jesus Christ if he is to be numbered among the godly who meditate in his teachings both day and night.

God's planted tree is always fruitful, bringing forth His fruit in his season. But not so with the ungodly. Jesus said, "You have not chosen me but I have chosen you and ordained you, that you should go and bring forth fruit, and that your fruit should remain..." The Lord's planted tree never has leaves that wither, for the special care of God is an abundant supply. The ungodly are not so.

And whatever he doeth shall prosper. For the steps of a good man are ordered of God. The ungodly are not so.

It must be emphasized that the special, abundant blessings of God to the godly, which the ungodly do not enjoy, is His presence. Not in the distant future, or after this life, but the godly enjoy the special providence of God here and now. The ungodly are not so. The ungodly are compared to the chaff. The chaff is so unstable and so worthless. It must be separated from the wheat, for it has no value whatsoever. God is interested only in the kernel of the wheat, and insists that the chaff be separated from it. This is the awful comparison that God makes to the ungodly. They are like the chaff which is driven away by the wind. The association of the chaff to the wheat is so very close until it could almost be said that the grain of wheat is born in the enclosure of the chaff. Yet God insists that it be separated from the grain. Various helpers in many forms of Christian work sit side by side with the godly—so very close to the grain and yet are only chaff. It takes only the gentleness of a summer breeze to drive away the chaff. And to where is it driven? Jesus Christ said he would burn up the chaff with unquenchable fire. What a sobering thought that we may be very religious and still neglect the Lord, and be numbered with the ungodly like the chaff which is driven away by the wind. Or you may be one of those who are numbered with the godly—one who meditates in the law of the Lord day and night. Which do you choose?

Notes of Praise

Dear Reverend Meares:

You have been wonderful to us to send us your Fellowship News for such a long time. My son and I enjoy reading it, for the news there means a lot to us. We go to the Woodlawn Baptist church near Fort Belvoir each Sunday where we are members. I want to send you a dollar a month for your work there. I know it is not much, but God can bless it for His cause. God bless you as you work for Him.

Mrs. Joseph E. O'Conor

Lorton, Virginia

* * *

Brother Meares, I shall never forget the wonderful sermon that you preached on the radio Monday, October 7, 1963. You preached about the man who did not forgive his servant, after he himself had been forgiven. You also spoke that many people were anxious and worried because they did not have a forgiving spirit. I am so glad I tuned in that morning, for truly I received just what I had been needing. I had been bearing with someone for many years and it was such a burden to me, because I did not have a forgiving spirit. You said, "someone listening has this unforgiving spirit." This was me, but through the grace of God He has given me a spirit of forgiveness. Thank you very much.

A listener

* * *

Dear Pastor Meares:

When I arrived home from work today I found the "Fellowship News" in my mail box. I always read it within the hour that I receive it, but even more so today. I just couldn't wait to get my jacket hung up and begin reading it. Today it seemed I found an answer to my problems as I read it. I am enclosing my tithes, and am believing God will solve my personal problems and needs. All I ask is that God will walk with me and help me to help others.

Dorothy Jackson

Washington, D.C.

* * *

I began visiting your church when you were on You Street and was so happy when you bought the building you are now in. I have been a constant visitor since, because I love the services. I love Brother Petrucelli's praise service, and then Sister Meares song before your preaching and then your sermons. It thrills me and every thing is so plain. We have something to carry us all through the next week.

I am 85 years old and have very little income, but I want to do my part in giving to God's work. I pray God to continue to bless you and the work at Evangel Temple.

Sarah Smith
Washington, D.C.

Article   —Robert Matthews

"Not by might, not by power, but by my spirit sayeth the Lord." I really saw these words come to pass as I went out to work in the evangelistic field. It started with my first revival in Luray, Virginia. My wife and I feasted and prayed for the saints to be encouraged and revived in the Lord, for doors to be opened, and for souls to be saved. We saw these results come to pass, not only in Luray, but in the revivals that followed in a five month's period.

Several wonderful things happened in our revival in Lexington, Virginia, which helped to open other doors for me. We were scheduled to hold outdoor meetings and night services for one week in Lexington, but on the Sunday the meeting was to close two or three hundred people gathered in the outdoor meeting. I was over-joyed and asked the people if they would like for us to continue the revival another week. Many hands were raised and we decided to extend the meeting. This very Sunday night twenty-five came to the altar and were saved. It was in this meeting also that God delivered an alcoholic lady. She would attend our outdoor meetings in the day time, but did not have the courage to come to the night services. However, she finally gained this courage and came and God wonderfully saved her. Two months later in one of our revival meetings in Waynesboro, Virginia, she was filled with the Holy Ghost.

I was impressed to set up an open-air meeting in Harriston, Virginia. Heretofore, my meetings had been sponsored by other churches, but in this one I was solely on my own. We had to start from scratch, without any materials, only $25.00 and two sisters from the Waynesboro area. The plywood needed to build the platform was given to us by a Mennonite who expressed interest in the work we were doing for the Lord. The microphone was supplied by the minister of the Lexington church and a piano was donated by another sister. Our chairs were furnished by the Dupont Chemical Company; the pulpit was supplied so everything we needed was ours. Praise the Lord! Some men put up a canvas over the speaker's platform to protect us from the rain.

On the first night of the revival only one person showed up at the beginning of the service. We sang a long time in which twenty or so came out. But during the week the audience grew until one week later every seat was filled and people standing around the grounds and sitting in their cars listening to the services. During the revival a little boy was brought by his grandmother to be prayed for. His legs were weak and crippled. As a result of prayer his legs began to grow stronger. When the grandmother saw how God had blessed the child, she came forth to give her heart to God.

I was in eleven revivals during the five months' period. I give the praise and glory to God for all that was accomplished. I have personally come to know that God works, "Not by might, nor by power, but by my spirit…"

Letters to the Pastor

As I was reading in the Fellowship News about the work you are doing in Missions in spreading God's Word, I was thinking, and said to myself, "I am going to send something to Reverend Meares to help in this work." At the same time, I received a letter concerning missions — the thing I was thinking about. So enclosed is my pledge or Fatih-Promise for $5.00 a month. It makes me feel wonderful to have a part in such a great cause.

Mildren McLean
4525 S. 37th St.
Richmond, Va.

* * *

Dear Bro. Meares:

I am writing to let you know we have been listening to your program on TV and they are a great blessing to us.

I have told my neighbors to watch next Sunday and they are looking forward to seeing your program. I was 80 years old last September, and am still happy in the Lord.

Mattie Edwards
Harpers Ferry,
West Virginia

* * *

Pastor Meares:

I have been a Fellowship member of your church for about three Sundays. I was saved there on July 14, 1963. It seemed that a still small voice said, "open your heart's door and let me come in." Then on September 8, I went to the prayer room and received the baptism of the Holy Spirit. I enjoyed your sermon so very much this Sunday morning on Isaac and Ishmael.

Paulette Duncan
Washington, D.C.

* * *

I do enjoy your weekly broadcast so very much. I know your ministry has the anointing of God upon it, for I can feel it. I will be 82 years old in December. I love God and feel so close to Him each day. Am sending you a little donation to be used for God's glory.

A servant of God
John Hutchins, Prince
Frederick, Md.

The Ministry of Radio   —Mary Lee Meares

Not long ago one lady wrote in and said, "The best part of my day is the fifteen minutes of the "Living Word" broadcast." A real child of God never tires of hearing the Word, but there is a constant hungering for more. It is Spirit and it is Life!

Very few countries are blessed with gospel radio programs as is these United States. In some countries it is next to impossible to have a radio program and tell the people what God can do for them. How long we will continue to have this freedom and opportunity I do not know. No longer can the Bible be read in schools or prayer offered. But thank God we still have the privilege of being on radio. I believe the radio ministry is vital in these last days. Hearts are troubled. Homes are broken. Boys are on foreign soil fighting. People are sick both in soul and body. The youth are rebelling against society. Dope and narcotics abound. Sex is no longer a sacred thing. And on and on we could numerate the wrongs of our day. People are searching and looking for an answer. If they will only hear and heed the gospel, they will find this answer.

Radio plays a part in spreading the gospel that the church cannot play. By-in-large it is the Christians that go to church and feed and grow upon the Word of God and the fellowshiping of the saints. But how many times does a person accidentally, and yet it is no accident, tune in to their radio while driving in their car, or while washing the dishes, and they hear a gospel program and something begins to stir within them, and they feel a need in their life. They begin to have hope for the problem they are trying to cope with. Or they feel faith rise in their heart as the Word is preached by God's servant. Life begins to take on a new meaning. They had perhaps not put forth the effort to find a church and there let God help them through the minister, but now they have turned on their radio and no matter if it is a Baptist minister, Lutheran or a Pentecostal, they are not thinking of a *preacher*, but now they are listening to someone tell them what Jesus can do for them. They don't see a church, but they see what Jesus can do for them. Even a Jew will many times, in the privacy of his home, listen to a Christian radio broadcast. And how much more, in light of recent world developments concerning Israel, will they be listening to learn more about the Messiah. There are many people that do not go to church, but they will listen to the radio. And then as the Word is preached under the anointing of the Holy Spirit, his spirit is arrested and he becomes interested in the things of God.

I remember as a young girl, I travelled with two other girls as a trio. We sang and went to different churches to minister in song. We were at Chattanooga, Tennessee in a revival and each morning we sang on the radio broadcast for the pastor of this particular church. One night there was a gentleman who came to our service and he said, "I am a dentist, and this morning while in my office I tuned in to your radio program. While you were singing I fell on my knees and the Lord came into my life." One never knows what is being done through the means of radio. Most of us, even though we enjoy a message or song we hear over the air, we never take the time to sit down and write to that person and tell them so. I believe that in these last days before the return of our Lord that radio is going to play a very important part in the spreading of the gospel.

Letters to the Pastor

This is to express my thankfulness for your radio ministry and for your love for all races. Some years ago you led a young Hebrew man to the saving knowledge of the Messiah. He told me of your patience and love for his soul.

Sarah Croswell
Fairfax, Va.

* * *

I am a regular listener to your program and find your sermons most inspiring. Please send me the book you wrote, "Faith Cometh by the Word."

Mamie Hill
Wash. D.C.

* * *

I am a stranger to you, but not to God. I was in service at the Temple the latter part of August and oh what a glorious time! I don't know when I have enjoyed being in the presence of such a devout and warm body of disciples of Christ. We were met at the door in such a warm christian manner. I was so much inspired and want to come again soon.

Rosa Evans
Arlington, Va.

~ ~ ~

Texas Evangelist Speaks of Evangel Temple —G. B. McDowell

Readers and members and friends of Evangel Temple: I have just closed my third revival for Rev. and Mrs. John Meares. My revivals have taken me in all 50 states many times and into Canada and abroad. But in all of my travels, I have never been in a church that was doing any more for the furthering of the Kingdom of God than is Evangel Temple in Washington, D.C. Not only does this church have the city of Washington at heart, but they help in many parts of the world to spread the Gospel. A few months ago Bro. Meares heard that I was going to Okinawa to minister to our thousands of servicemen before they went to Viet Nam. He wrote and said his church wanted to have a part in sending me to Okinawa for a great revival.

I only wish as I travel across America, I could set some of our many churches who have lost the vision down in Evangel Temple and let this congregation inspire them to work for God as they have inspired me. This is a church holding out for the faith that was once delivered to the saints. If you readers of this magazine who live outside of Washington ever go there, you owe it to yourself to go hear Reverend Meares preach and to also hear his wonderful choir. They bring heaven down to the people and you feel as though you will be lifted off your feet.

God bless you Pastor Meares and your church. Please have me back again.

Editorial

—Mary Lee Meares

The song says, "It is joy. unspeakable when I look and see what the Lord has done for me." That is not only true for the year of 1962 that is now history, but that is my testimony as far back as I can remember. Sometimes I look at those around me and wonder why it is that they, even though good Christians, seem to have so many trials and heartaches, while I have so many blessings to come my way and literally "the windows of heaven are opened." Is it because one person lives better than the other? I don't think so. I think our attitude and our faith or expectancy has to do with what comes our way. I once read of a group of people who wrote letters to themselves on New Year's Eve and instead of writing a lot of New Year resolutions and good intentions, they wrote what they expected to happen to them in the new year. Then at the close of the year they opened those letters and almost to their surprise, as they read their letters to each other, what they had expected was what came to pass in their lives.

Some people always speak in the negative and think in the negative, but why not during this coming year of '63 speak positive and act positive-expect everything good to come your way. Even when something is thrown in your path to obstruct and destroy and discourage, look beyond and say in your heart," God, you're with me, I need not fear. You are my victory." When you begin to see in this manner, your trials will take a different light and meaning. You have seen people who seem to be happy all the time, and you wondered how they could have such an attitude of joy when you knew their actual circumstances. It is because they have an abiding faith and assurance that Christ is their victory. The same trial could come to another person and they be overcome by it just because of their lack of faith and trust in the Lord. They fail to believe positive.

This new year lies before us unknown. We know not what it holds and each day is an adventure into the unsoiled. Both the good and bad facts of life will come our way. Let us be sure that we are fortified from within with the power of God to be overcomers and victorious in whatever the year might bring. There is power in our thinking. If we will only meditate on the greatness of God, we cannot help but believe right and know that God will meet our need in every situation. God will become bigger and bigger to us as we are aware of His presence in our lives and that He is concerned with everything we do. For myself, I believe 1963 will be my best year. I believe that no matter what comes my way, I will be the victor. My God is good-great-loving and these are not only words but a firm belief, I am sure of a victorious new year in the Lord.

Returning with Joy — John Meares

"He that goeth forth and weepeth, bearing precious seed, shall doubtless come again with rejoicing, bringing his sheaves with him." Psalms 126:6

Everyone wishes for success. Whatever errand one sets out upon he wishes to come back having been successful.

This verse of scripture gives the recipe; of success. It speaks of success in the most urgent field of endeavor that one can possibly work in. The wise man said, "he that winneth souls is wise." There is no greater work in all the world than that of being a soul winner. Then the next question is, "how can I be successful in the most important work in all the world?" The above scripture gives the road to success in soul winning.

First, one must have a goal. You cannot win souls by just thinking how wonderful it would be for people to be saved. You cannot win souls by just merely planning for souls to be saved. You must make an effort. One must go forth, and we have many promises in the scriptures that the Lord Jesus will go with us as we go. So the first step is to go forth.

Next, "to go forth weeping." What does that mean? This means that to win souls is not an easy, carefree task. It is a task that sobers the heart and sobers the mind. When one is willing to go forth, and carry the burdens that are necessary to do this work, then God will honor such a one. Many times there are those who think how great it would be if they were to go out and evangelize. But after having gone out, they find that the burden is heavier than they choose to bear. They cease to carry out what they thought they desired to do because the burden was too great.

Third, as we go with the burden upon our heart, let us be sure we have the right thing to give. "Bearing precious seed..." is essential.

One may go and entertain people and still not have sheaves to bring back. One may go and enjoy themselves in their work by visitation and conversation, but still be unsuccessful. The third requisite is a very prime one . . "bearing precious seed." For it is the gospel of Jesus Christ that saves and nothing else. For it is the power of God unto salvation. To be able to sing beautifully or to be able to speak words of wisdom, may be well; but without the Word of God—the Truth of God, it is impossible to be successful in soul-winning. *(Continued*

The Bible declares that the angels of heaven rejoice over one sinner that repents. What great joy it brings to the heart of a person who has gone in the name of the Lord and successfully led souls to the feet of Jesus Christ. It is joy unspeakable and full of glory. In fact, if you do not have the joy in your Christian experience that you should like to have, I suggest that rather than fasting and praying to have your joy return to you, or rather than perhaps making some new consecration, go out in the name of the Lord and win a soul for Christ, and you'll find the joy springing up in your heart that is greater than you're able to contain. So then, the promise is that one shall return with joy and shall be bringing his sheaves with him. You will have fruit to show for the labors of your hands. God will make you successful in the most important business in the world, if you will follow the steps of this scripture.

—Mary Lee Meares

Wouldn't it be wonderful if we would let the Lord help us with our problems? You say, "Oh, I do." But do we really? The other day I received a letter from my daughter who is away in school, and she began by saying, "Mother, I have a problem, and you are the only one that can help me with it." Now, I wasn't happy that she had a problem that was too big for her and she needed help, but I was happy that she had confidence in me as her mother and would come to me with it. To me she was saying, "Mother, I believe you can help me—Mother, I trust you." Then it occurred to me that the Lord was pleased with us as His children when we come to Him with our problems and our needs. We are saying, "Lord, I trust you—I believe you are not only able to help me, but will help me." Did Jesus not say, "Come boldly to the throne of grace." He has told us to make our requests known.

One of the greatest lessons we can learn is how to simply trust God. I know people that have been saved for years and still have not learned how to trust the Lord with their problems and their needs. But they are still trying to labor and work them out themselves. They might ask the saints to pray for them, but they certainly have not cast their burdens and problems at the feet of Jesus. So many Christians go trudging along under the load. It was my joy to help my daughter with her problem. To know she trusted me and would confide in me made the bond of love between us even greater. Oh, that we would trust God with the every day cares of our life. Certainly a God that loved us so much that He died that we might be saved, is concerned with every other detail in our daily affairs. Not long ago I was becoming anxious over something that I had asked God to do, and felt like it was His will to do. However, my faith began to waver just a little whether it would be done. Then God spoke to my heart and said, "Don't you know I am more interested in that being done than you are?" This gentle rebuke did me good. My daily prayer is for God to help me to trust Him and realize His great love and concern for me as one of His children. As the song says, "Trust and obey, for there is no other way to be happy in Jesus, but to trust and obey."

Himself He Could Not Save

—Mrs. John L. Meares

When someone says to you, "show me" in a manner that means if you could you would, it is a temptation, to say the least, not to show them.

Jesus was human the same as He was divine. And I believe if He had not already obtained the victory in the garden, He would not have been able to withstand the temptation of showing those that were mocking and making fun that He had the power to come down off the cross, thus proving to his enemies standing around that He was the Son of God.

Early in His ministry He was tempted to prove Himself the Son of God. Satan had said to Him, "if you're the Son of God, turn these stones to bread. If you're the Son of God, cast yourself off this mountain, it won't hurt you." But Jesus had again already overcome the temptation. He had just fasted for forty days and was full of the Spirit. Throughout His ministry He was tempted even as you and I are.

Never did the Son of God manifest His power or the divine just to show people. He only manifested power to glorify His heavenly Father. Perhaps, you some time or other, have had someone to do evil to you and the human within you said, "I'll show you," but the divine said, "that would not be Christ-like, and I cannot afford to do it." Any power that is manifested through our lives should be for one reason and that is to glorify God, never ourselves.

Jesus said, "I cannot save myself, for if I did, then I could not save others." He was thinking of you and me. The principle of the salvation of the world is a divine law that still lives. Jesus said, "he that would save his life would certainly lose it, but he that will be courageous to lose his life for my sake and the gospel shall certainly find it." Christ could not afford to show His power and come down from the cross. It was not the nails that held him there, but His love for you and me. No doubt, some that were standing by said,

"Is not that the man that has healed so many sick people?" Another said, "He is the one that spoke and made our hearts burn within us. Why does He not show these people. Anyone that can raise the dead can come off that cross." But as surely as Christ would not save Himself, neither can we afford to save ourselves. We must give ourselves — lose ourselves in Christ, that others might know that He gave His life that they might live. I am glad that I have a life to give to Him.

Letters to the Pastor

I was in Washington recently visiting my sister. I had a longing in my soul to come to your church, so I got a taxi and came. I know the Lord sent me there, for I was so burdened and low in spirit when I came. The devil had been telling me I wasn't saved. In your sermon it seemed that you read me as though I had written a note to you and given it to you asking for you to pray for me. When you got through preaching you had covered all my requests. Even though I went in burdened, I left so uplifted. I also enjoyed Sister Meares' solo. It was all meant for me. Thank God for a minister that can lift others when the are down low in spirit.

A visitor

* * *

Greetings in the precious Name of our Lord and Saviour! I always enjoy the timely messages and testimonies in Fellowship News. I was saved in 1914 in Buffalo, N. York, and then lived in Washington most of the 20's before coming to New York. I enjoy the Temple every time I have a chance to visit to D. C. I retired a few years ago so my donations are small, but I am happy to have a small part in Evangel Temple.

Rev. David Green
Brooklyn, N. Y.

I want to give my testimony of how God blessed me on last Tuesday. My job requires that I work one Sunday a month, so am on the job today. On the last Sunday Reverend McAlister was asking for contributions for a Volkswagon car to be used on the missionary field in Brazil, I was quite low in finances, but the Spirit spoke to me and told me to give $5.00 on the car. I was obedient to the Spirit and gave the $5.00 that I had really needed for something else. On Tuesday of the following week I attended our annual credit union meeting during my lunch period. A few $10.00 bills were given as door prizes. To my surprise and joy, I got ten dollars. The Lord gave me back the five dollars I had given so freely and five dollars more. Isn't God wonderful!

Jamie Pinckney
No. Englewood, Md.

* * *

Enclosed find $2.00 for the radio broadcast. I started visiting Evangel Temple last New Year's Eve. I felt so good just to be in the house of the Lord. I had not been in a church for quite some time, but I have been coming ever since New Year's. Thank you for sending me the Fellowship News. It has been most helpful and always seems to come at just the right time.

Bertie Walker
Washington, D.C.

Eyewitness Account of the Trinidad Harvest

Trinidad was shaken by the power of God through the anointed ministry of the Rev. John L. Meares and Morris Cerullo. Those precious days will never be forgotten by any of us who attended the meetings. It was the first time we have had a meeting of this nature. Notice of the intended visit was very short. Within two weeks we had to make all the arrangements for the meetings. However, from the time word reached us that he was coming, we started working around the clock to have things ready. We were told that the Rev. Meares would come a few days prior to the meetings to assist us with the arrangements for the campaign. As soon as he got there things really started to move; permission was granted for us to have service in Woodforde Square, in the heart of Port of Spain, the main city of Trinidad. This was a direct answer to prayer. No religious group was ever given permission to use this Square for more than one night, but God gave it to us for ten nights. This confirmed that the services were prearranged by God. I am quite sure that if Rev. Meares had not been with us at this time we would have never been able to complete our arrangements for this great campaign. On behalf of our people in Trinidad, I would like to thank him for all that he has done for us. During the day time we worked building the platform, putting in the lights, the loud speaking system, making arrangements for the printing of fifty thousand handbills, also radio announcements, and ads in the daily papers.

We had as many as fifty-thousand attending a single service. This was indeed the Trinidad Harvest. But the greatest was yet to come. Jesus, the miracle worker, visited us each night as we saw hundreds healed by the power of God as the prayer of faith was prayed. The blind received their sight, the lame was made whole, the deaf heard, and all manner of sickness was healed by God's power. We praised God for this mighty visitation. As a result of these meteings, we now have a large gathering in the city of Port of Spain. This is something we have been praying about for forty years. About 700 attend services each week. All of our churches have had an increase in their attend-ance. We praise God for this revival and for His servants he used in bringing it to us. During the day of preparation for the campaign our church at San Juan was honored with a visit from Rev. Meares. As he spoke to us in the service God's spirit came upon us in a very precious way. Truly our hearts were richly blessed. Bro. Meares told us of his church and the wonderful people of Washington, D.C., and extended an invitation to me to minister to his people at Evangel Temple. I want to thank the pastor and people of Evangel Temple for the kind invitation and the ticket to come to the U.S.A. I have enjoyed ministering to the people of Evangel Temple. May God continue to bless you in your missionary outreach for His glory. In the West Indies you will find a very grateful people praying for your pastor and the people of Evangel Temple, for making possible this great Harvest of souls in Trinidad.

Have You Heard Him?   —Mary Lee Meares

To me, one of the things that makes the Word of God so wonderful is the constant new truths that are revealed as I read it. The other day as I was reading the account of the resurrection of Jesus in the 20th chapter of John, I saw something that I had not seen heretofore.

Mary came to the tomb at early dawn to anoint the body of her Lord. How she loved Him above all others. He had changed her life, brought her peace and joy, and His words had found a lodging place in her heart. But now, His eyes were closed in death; His hands of mercy lay still, and no longer could she hear Him teach and preach the Words of Life. So she had come for her last time to show her love and devotion. On entering the garden, and finding the stone rolled away, she ran with haste to tell Peter and John. Her words seemed as idle tales and the Bible says they believed her not. However, Peter and John, out of curiosity, ran to see if it could be so. Jesus had told them many times that He would arise on the third day, but they did not understand. Has the Lord ever told you anything, and you did not understand until it happened?

Now as Mary was standing before the sepulchre, weeping and wondering where they had taken her Lord, Jesus, Himself, appeared unto her. Strangely enough, she did not recognize Him. Has this ever happened to you? Have you failed to recognize His presence because you were blinded with tears of grief and disappointment? Have you forgotten His promise, "Lo, I am with you always." But, the moment He spoke, "Mary" she knew—yes, she knew that voice.

Was it not also true that as the disciples were fishing one evening, they saw Jesus walking on the sea and knew Him not, but when He spoke, "It is I, be not afraid," then they knew Him. Learn to know that voice. He said, "My sheep know my voice." The best guide anywhere for our life is the voice of Jesus. We do not have to see a physical presence or hear an audible, voice, but we can know He is near us; we can hear Him as He speaks. And this is the reason we are certain—we are positive—we are sure of His resurrection; He lives today! We hear Him speak each and every day to our hearts.

Eyewitness Account of the Crusade in Barbados

To feel the mighty power of God grip a whole nation is a strange and wonderful experience. This was my privilege during the month of January when Brother Morris Cerullo, Brother Clara Hutchins and I were in Barbados, B.W.I. Many precrusade preparations were made. Thousands of hand bills were given out over the entire island. The large, beautiful Queens Park was secured and at one end of the park a large platform was built and a ramp where thousands who received a miracle from God came and gave testimonies of the wonderful power of God. It is always a thrilling adventure, after having made preparations, prayed and believed God, for the first night of the crusade to come. Every moment of prayer and faith was gloriously rewarded as we saw 10,000 people gather to hear the Word and experience God's miracle working power the very first night. There was a hunger written upon the faces of the people as they stood reverently and silently throughout the service. At the close of the sermon one could sense the power of the Spirit of God as it enveloped the multitude with conviction. The conditions of receiving Jesus Christ, as Saviour, was simply and clearly stated. Then a challenge for those who wished to accept Christ as Saviour to make it known by raising their right hand. Thousands of hands in one second were raised eagerly above the sea of humanity. With a sound of many voices they prayed the sinners prayer. Heaven bent low, angels rejoiced; the eyes of the cooperating ministers were filled with tears, mingled with compassion and thanksgiving for the beginning of the greatest harvest of souls that Barbados had ever witnessed. Then there was worship, praise and adoration from the newborn babes in Christ. This was the beginning of a river of thousands of written testimonies that came to us telling how Jesus had changed their lives and given them a new hope.

The afternoon services for the new converts was attended by hundreds who were eager to learn how to become a disciple and follower after the Lord Jesus Christ. As I preached to them, it seemed they would literally take hold of every word and plant it within their heart.

On closing of the crusade in Queens Park, a large building (the same that was used for the afternoon services) was made available to establish a great Evangelistic Center. On the Monday night following, this building was dedicated and a young Barbadion, who was an officer in a local bank, Rev. Williams, was installed to carry on this work. At least 2500 people crowded into the building while thousands more completely filled the yard and surrounding streets. Rev. Williams had been prepared by the providence of God for such an hour as this. For over a year he had been having prayer meetings in his home and leading people to the Lord. He resigned his position in the bank and dedicated his life anew to reaching the lost.

≈ ≈ ≈

The Hand of God   —Mary Lee Meares

I have a plaque that hangs above my desk which says:

> "And I said to the man who stood at the gate of the year:
> Give me a light that I may tread safely into the unknown!
> And he replied, Go out into the darkness and put thy hand
> into the hand of God. That shall be better than light and
> safer than a known way."

Every time I read these words there is something within me that
says, "Mary Lee, keep your hand in the hand of God and you will
always be alright."

I can remember as a child of only five years of age, I would
wake up in the night and be afraid. My mother would let me get
up out of my little bed and climb in bed with her. As soon as I felt
her arms go around me and her hand slip in mine, I was no longer
afraid, no matter it was.

I find each new 24 hours just as full of problems as the day before,
but inside me there is quietness and security and the strength to deal
with those daily problems. This strength comes from the assurance
that my hand is clasped with the hand of God.

There is no independence between God and man. We need Him,
He needs us. So Let us walk hand in hand together that we might
not stumble and fall, and in turn the kingdom of God will be lifted
up in a dark and sinful world.

May you never fear the morrow-only put your hand into the
hand of God. It will be better than light and safer than a known way.

Our American Heritage   —Mary Lee Meares

Time has a tendency to make one forget the price that was paid for the freedom you and I enjoy in our day. However, each new year that we celebrate Thanksgiving we are reminded that our forefathers came to this country and endured many hardships in order to enjoy religious freedom.

Not only did our forefathers pay a price for our freedom, but many wars have been fought since that time and multitude thousands have paid the supreme price that we might live in a land where the flag of freedom still waves.

Faith in God gave America this heritage, and the only way for it to be maintained is for us to keep our faith in God. With our freedom once again being threatened, let us not forget to acknowledge God as the One who will fight our battles for us. No matter what power our country or any other country has, the greatest power is the power of God. The greatest security in all the world is "Under His Wings." The greatest trust is "In God We Trust." He sees down within our hearts and knows whether or not we have our trust in Eim. He knows whether or not there is a praise in our hearts for His protecting hand and His loving care.

I have found that a real faith in God causes one to live in an attitude of praise. As long as we praise God for His blessings and goodness, the devil has a hard time getting us to become discouraged and believe his lies. An attitude of praise is the best way to live a victorious Christian life. It is impossible to number our blessings without losing count. As I begin to praise God for one blessing, another will come to my mind. I am sure you can say the same. Some Christians are always "asking God" while others are always "praising God." There is a vast difference in the two Christians. Which kind are you?

The Bible says, "Every good and perfect gift cometh down from the Father above..." Do you recognize this Giver of blessings? My prayer this Thanksgiving is, "Lord, help me to use my blessings each and every day for the glory of God." I shall never fail to praise Him for my American Heritage of freedom. To worship God as I choose, the One I love above all others, is the greatest blessing that I know of.

Gospel Stirs Haiti　　　　　　　　　　—John Meares

"Behold ye among the heathen, and regard, and wonder marvellously: for I will work a work in your days, which ye will not believe, though it be told you." Habakkuk 1:5

The Lord is working marvelously in this day. This is the opportunity that many have looked forward to when the Lord shall pour out His Spirit on all flesh, Certainly today, unparelled with any other period in the history of the world, the Spirit of God is moving throughout the earth.

My recent trip to Haiti was one of the most blessed, heartwarming experiences that I have ever had. For Jesus Christ opened this nation for the hearing of the gospel in perhaps the greatest way in its history. I say this first of all because of the attitude of the government. For years Haiti has been ruled by dictators. In the last thirteen years there has been sixteen different presidents or dictators, along with sixteen revolutions which brought them into power. These dictators were not favorable toward religious freedom. But just recently the Lord has raised up a government which grants religious freedom. This is the work of the Holy Spirit in this last day. Moreover, it was not the missionaries nor was it the local Christians or pastors who invited this great revival that is now history. It was none less than the government itself. President Duvalier sent a personal representative, Senator Bonahomme, who is the leading Senator of the government, to invite a group to come and conduct a revival campaign. Brother Morris Cerullo was chosen by this group to be the evangelist. Some Christian businessmen went first to make the preliminary arrangements for the meeting, as well as to witness for Christ. As a result of this effort, there were each night on the platform, high government officials and businessmen to see the wonderful works of the Lord. Many of them had no real religious faith or background as we who are Christians have. It must be acknowledged that this is not the doings of man, but the work of the Holy Spirit.

The meeting in Haiti was a glorious success because of the unusual manifestation of the Spirit of God. I have been in many great evangelistic campaigns, and I have seen the Lord do marvelous and wonderful things. But here in this nation night after night tens of thousands of people turned out to the services. In one of the Sunday afternoon services, it was estimated that at least 35,000 people were present. The majority of these people were considered to be devil—worshippers or worshippers of the Voodoo religion. Yet, their response toward the preaching of God was certainly heartwarming. They seemed to be so eager for the truth of the gospel and would accept it with an open heart. Thousands each night would make a response for the acceptance of the Lord Jesus Christ as their Savior. To try to determine how much permanent good was done by the work of the Spirit would be impossible, but to say the least, thousands came in contact with the Lord and was keenly aware of His presence. I firmly believe there will be a host of people in heaven as a result of this great meeting. Each night the services were broadcast for two hours throughout the nation.

Haiti is a primative country. Above is an open slaughter house. There is no evidence of water or sanitation. In foreground are the entrails and refuse of the animals.

In addition to the people accepting and receiving the Lord into their hearts, there were many miracles of healing. One young lady was brought who was chained and led like a wild animal. Another young lady, who was mightily exercised by the evil spirits of Satan, was wonderously delivered. Then there was a voodoo priest who came to the service and said he would like to burn his voodoo idols and give his heart to Jesus. The next day we went to his house and there all of the idols and pictures, etc. he had blessed were broken and carried out of his house. All that was burnable was burned as several saints of God gathered with us around the fire and we began to sing "There is Power in the Blood." This priest fell on his knees and lifted his hands calling on God. He was soon rejoicing in his heart and soul because he had found the true Savior. The bonds of Satan were broken, and he was set free to give glory unto God.

Our Great African Convention

Rev. & Mrs. Bhengu & daughters

Since coming back to Africa the latter part of last year, I have been extremely busy. The first two months were spent in visiting various Assemblies of our connection. My wife and I were on the road daily in order to fit into the schedule. The people were happy to see us back and the Lord poured out His Spirit in every meeting.

We proceeded to East London for the annual convention at Christmas. Our guest speakers were Reverend John L. Meares and

John Petrucelli of Evangel Temple, Washington, D.C. Never such speakers! Never such blessings! They became one with us in everything and never have we loved white people as we did—our people could have swallowed them alive. Showers of blessings, riches of Grace! Blessed men of God! We had over 7,000 delegates at the convention and never have things gone so well. The presence of Jesus was real, and we revelled in the sunshine of His blessings.

The convention usually lasts for five days, but this one could hardly stop on the ninth, and finally dispersed on the tenth.

On January -16th the Meares-Petrucelli Crusade started in our big tent at the Plantation Square, Orlando, Johannesburg. We had over 2,000 the first night and miracles of healing and conversion did not wait for the second night. Wonderful Jesus. Crutches piled up, the blind saw, the deaf and dumb heard and spoke. Our people still sing the song Bro. Petrucelli taught them, "Jesus is the Light of the World." The meetings are still going with signs and wonders. Orlando is moved mightily and rocked by the power of God. We will build a church, for we will lose them if we have no building. Evangel Temple has started a fund for the building of this church.

We said "farewell" with heavy hearts and there was experienced a sense of bereavement at their departure, but praise God we can look back on many blessings and a shared fellowship in His vineyard. We still revel in the many healings and new converts. The tent is filled to capacity for the evening services. Yesterday, February 21, we had approximately 300 new converts.

Thank you for the love and interest in the African people. I reciprocate all your kind thoughts and your prayers.

The Lord bless you.
Nicholas Bhengu

Letters to the Pastor

During the crusading campaign when Bro. Popoff was at the Evangelistic Center, two of the ladies from your church came to my home and prayed for me and my family. I was saved and have been attending your church ever since. I would like to become a Fellowship member. Since I have been saved I have been blessed in so many different ways.

Regina Hawkins,
Washington, D.C.

* * *

I would like to tell you about the wonderful Easter I enjoyed at the Evangelistic Center. I was there Sunday morning, noon, and night. The services, play, singing, film, and everything was wonderful. It was the best Easter I have ever had because I accepted Jesus Christ as my personal Saviour. I am born again through faith by the Word of God, which liveth and abideth forever. I believe Jesus bore my sins and I am now forgiven. I cannot be at the Center often because I work in Easton, Maryland, but will come when I can. I want to send you $10.00 a month to help in your ministry.

A new-born babe in God's family,
Viola Amos,

* * *

Thank you for the prayer cloth you sent me. As soon as I received it I put it on believing God would heal me and He did. I was going about the kitchen fixing supper, when all of a sudden I discovered all the pain and misery in my back and hip was gone. Praise God.

Addie Simpson
Washington, D.C.

* * *

My husband had a stroke on the left side and could not talk, walk or use his left hand. He was committed to Mt. Alto Hospital. I requested prayer at the Center, and now he is talking and using his left hand and leg. The doctor says he can come home soon. I praise God for answering prayer. Thank you for the FELLOWSHIP NEWS. Don't ever stop it.

Mrs. Jefferson Wood
Washington, D.C.

* * *

I am so glad that you sent me one of your books. I read the book over and over, fasted and prayed and God has healed my hands. I can do anything that I want to now. Thank God for being so real to me.

Geneva Buddin

Being Thankful —John L. Meares

Thanksgiving is in the minds of most people a day that we set aside to be especially thankful for material blessings, plenty to eat, plenty to wear, shelter over our heads, etc. And the majority of these people do not really realize where their many blessings come from. They just know we live in a nation that has plenty and we are not suffering hunger and poverty pangs like many other nations of the world. They are glad that the war we are presently engaged in is being fought in Viet Nam instead of America. They are glad that we aren't under communistic rule. Many other things could be enumerated that we are glad of. But when one thinks of these blessings without giving thanks to the Giver or acknowledging that "every good and perfect gift cometh down from the Father above... " then I feel that they have not really learned the meaning of Thanksgiving. It is not a day that we do not have to work and can stay home or go to a football game or have a big dinner with our friends, Thanksgiving is our attitude every hour of every day. Thanksgiving is giving praise to Almighty God for all the blessings that He bestows upon us. Thanksgiving is not waiting until God delivers us from some calamity to give thanks, but thanksgiving is praising God for keeping us from the harms and hurts in this life. Thanksgiving is being able to make a praise in your heart when you are walking through the valley—knowing that you don't walk alone but have One walking by your side.

Thanksgiving is being able to see good instead of evil all the time. True we live in a world of hate, war, riots, prejudices, sin and debauchery. On the other hand we live in a beautiful world, and God manifests His love to His children constantly, in so many, many ways. And when one offers up a prayer of praise, it somehow fortifies our faith in a living God, and faith is not only acceptable to God, but is the channel through which all of God's blessings flow. God inhabits the praises of His children.

One thing that has been so noticeable in the six o'clock morning prayer services at the Temple is that everyone praying seems to be spending practically all of the time on their knees praising God instead of begging God. No wonder there is such a wonderful spirit when you walk in the prayer room. Some are praising God in the Spirit, while others are reading the psalms of praise. All are mindful of the Giver of all blessings in this life.

One of the Psalms read, "Bless the Lord O my soul, And all that is within me, bless His holy name." Let all that is within you praise the Lord. When your heart is truly thankful your lips will speak joyfully. Your expression will be one of joy and gladness if there is a true praise "within." Lip praise without heart praise has a dull ring. Lip service without action or service is only a form without any true meaning and which the heart has never entered. Real thanksgiving is backed by deeds. Each of us has our own way in which we show gratefulness, and we have different reasons for our thanksgiving. The Psalmist David said. "Whoso offereth praise glorifieth Me, and maketh a way whereby I can work." So if you want God to be real to you and to work in you, then give Him praise in all things and He will begin to do things for you that will even amaze you. You will begin to wonder at His goodness to you.

So Thanksgiving is not one day we set aside to catch up on being thankful, but it is the life we live 365 days in the year. It is the greatest life one can possibly live—the fullest and richest. Are you living this abundant life?

"I will bless the Lord at all times: his praise shall continually be in my mouth

My soul shall make her boast in the Lord: the humble shall hear thereof, and be glad.

O magnify the Lord with me, and let us exalt his name together." Psalm 34:1-3

THANKSGIVING SERVICE

Thursday Morning

November 23

8 o'clock — 9 A.M.

EVANGEL TEMPLE

COME...

Where Jesus Was Born — Mary Lee Meares

In 1955 it was my privilege to walk down the narrow cobble stone streets of Jerusalem — the streets where Jesus once walked, where He stopped along the way to heal the sick; to bless a mother's child; to speak a word of cheer.

It so happened that at the time I was there, there was much rioting going on between the Arabs and the Jews. Several young people had been killed and there was a tenseness that filled the air. We were told it was not safe for an American to be on the streets for the Arabs felt hard toward the Americans. The United States had helped the Jews become a nation again. Israel had been reborn and many Arabs had had their property and homes taken from them. I stood on one of the hills of Old Jerusalem with my guide, Mr. Monsueir, who showed me a home he owned over on the Israeli side just a few months before, but now it had been taken away from him. Guards were standing by barbed wire fences to keep anyone from crossing Jerusalem to Israel. No doubt the Arabs had a right to feel bad toward American for helping Israel become a nation, I do not know.

Even though our guide said, "You had better stay in your hotel room or you might be stoned," I had come to Jerusalem to see the places I had read so much about in the Bible, and after one day of looking at hotel walls I ventured outside.

I so much wanted to see the birth place of our Lord, so from Jerusalem our guide took us over some back roads to Bethlehem hoping not to draw any attention as a foreigner. We came to a large stone courtyard where the Church of the Nativity was. This church had been erected over the site of the inn at which Mary and Joseph sought lodging. There was a large mob of people not far from the church, but we slipped inside without being noticed. Descending down a steep flight of stairs we came to a group of flickering candles. In the floor a silver design of the star of David marked the place of the manger. It was a little hard for me to picture in my mind this exact spot as being where the Christ child was born. The candles and altar did not make me think of a lowly cow stall with the smell of hay; however, Mr. Monsueir assured us this was the place. As I stood there one thing I was sure of, and that was Christ had been born in my heart. I had welcomed the Christ child in my life. He now was living within the temple of my heart.

On my way out of the Church of the Nativity I stopped to talk to a number of elderly robed priests. We discussed the customs and characteristics of their people. Passing by were men on their donkeys carrying trinkets they had made of olivewood. This, to many of them, was their way of making a living.

As I looked out over the Judean hills, there were some shepherds tending their sheep, and it seemed as if I could hear the angelic chorus singing "Unto you is born this day in the city of David, a Saviour which is Christ the Lord." Not only a babe was born, but a Saviour. Chirstmas has no real meaning unless He has become your Saviour. He no longer is to be worshipped as a babe in a manger, but now we worship Him as Lord and Saviour and our soon coming King!

* * *

The devil cheats so many good Christians out of that close communion with God just by presenting the everyday, pressing duties of the day. True, they must be taken care of, but I think one will still be able to get the job done if first he will take out time to "just love God." Not long ago I moved into a new home and I found myself so busy trying to get fixed up until I let my devotion to God go slack. One day while in the laundry room, I just stopped and said, "No matter how busy I get, I am going to stop and tell the Lord how much I love Him; and when I said it, the sweetest presence filled my heart. That's what the Lord wants—our love—our spirit to commune with His Spirit.

Do not try within your own strength to work out all the problems that you will encounter during this coming year. Realize that as you commune with God and praise and love Him, that in turn He will solve your problems for you. This is the better way and the pleasing life to God. May your devotion not just last for the first few weeks of this year, but may each day bring you into a closer fellowship with the Master, and by the end of 1962 you will be able to look back and rejoice over the moments and hours you have spent in "just loving God."

Now, as is often the case, when I try to express myself, words seem inadequate. So please just try to see my sincerity in what I shall try to say. I am grateful and deeply appreciate your humility, unselfishness, and genuine interest in both the members and visitors of Evangel Temple.

I can see why Brother Petrucelli enjoys his work as co-pastor and why he never shows he is tired. Sometimes I think of you and Brother Petrucelli as father and son; again, you remind me of Elijah and Elisha. Finally, I see you as two Spirit-filled men whom God called to work together to minister to people who desire so much to grow in grace that little else matters. I am sure God is pleased with your labors.

In studying any subject, the more we learn about it, the more we realize how little we know. So it is in our spiritual lives, as you preach and teach and unselfishly permit other men who are Spirit-filled evangelists to preach and minister to us at Evangel Temple, we hunger and realize the more our great need of God. As we seek to know Him in a greater way, we remember He has said, "Blessed are they which do hunger and thirst after righteousness: for they shall be filled." Pastor Meares, I pray daily for you and Brother Petrucelli and pray God to richly bless you both.

A fellowship member

Chapter 5 – 1963

A New Thing
—John L. Meares

"Behold, the former things are come to pass, and new things do I declare: before they spring forth I tell you of them."

—Isaiah 42:9

If one would reminisce for a few moments of the mighty acts of the Lord here at the Evangelistic Center, we could find nothing but thanksgiving and praise in our hearts. These past six years have been the shortest years of my life. God has moved upon multitudes of people who have found salvation for their souls, healing for their bodies, and an experience of the baptism of the Holy Ghost. There is no question about the revival fires burning. All of this, with the Psalmist David, makes us exclaim, "Praise ye the Lord." His name is certainly worthy.

However, in spite of the great things God hath done, it is not a healthy thing to live on past glories. If one should only consider the great things of the past, they would cease to longer be used of God. Apostle Paul declared, "forgetting those things that are behind, I press toward the mark." We cannot tarry too long at the victories for there are yet new battles to be fought. My constant prayer is that we will not become at ease in Zion. The greater the blessings of the Lord, the more is required of us.

In the last few weeks God has been speaking to my heart concerning His glory and anointing that He is beginning to pour out upon the worshipers at Evangelistic Center. There is no doubt that because of our faithfulness and desire toward the things of God and His kingdom, God has brought us to a new place in His grace with a new anointing upon our lives, and a new vision in our souls, and a new courage to go forth in the power of His might. In the most recent services, God has confirmed this by pouring out without measure, His glory. It seems that the services have had the greatest anointing that has ever been experienced at Evangelistic Center. This has not happened accidentally. It is after the hearts of the people have been prepared that God pours out His glory.

For many months God has been speaking to my heart. There were seasons of disappointments and seasons of longings. However, as I look back, I can see the hand of God as He was preparing the life of His servant for a new visitation. God recently made known to me, that which He is wanting to do. In a most unusual way, He confirmed this by others. There has been a number of circumstances that God has wrought by sending others who had no knowledge of the preparation that God was doing in my own heart, but came and confirmed in marvelous ways the mind of the Spirit.

While He was preparing the heart of His servant. He was also preparing the hearts of the people so that as a mighty army we could rise up in this great city as never before to do the works of Him that sent us. We have been declaring our desires to have this city for Christ and now God is preparing us for the greatest offensive against the powers of the evil to the tearing down of strong holds and spiritual wickedness, that the kingdom of God might triumph for holiness and righteousness and peace in the Holy Ghost. This is a work that must be done through dedicated vessels filled with the Spirit of knowledge, the Spirit of wisdom, the Spirit of love and the Spirit of courage and power.

Letters to the Pastor

Dear Bro. & Sis. Meares:

May God bless and keep you strong to do His mighty will.

At this time I want to thank you for all your sincere prayers and warm handshakes from which I have been blessed. In the time of my trial, when my son was in serious trouble, you will never know what it meant to me to have you remember me out of the hundreds of requests, and give me the assurance of your prayers for my son and me. I just never can express what it meant and how thankful I am. Thanks again and again.

A member

* * *

I was reading one of your magazines, "The Fellowship News" and do thank the Lord for it. I obtained it from my mother-in-law. It was so uplifting to my soul. Rev. Meares, I am greatly in need of healing for my body, and am asking your prayers. Enclosed is $1.00 for your broadcast.

Margie Thomas
Virgilina, Virginia

* * *

I was so happy to meet you and Mrs. Meares while in Washington, and also your wonderful members. I hope I can come back soon. I got filled up with good things, and feel like a different person. I know I have been in touch with the Holy Spirit. I am a member of the Presbyterian church of South Carolina.

—Rosa Cooper
Mayesville, S. C.

≈ ≈ ≈

The Full Responsibility

For the past few months God has dealt with me in a new way. I have seen the Lord in my ministry in the past 20 years accomplish many things for His glory. Several churches and congregations have been raised up which are still carrying on His work. However, God's direction has been the clearest recently than any time of my ministry heretofore.

Since God called me to Washington some 6½ years ago my heart has constantly reached out with a burden for this great city with its three million souls. We have, with God's blessings, established many outreaches which only eternity will reveal the accomplishments. Bible Adventure Land has reached the hearts of hundreds of children. Camp Adventure Land has helped us reach children of every background and home environment. The teen-age effort has molded the lives of a number of young men who will be mightly anointed of the Lord as ministers. The Crusaders have brought the presence of the Lord into many homes. In addition to these outreaches, we have sponsored several campaigns in the city to try to reach the masses, and all of these efforts God has blessed. However, in our effort at the fairgrounds it seemed that hundreds would be moved for God, but down came the April showers in the month of August. Then more recently it seemed God's time to send a great revival and we went to the Uline Arena where the altogether unexpected became an impossible barrier. The sound was so bad that the people who attended could not understand because of the echo.

I began to ask God why? God knew my desire and like David I was after the heart of God. Then recently God spoke to me and answered my questions. He said, "son, I have called you and laid the burden of this city on your heart. I have waited for you to accept the full responsibility of this call. I will open the door so your ministry may be a witness to the people of this city."

This is the beginning of a new move of God's Spirit in this city. To realize that you and I can share in God's plan to reach Washington for Christ humbles my heart as I thrill to be a vessel for His glory.

Evangel Temple's Ministers Association

Realizing the need for more unity and closer fellowship among the ministers of Evangel Temple, Pastor Meares called a meeting of all the ministers on October 8, 1962. From this meeting much was to be accomplished for the Kingdom of God. Some twenty-five ministers of the church came out and rededicated their lives and their ministry, thus THE EVANGEL TEMPLE MINISTERS' ASSOCIATION was born. The first meeting of the association was a real blessing to every one present, with the Lord's Supper and feet washing.

Through the efforts of the Helping Hand, there was $60.00 raised for the ministers. Instead of dividing the money among themselves they voted to put the money to some good use. Several suggestions were made on how the money should be spent. It was finally agreed on that the money should go toward renting a building in which one of the brethren could hold services. True, sixty dollars seemed like a small amount when it came to renting a building, but only the Lord knew how this small amount was going to be blessed and increased for His glory. Before the meeting was over, the Ministers had pledged $180.00. Pastor Meares made it known to all present that Evangel Temple would give dollar for dollar in the pledges. He, above all realizes the great need here in the Washington area for more Soul Saving Stations. It is his heart's desire to see all of the young ministers of Evangel Temple step out with faith and start a work for the building up of the Kingdom of God. Our Bro. Fred Hall, Pastor of The People's Church said his church, by faith, would make a good size pledge. All in all, after the pledges were made the total was $540.00.

Editorial   —Mary Lee Meares

"I will lift up mine eyes unto the hills, from whence cometh my help. My help cometh from the Lord, which hade heaven and earth." Ps. 121:1-2. This is a scripture that cannot be erased from my heart. It is one that I have depended upon many times in my serving God. It is a verse that I will lean upon in the year of 1965. More each day, I realize that man's ability is not sufficient to live a victorious chrisian life. But thank God there is a source of help from One above, and all we have to do is simply look up and ask for His help—His guidance. The third verse says that He will not let our foot be moved, or He will not let us fall. When our way becomes a little shaky, God will be there to strengthen. He is watching over us and He is a very present help in the time of need. How precious are the promises of God in these present days. When David wrote the psalms, he had learned first hand that God was his help, and no matter what or how many times one fails, God is a merciful and loving God and ready to help. Maybe you feel that in 1964 you made so many failures, and failed to do so many things a christian should have done. But forget the past and look to God and let Him know that your trust will be solely in Him in '65.

God was very good to us at Evangel Temple in 1964. Needs both spiritually, physically and financially were met; victories were experienced, and the guiding hand of the Lord was felt. Our help came from above! Many were the times we "looked up." Victory never comes by looking down. There will be times of temptations, but let me assure you "God tempts no man." It is the devil who tempts. God tries the heart. Always the devil tempts the flesh, or our five senses. It may be sickness, or lust, or covetousness, pride, or a hundred other things that have to do with our senses. These will not be temptations to some of the children of God, but there will be those times that God tries our heart. He will see just how much you love Him. But thank God you can be tried and come forth as "pure gold."

In the old Testament we read of Abraham and Lot and the decisions they made. Lot was tempted by the material wealth of the world, and chose such. Abraham had risen above being tempted by possessions. Even though he was a man God had prospered with an abundance, he did not let his wealth come before God and being obedient to Him. God tried Abraham's heart. He said, "Abraham, give me your only son." This was something that was near to his heart, but he came out of the fire as pure gold. God said, "I see that you love me." What is a temptation to one child of God will have no effect on another child of God. The world has no allurement to some of us, but then there are those times we must have God's help when our hearts are tried. There is a place in God we can live, not a struggling christian life, but a victorious life. We just realize our help comes from the one who made heaven and earth. Come boldly unto the throne of grace. Sometimes we aren't aware what is really in our hearts. The heart can be deceitful. But God knows! God tries! God proves us!

East Berlin

America is called the land of the free and the home of the brave and I believe it to be just that. Especially after a visit to East Berlin some months ago do I feel this way. I am sure none of us really know what freedom means until it is taken away from us. No doubt, very few of us have ever stopped to think how it would be if we couldn't express our thoughts, or write as we desired, or go where we wanted to go or do as we wished. The majority of us are individuals and live as we please.

When Brother Meares and I were on our way back from the meeting in Celingy, Switzerland, we stopped in West Berlin for a couple of days. One would hardly believe that it had ever been bombed and the the city practically destroyed during the last World War. It has been rebuilt and is now a bustling, gay and lively town with people everywhere. It is much the same atmosphere as you would sense on the streets of Washington, D.C. But how quickly this atmosphere can change!

I have heard much about the East Berlin wall and wanted so much to see the things I had read about in our newspapers. Even our papers carry propoganda, so I wanted to see first hand for myself. Of course, West Berliners are not allowed to cross the wall into East

Berlin, but there are touring buses on which a foreigner may go any day of the week.

At the time of our visit it was only two days away from the first anniversary of the wall. You might say, "Why didn't the people get out when they saw the wall being built?" The wall was up and finished before the people hardly realized what was going on. Certainly now, though, it is there to remind them that they are in captivity and with little hope of escape. It winds some 38 miles separating East and West Berlin.

There are some 20,000 guards patrolling the walls and two guards are placed together and usually changed every three weeks. The reason for this is they do not want the guards to become good friends and perhaps try to escape. The way it is now, one doesn't have time to really learn the other and if he spoke of escaping, he might be talking to the wrong person and be turned in. Also if one guard allows the other to escape then he can be held and punished in his stead.

At Check-Point Charlie, the border crossing, our bus was stopped and our passports taken by the East Communist guards. We had some papers to fill out and then allowed to go on through the gate. Our communist guide was very nice and tried to make the tour interesting and show places of interest, but there was nothing to see. It reminded me of a ghost town, (if there is such a place)... There was hardly anyone on the streets, no one shopping for there is very little one can buy and if it were in the stores it would be too high for their income. A car there costs twice what it would cost here, and it has to be bought on a cash basis. Then even if you would order one, it may be two years before it would be delivered.

I asked our guide why no one was on the streets and he said, "Well, this is Saturday and they are either enjoying their homes or are at the river in their yachts." I suppose he expected me to believe him. When I was back in West Berlin I asked the guide what excuse they gave during the week for no one being on the streets, and he said they would tell you they are all at work.

A few hours tour and I was ready to get back to West Berlin. I began to think and think hard what freedom really meant. If just a few hours in a communist territory made me feel as I did, just how did those precious people really feel inside? When their freedom will come, one does not know. My thoughts were turned to the scripture, "Ye shall know the truth and the truth shall set you free." Even if they were captives, if they just knew our Lord they could be free in Spirit.

A Constant Reminder of   Russian Guards Along
No Freedom   the Wall

Missions   —John L. Meares

This month we want to give you a little idea of what your mission money is doing. We here in the homeland give our dollars that the "heathen", as we call them, might hear this glorious gospel that you and I have heard and enjoyed for such a long time. Most of us will never be able to visit any of the places where our mission money goes, but as you read the reports of what God is doing, I am sure you will be blessed and wish in your heart you had more to send to those on foreign soil.

One of our young ministers here at the Temple recently visited Jamaica and preached to the people there. When he returned, he said, "Bro Meares, one does not know how to appreciate America until they leave it. I am so glad I was born here." Yes, we are a privileged people. Why you and I are blessed so abundantly above people in other lands, I will never know, but we are. What little I have been privileged to travel has made me so very grateful that God has not called me as a missionary to some other country, but allowed me to serve Him here in this bountiful country. I am reminded of the time I visited India and at night I would look out my hotel room and there on the sidewalks were multitudes of people sleeping, as they had no homes, or no beds in which to sleep. You could not walk down a street without being followed by many small boys and girls begging for just a penny for bread. This is their way of life. One must have a real missionary call from God to enjoy laboring in a foreign country. It is no glamorous adventure as some might think. However, I have seen many missionaries come home on furlough and they were so anxious to get back to where God had called them to labor. This country was no longer home to them. This is when you can know a real missionary. It is one thing to visit a mission field, and another thing to live there. It is much, much less sacrifice to give our money and our prayers rather than our lives.

"Out there is a gold mine... I must go down, but you must hold the rope." These were the words of William Carey, a great missionary, to his pastor. It takes both. So here at Evangel Temple we are trying in a small way to hold the ropes while others go out and dig the diamonds in the rough, and present them to the Master to be polished and shine for Him.

Editorial

—Mary Lee Meares

Four years ago this December the first issue of the Fellowship News was published. It has been a joy to come into your homes by way of magazine. We are now mailing out 3600 copies each month. Your letters and words of comment are always appreciated, and we trust that the paper will continue to be a blessing to you.

As the Christmas season is approaching, you, no doubt, have begun to think what you are going to do, where or whom of your relatives you want to visit, what you are going to give someone, or have started planning for the many, many preparations that accompany the Christmas holidays. This is good, and only natural; however, along with our plans I trust none of us will become so busy we will fail to find time and even extra time to worship the whose birthday we celebrate, in every act of giving, or planning, we should have a gladness of heart because Christ came to be our *Saviour*. This was his purpose of being born in the flesh. Every song we hear about the Saviour's birth should make us tingle wtih excitement. He is our Saviour, so we cannot help but be happy. Yes, Christmas is a time to rejoice, not only because of what we can give one another, but because of the Gift that has been given so freely to us.

Mary, Joseph, Elizabeth, Anna, Simeon, the shepherds, the angels and the wise men all rejoiced because a *Saviour* had been born. This is the meaning of Christmas. If we want to give a real gift to someone, lead them to the Saviour. As the choir sings, "I've seen the light," Lord, let us shine bright enough that someone else might see the Light. Your light can make a heart glad this year, and a burden lighter. You can be the star to lead the lost to the Saviour. So if we really want to rejoice this Christmas and make the heart of our Saviour glad, and the angels in heaven rejoice with us, let us spend our time praising God and magnifying Christ to others. He is our Saviour and our Redeemer!

Remember **CHRIST** *this* *Christmas Season*

"A New Beginning" —Hazel Holley

MRS HOLLEY *is a dedicated Christian worker that has a great desire to see the Kingdom of God furthered, not only at home, but in foreign lands as well. She attended Bible College when a young lady, and ever since has been a devoted worker for the Lord in the New York area. Besides her interest in her local church, she is promoting many missionary endeavors in Africa.*

A "new beginning" has lifted our spirits and the praises of God are still ringing in our hearts because of the great missionary challenge rendered us throughout five days of the anointed ministry of Rev. John Meares in the Manhattan, Queens (New York) and Connecticut areas.

Rev. Bhengu of South Africa had written me to contact Rev. Meares for our next missionary meeting for Africa, and as a result, our group, The African-American Back To God Crusade, arranged an itinerary for Rev. Meares among five of our churches. This was most certainly the directive will of God, because we had been praying and waiting for additonal, first hand information from Africa for some time. The visit by Bro. Meares filled this need. We were anxious to hear about the indigenous ministers of the various churches raised up under the capable leadership of Rev. Bhengu, and Rev. Meares gave us informative, enlightening, and spiritually potent missionary reports which really opened the blinded eyes of many. We are praying for God to give more people a vision for the urgency of the needs in Africa, but are grateful for a "new beginning" among our churches. The reports from Rev. Meares were saturated with great christian love, warmth and sincerity. Tears would come to his eyes, and ours too, as the spiritual and economic needs of the people were unfolded, and also tears of joy came as he stirred our souls with the declaration that a great revival is going on in the Republic of South Africa with souls being saved!

We enjoyed the grand, gospel messages which brought about a spirit of revival in each of our services. The anointing was great and the power of God was heavy among us. I am constantly being asked, "When is Rev. Meares coming back?", and I can only reply, "I hope very soon." I can now readily understand this quote from Rev. Bhengu's last letter to me, "… You will enjoy him. He is our own. We do not just like him, but love him. The crowds literally weep and sigh whenever we pass greetings to them from Bro. Meares and also Bro. Petrucelli. They have become part of us here."

Rev. Meares worked overtime by giving reports, preaching, showing the African films, and taking monthly pledges and offerings for the support of God's messengers in Africa. The people accepted the call of the missionary challenge an as a result, a number of additional African workers will be supported in Malawi, Southern Rhodesia, Zambia, and the Republic of South Africa. Now you can understand why we are praising God for these nights of a "new beginning."

Chapter 6 – 1964

Report

—Mary Lee Meares

on Pastor and Mrs. Meares' recent trip to Switzerland

The home of the Ecumenical Institute.

The ten days spent in Bossey, Switzerland were of great value to me in my Christian experience. I went, not knowing what to expect at this gathering of ministers from every continent. Heretofore, in my mind, the World Council of Churches was a church organization that only represented a religious shell and emphatically wanted nothing to do with the real power of God. How wrong I was! I do not mean to imply that all the ministers attending this conference care about the moving of the Holy Spirit as we Pentecostals do. Some are satisfied to worship a structure and a tradition of man, and to have only a form of worship. But on the other hand the questions asked by so many, and the desire that was shown to know of this experience of the baptism of the Holy Spirit, to me, indicated clearly a burning within many hearts for a deeper experience with the Lord. Many of them readily admitted the coldness in their church and their need of the move of God. It was a joy to tell them that the Holy Ghost would endue them with power, and that the day of revival was not just a thing of the past. Many of these theologians had the idea that the apostolic ministry was not for us today. But as the days went by and the scriptures were explained from a Pentecostal viewpoint, you could see their thinking being changed. Many had only heard of "the Pentecostals" and usually what they had heard was the "faults" (Pentecostals do have some). They had not first hand knowledge of this wonderful experience. I have no doubt in my mind that seed has been sown that will bring forth a harvest. There has definitely been an awakening among many of the ministers. It was not just a time of debating of the scripture of this church believing one thing and another denomination believing something else. It was a time of discussing and learning and desiring to be enlightened. As I heard one minister say, "I never knew until I came here that there was any difference in the Holy Spirit being with you and the Holy Spirit being *in* you."

My heart was touched as I heard one minister from East Africa tell of the revival that his country was enjoying. He said everyone that had accepted the Lord as their personal Saviour always greeted each other with, "Praise the Lord." Even though there were many persecutions, still the constant phrase was "praise the Lord." As he spoke, love flowed from each word. He would readily put many of us who are filled with the Spirit to shame in comparison with the burden he felt and manifested for the salvation of his fellowmen.

I left Switzerland with a joy in my heart for what I felt had been accomplished for the kingdom of God. The world must know of the Pentecostal experience with power, and many have now heard that heretofore were in darkness.

A Shield in 1964 —John L. Meares

No one knows what Nineteen hundred-sixty four holds. We do know, however, that we are living in momentous days when death and tragedy can sweep the whole world in a wave of destruction that could not have been imagined a generation ago. With all of the efforts that are being made to bring peace in the world, yet our peace is the most insecure in history. There are those that even seek to go to the remote areas of the world to find safety. Others build underground shelters in search of safety.

Abraham believed that God was his hield, for God promised to him, "I am thy shield." (Gen. 15-1). The Lord spoke this to him in a vision and Abraham knew the Lord would not fail him. God was faithful and throughout all of Abraham's life, God shielded him: No evil coming near him, he enjoyed the Divine Presence and the favor of the Divine Friendship. However, the promise need not be to Abraham alone, but indeed to all of His spiritual seed. For the righteous require a shield. There is evil on every hand, seeking to destroy those who trust in God. There are evil spirits as well as wicked men that combine under one mighty persevering and powerful adversary, the devil. He is referred to in the scriptures as going about like a roaring lion seeking whom he may devour. Again, he is pictured as throwing fiery darts to destroy the faithful. We are not within ourselves sufficient to withstand the diabolical powers. Consequently we are in a position of great need. Were it not for God's gracious mercy and protecting Shield, certanly we would perish. But thank God He still declares, "I am thy Shield."

A shield is a piece of defense armor to ward off the arrows or strokes of the enemy. God is this Shield to His people in many ways.

He is a Shield of their substance. The Bible tells how God put a hedge around all that Job owned, so that satan could not injure his property. And so it is that God will protect our substance as we commit all that is ours unto Him. God promises that no plague shall come nigh our dwelling place, for He is the Shield of our bodies. He holds the life and breath of His saints in His hands. He gives His angels charge concerning them. He is a Shield of our souls, for He guides, He keeps and upholds the souls of His people. He watches for their safety. He preserves from satan's attacks, from the world's snares and from the weaknesses of the flesh. So then God is a Shield of the righteous in all they are and over all they have.

The wonderfulness of this Shield is its great power for the mighty power of God is the Shield and defense of our righteousness. This is an all sufficient Shield that has never failed. It is a perpetual Shield at all times and at all places. Throughout life in every age and season, and even in the valley of the shadow of death, the Lord is the only Shield.

MOTTO FOR 1964

And as ye would that men should do to you, do ye also to them likewise. Luke 6·31

In the coming year ahead, we need to recognize that there is none other to help us. All our human efforts are but sinking sand without God. He is the only sure and everlasting defense and Shield of the righteous. Therefore, let us cleave unto the Lord. Let us look into the New Year with great confidence, for our hope is in the Lord. Let us look into the New Year without fear, knowing He will not fail us for a minute. By faith and prayer, God's protecting and persevering power will encircle us. Then let us not for a moment be forgetful of God's protection, but constantly give heart-felt thanks for it and rejoice in His protecting power. Nineteen sixty four will be a great and wonderful year. Of this we can rest assured, for we have a great and wonderful God.

Home Missions Glendale
—Mattie Bowie, Katie McAlister and Juanita Turner

We praise God for His goodness to us. For the past four and one-half years a group of us from Evangel Temple have been holding missionary serviecs at Glen Dale Hospital. The majority of these patients are either paralized, blind, deaf or dumb. When we began these services, there was not much response from them. But praise God, he is able to do the impossible. God has saved so very many. Only last week we saw one person gloriously saved. He has caused those who could not move their limbs to raise them, and the lame to walk. Others who had lost hope of ever returning home again have been sent home. These patients are testifying themselves of the goodness of God and what He has done for them. The nurses have come and ask for prayer and then come back to us and told us how God has answered prayer. God has done so much for the patients and it has been inspirational to us. It has made us more deeply grateful and thankful for our health and salvation.

There have been many of the saints at Evangel Temple that have been a great blessing to these people either with their presence or their prayers and we wanted to share this testimony with you that you might rejoice with us. This is a part of the labors of Evangel Temple. Thank God for the moving of His Spirit at Glen Dale Hospital.

Witnessing   —John L. Meares

A mystery the angels never cease to wonder about is the redemption of the soul of man; how that Jesus came, was born and lived among men. "He came to minister, not to be ministered unto, and to give His life a ransom." This is a mystery that staggers any reasoning mind. It can only be explained in the words of St. John, "For God so loved that He gave."

As we contemplate upon the wonderful mercy, grace, and gift of God, we then should not take lightly His blessings upon our lives. We accept salvation and all the benefits of the Lord many times without returning the adoration and praise to God that should flow from our hearts. To be forgiven of our sins, saved—borned a child of the Kingdom, we accept as a common place experience. However, the Bible is very plain to state that an individual is not saved by the grace of God for himself alone anymore than Jesus Christ was raised from the dead for Himself alone. He was raised to become the first-fruit. Likewise, this life-giving grace of God comes to the heart of a mortal that he may share it with others.

There are many wonderful promises that we like to claim and accept, but most of the promises are on condition. One such promise is the continual presence of Christ with us, for Jesus said, "Lo, I am with you always, even unto the end of the world." If you will notice, this promise is conditioned on the basis of declaring to every creature the wonderous story of redemption. For one to live a victorious Christian life is not only abstaining from the evils of the world or the appearances of evil, but it is living a life that causes men everywhere to know that Christ lives within. It is a life that witnesses to the saving grace of our Lord and Saviour, for we are given God's grace to declare what He has done for us. When we fail to witness for Christ, we no longer can be so keenly aware of His presence-His nearness to us, for the promise is to those who tell every creature.

The promise of Christ to His followers that the Father should send another Comforter again is for the sole purpose of witnessing. Many of us wish to receive God's Spirit without measure for our own enjoyment and spiritual pleasure, but this cannot be. When the one hundred and twenty, in the upper room, were endued with this power, the very first thing they did was to tell all Jerusalem. Here were those who had recently denied the Lord endued with power and speaking with boldness. Jesus declared that, "After the Holy Ghost comes upon you, ye shall receive power," but there is a price for this power. It is not given to us to lavish upon ourselves for our own selfish interest, but is given us to bring glory to God and to further His Kingdom; for He said, "Ye shall receive power to be witnesses unto me." Therefore, to be in the constant presence of the living Christ and to have the power of God flowing in our lives, we must be witnesses unto Him.

Editorial   —Mary Lee Meares

An anniversary, according to Webster, is a notable event. And so it was that eleven years ago this July that an event took place here in Washington that was to have effect on countless hundreds of people. Something began that is still in action, and this was a church now known as Evangel Temple. Each year that passes, we feel that we have just begun — just laid the foundation to do the work which God placed upon the heart of Brother Meares for the city of Washington.

About six years ago we wrote an article in Fellowship News telling how the Lord spoke to Brother Meares, and led him here. There have been so many, many people added to our mailing list since that time that I thought you might like to know a little more of just how and why Evangel Temple began.

It was in the winter of 1955 in Memphis, Tennessee that Brother Meares woke me up one morning around 3 o'clock and said, "honey the Lord wants me to make a move in my ministry." I thought to myself, perhaps a year or so and we might move so, I just said, "O.K." and went back to sleep. A month later my husband came in from a convention out west and said, "Put the house up for sale." I knew he was serious and meant NOW. For a day or two I went around in a daze. I was happy in Memphis. The Lord had helped us establish a good work there, and had given us a wonderful congregation of people to pastor. On the material side, we had a lovely home to live in, so I could think of no reason for leaving and going somewhere else. There was none — except that the Lord wanted us to work in another field of labor.

Brother Meares felt that the south had been blessed with gospel preaching more than the north, and that it was time to go north with the message of "Faith and Power." In July we tearfully — yet with an assurance of God's will, said goodbye to Memphis and moved to Washington, D. C. So it was that Brother Meares, our three children and I began our venture of faith. I say 'faith' for we knew no one in Washington, nor had an invitation from anyone to come to Washington; yet we were sure that God would have an interdenominational church for all people of all races in the nation's capital.

It was not easy to find a building in which to have service — especially if one wanted to have service every night. But finally, for the sum of $2000.00 a month, we secured the Turner's Arena which seated around 1500 people. This was not at all a desirable place to worship. On Wednesday and Saturday nights there were boxing matches and dances respectively, so we always had to give up these two nights of the week. However, the other five nights found a great crowd worshipping the Lord in Spirit and Truth. Many sin-sick souls found their way to the Saviour, while many, many more found Christ as their Healer.

Just five months later we rented a large, unused warehouse at 1331 'U' Street, N.W. Neither was this the building that we wanted, but after a lot of cleaning and installing of seats, we moved in. At least we could have service every night. We moved in Thanksgiving week and had a Thanksgiving celebration. Everyone was happy to be able to sit in a comfortable seat instead of the bleechers that the arena afforded.

Brother Meares brought in some of the best evangelists week after week to preach and minister to the people. For sixteen months we leased this building, but then one day a notice came that we must vacate. The government wanted to use it; and since they would pay $70,000 a year for it, we decided there was no use for us to make an offer. Once again we were faced with the problem of a place to worship. Our people began to pray about a place of our own—not just a place to rent. The Lord opened up (just in time) the York Theater at 3641 Georgia Avenue. It was necessary to vacate the 'U' Street building by the 18th of March. The last movie at the York was shown on the 17th, and we had our first service in our new home on the 18th. The down payment of $25,000 was raised by the many fellowship members and friends of the then 'Evangelistic Center.' So very, very much has been done in remodeling the old theater into a lovely sanctuary in which to worship. Such a transformation! But the greatest transformation—the greatest miracle has been that of the harlot, the drunkard, the church member, or that person who had simply lost their way and felt there was no purpose in living. And our heart rejoices that these miracles still take place every week.

We must have larger facilities to take care of the vision that has been laid upon Pastor Meares heart, and plans are in the making for such. These have been eleven exciting, joyous and rewarding years. Never have we had the privilege of pastoring a sweeter, more dedicated congregation of people than you find at Evangel Temple.

They are always ready to pray and stand with you in any need that is presented. The little chorus that Brother Petrucelli brought back from South Africa has become the prayer of this congregation.
If you believe, and I believe And we together pray
The Holy Spirit will come down And Washington will be saved.

Involved

— Mary Lee Meares

Not long ago, for 42 minutes, twenty-four people watched a young Italian girl in New York City stabbed and raped without once offering any help or driving away her assailant. She screamed for help, to be sure, but yet people just peered out their windows and doors and watched, but never answered her cries. The assailant fled, but after seeing no one was coming to the rescue of her screams, returned to finish his job of stabbing her to death. When policemen came and questioned those who had watched, and asked why they had not gone to her aid, or why had they not even phoned earlier, or done something, their replies were, "I thought it was a lover's quarrel." Another said, "I didn't want to become involved." And such were the excuses of letting a girl die without any help of the twenty-four who looked on and watched. None of them wanted to get INVOLVED. Not one.

How many Christians, yes Christians, just stand by from day to day and watch a boy, a girl, man or woman die that are on their way to hell. We know it, and yet by our actions we are saying, "I don't want to get involved." We never go to their rescue or tell them there is a Saviour that can save them and give them Eternal Life. We seem to only be interested in getting to heaven ourselves. Perhaps, you aren't aware that this is your attitude, but can God judge otherwise?

It is time Christians became involved in the saving of souls. Even though we live in perilous and dangerous times, we live in a golden opportunity of spreading the gospel to the lost, dying world. The radio ministry is a vital ministry in these last days. A radio message reaches much more of a diversified audience than does a message preached in a church building. Perhaps this is one of the reasons. When one sees a church building with the sign "Baptist," "Methodist," "Pentecostal," or any other denominational name on it, you at once think of a certain group of people that believe a certain doctrine and attend their own particular church. If that is not your faith, you usually do not think of attending their services. But with radio it is different. You see no sign on a building, not even a man. You only hear a voice telling what Jesus can do. In the privacy of his home, even a Jew will listen to radio preaching, since he is free from the effects and influences of the building, people and surroundings. The same is true of a sinner. Perhaps, he will not go to church, but he will listen to the radio.

This is why I am asking you to be a faith partner in the radio outreach in 1965. Reverend Meares has been preaching each week for the last nine and one-half years here in Washington. The program reaches out into Maryland and Virginia and the surrounding areas. Letters each week come in as a result of the broadcast. Will you become INVOLVED in the winning of souls by means of radio? Do not stand by and watch a person die without offering help—Jesus Christ. On the last page of Fellowship News is a coupon that we pray you will fill out and return to our office. Thus, you will be saying,

"God, I want to be one who is involved in the winning of souls for your kingdom." The Lord help you to be obedient to His voice.

Testimonies

Rev. Meares and Rev. Petrucelli and Members of Evangel Temple:

I am writing to let you know how much I have appreciated the wonderful things you have done for me since the death of my husband. The Lord has been wonderful to me. I just cannot thank Him enough. I really miss the services there even though I did not get to attend as often as I would have liked. You could always feel the presence of the Lord in the services.

I enjoyed reading the Fellowship News and wish that you would continue to send it to me. Though I cannot be in the services with you, when I read the Fellowship News it makes me feel like I am there. Whenever I come to Washington I will always come to Evangel Temple. Pray for me and the children and may God take care of all of you.

Mildred McLean
4525 S. 37th St.
Richmond 31, Va.

* * *

"God's Tenth"

"He asks of you?" I had never said this to anyone before, but if I can help someone by telling them a truth in God's Word, then I am doing wrong by not doing so.

I read a clipping recently that impressed me. A pastor wrote to a business man in the city and asked for a donation for some project that they were undertaking in the church. The business man's reply was, "give, give, that is all I hear from the Christian church." The pastor sat down and wrote the business man a letter of thanks for the best definition he had ever heard of the Christian life. He said, "yes, this Christian life is just one continual big 'give, give'."

Oh, that I can have the priviledge to give to God who owns the cattle on a thousand hills and everything there is — that He will accept my gifts, my tithes, my offerings, however small as expressions of love. Then He in return pours out blessings upon me that cannot be numbered. How could I ever afford not to be a "tither?"

I was baptized by Pastor Meares out on Benning Road in Jack Coe's meeting. Then I went to the first service at Turner's Arena and have been in the services ever since. God has healed me so many times and blessed me so until I just can't begin to tell it all.

Marie Morris

* * *

While attending Brother Jack Coe's meetings, I heard that Reverend Meares would be preaching at Fourteenth and W Streets, so I went to hear him the very first night. I had been looking for a place where I could really worship the Lord, and here I found what I had been seeking. I am thankful indeed for what Pastor Meares has taught us about God, and for sending him here to find the lost sheep.

Lula Baldwin

High Blood Pressure Healed

I must tell you how I was healed the Friday night you prayed for me. I had been so weak and tired for months. My daughter insisted I see a doctor, and he said my blood pressure was a hundred above normal. My heart was also bad, plus other conditions. I just can't tell you how bad I did feel. After you prayed for me. I went home and slept like a baby. I went back to the doctor and he said my blood pressure was normal, and my heart much better.

I am praying that you will be my pastor the rest of my days here on earth. I heard you preach your first sermon here in Washington on W Street, and I want you to preach my last sermon.

Georgia Houchins
816 Farragut St., NW

≈ ≈ ≈

The Inner Circle — John L. Meares

Was there an inner circle among the disciples? Was there anyone of the disciples who seemed closer to Jesus than the other? If so, why? In Matt. 17:1-5 we read of the transfiguration of Jesus on the mountain. Here we find three of the disciples, Peter, James and John, on the mountain with Jesus to witness this wonderful event. Jesus had taken these three with Him. They had heard God say, "This is my beloved Son, in whom I am well pleased." A very unusual wonder came to pass. They saw before their eyes Moses who had died almost 2000 years before. They saw Elias, the great prophet, that long since had passed the scene of action on earth. They saw Jesus, their Master, transfigured and appeared in all the glory that He had after His resurrection from the dead. Why did Peter, James and John see the great phenomena on top of the mountain, while the other nine were down at the foot of the mountain? They were all apostles, called of the Lord.

At the raising of Jairus' daughter from the dead, Jesus was accompanied into the closed room by Peter, James and John as He took the little girl by the hand and said, "Daughter, arise." The other disciples remained outside.

Again, when Jesus was experiencing His most severe trial of His earthly life, and He went into the Garden of Gethsemane with all of His disciples, He asked Peter, James and John to come a little closer to Him, apart from the others. During the agony in the garden, He went back twice to these three to converse with them. He seemed to desire their presence during this time of intercession.

Peter was a rough, swearing fisherman with a bad temper, but the Lord called him. He calls the least of us and makes something out of us! But Peter had a characteristic about him that God certainly did love. Even of the three — Peter, James, and John — Peter seemed to stand foremost above all. He had many faults. He denied the Lord.

He got mad and jerked his sword out and cut off the ear of the high priest's servant. It seemed he made more blunders than the rest of them put together, but God chose him to preach on the day of Pentecost. What was it that God saw in Peter that made him a very special vessel? Peter had the courage and boldness of a lion. This was it. You cannot be a follower of the lowly Nazarene unless you have a little bit of courage. Some Christians don't have enough courage to witness for the Lord. When I was a young man I attended a Bible school in Cincinnati. There was also a young man there with a car and a lot of money, and was a sinner of sinners. A group of us had been praying for him. One night he was gloriously saved. God's glory was upon him until he did not know what to do. I said, "let's go to the park and you tell what the Lord has done for you." It was about ten o'clock at night and a group of teen-agers came to see what was going on. One at a time we began to testify and then we pushed this boy out and told him to testify. Whereas he had been ashamed before, he now had courage and was glad to tell what Jesus Christ had done for him. You need to have a little courage to tell others about your salvation, and about Jesus Christ your Elder Brother, and God your Father. Peter did a lot of things wrong, but at least he had the courage to do something. I would rather see people try to do something and get mixed up doing it, than not to try to anything at all. As surely as you try to do something, you will do a few things that will not be just right, but God will be there to help you when you fail. Peter saw the Lord walking on the water, and he asked the Lord to let him come to Him. Jesus said, "Come on." The water held him up until he took his eyes off Jesus, but the Lord was right there to pick him up. He was the only one who had enough courage to try to walk on the water. The rest of the apostles sat in the boat scared half to death, thinking they had seen a ghost. Peter had enough courage to take God at His word. God puts a premium on a person who has courage. I have seen people go out on the street corners and do things that maybe you would be ashamed to do, or to be with them, but at least they won souls to God.

In the garden of Gethsemane, soldiers came to take the Lord. Seeing this, Peter pulled out his sword and cut off the ear of the servant of the high priest. The other disciples were standing back with their knees knocking. He made a bad mistake, but Jesus was there to pick up the ear and put it back on. The devil will keep you from taking a step for God. He will try to bluff you, but remember only those who declare God with courageous hearts will get anything or anywhere with Him. You say, "But Peter denied the Lord." That is true, yet he was the only one who had courage enough to even go to the back of the hall at the trial of our Lord. The rest of them had run and hid somewhere. After he denied the Lord he went out into the darkness and wept like a baby, and he was forgiven. It may be that you make a lot of mistakes, but have enough courage to do something for God. If you had a child who never made an effort to walk, and you would not allow him to try because you were afraid he would fall and hurt himself, he would become an invalid. A lot of people who call themselves children of God are invalids. They do not have the courage to walk by faith. They are afraid they will fall. If you do fall, remember the Lord is there to pick you up. The Lord performed a miracle when the high priest's ear was cut off. The Lord can take your mistakes and make miracles out of them.

Faith Toward God —Robert Matthews

Paul tells the elders of the church that everything that was profitable unto them be publicly taught from house to house. He testified both to the Jews and the Greeks repentance toward God, and faith toward our Lord Jesus Christ. Acts 20:20-21. He let the elders know that they must have faith toward our Lord. Faith toward God is the way we come to the knowledge of salvation. Ephesians 2:8-9. There are many who will try to change the way of salvation by working their way into the Kingdom. They try different methods, but the Apostle Paul declares if an angel from heaven preach any other gospel unto you, let him be accursed. Galatians 1:8. The gospel that Paul preached was a gospel of faith. The word is in thy mouth and in thy heart, that is the word of faith which we preach. Faith toward God is being obedient to what the word of the Lord is saying to us, and believing that God is a rewarder of them that diligently seek Him. Abraham obeyed God and went out, not knowing whither he was going. He was looking for a city whose builder and maker is God. This man of faith believed God, and he staggered not at the promise of God, but was mighty in faith. He knew that whatsoever God had promised, He was able to perform it. Faith toward God is when we as God's people will obey and believe His Word and all of the promises that are in His Word—knowing that God will perform His Word as He did for the patriarchs of old.

The POWER of the Gospel —John Hedgepeth

I was born in Hollister, North Carolina in 1934 and was reared in the Halivar Indian Tribe. There we had our own church and school which I attended until I was sixteen. I was something like the prodigal son—I wanted to see the world. I went to Rocky Mount, North Carolina, got a job as a waiter, and made good money. However, I wasted it on riotous living. After being there for two years I went back home and got a job.

I became restless and came to Washington where I had a sister living. This was in 1951. By this time, I had became a drunkard, and soon was unable to keep a job. I began to drink more and more and finally became an alcoholic. I was unable to pay for a room, so I lived in parks, alleys and jail houses. I cannot count the times I was locked up. There were as long as five months at a time that I had no home to stay in, hardly any food and so weak.

I was unable to talk. But thanks be to God, who is able to deliver from prison bars and a life of sin. I can say like the Apostle Paul in Tim. 1:15: "This is a faithful saying and worthy of all acceptation, that Christ Jesus came into the world to save sinners; of whom I am chief." In April, 1955 I was walking down "U" Street under the influence of alcohol. As I passed 1331 U Street, I heard singing that sounded like angelic beings singing. The Lord stopped me in my tracks and led me inside. God, alone, knew how miserable I was. Reverend Meares was preaching and never in my life had I seen a man so full of the power and the glory of God. When he gave the altar call I went forward and found the Lord as my personal Saviour. I pray that every drunkard, harlot and every person out of the ark of safety can find an experience like I had with the Lord that night. About a month later the Lord filled me with the precious Holy Spirit. He spoke to me through a prophecy and called me into the ministry.

I have begun in full-time ministry and count it a privilege to work among the lay ministers of Evangel Temple. We anticipate a great harvest as we labour in His vineyard.

John Hedgepeth

Let's Save Our Youth —Mary Lee Meares

One of the first scripture verses that I ever learned was, "Remember now thy Creator in the days of thy youth..." Ecclesiastes 12:1. I not only learned to recite it, but followed its advice and accepted the Lord as my personal Saviour at the tender age of eleven. I have often thought how good God has been to me to keep His hand upon me since a mere child and to keep me from the many pit-falls that Satan has for every boy and girl born into this world.

Each week without exception, we receive at least one letter from some desperate mother saying, "please pray for my boy or girl, I cannot do anything with them." So many times the child has not even reached the teen-age stage. Should we not become alarmed that there are so few that are remembering their Creator in their youth? Wherein does the fault lie? Have the parents failed—has the church failed? Perhaps both are to blame. The Bible says, "Train up a child in the way he should go…". This is speaking to the parents, but how can parents train a child in the way they know not? There is only one way they should go and that is the Christian way. Then if the parents do not teach them by example of Christian living, does not the responsibility rest with the church to lead them in the ways of the Lord?

This is the responsibility that we have felt here at Evangel Temple for the last few years. When one carries a burden for teen-agers, he is carrying a burden with many problems attached—problems which are not solved without much prayer, effort, time and money… Perhaps this is the reason the church too often shifts the responsibility.

We have watched the young people of Evangel Temple grow from a mere handful to about a hundred or more. We have seen young boys and girls mature from babes in Christ into strong Christians in the Lord. You would think that some of them have been serving the Lord for many years. There are a number of our young boys who are planning to enter the ministry, and numerous girls who are serving the Lord from the deep of their heart. One night each week it is their joy to go out witnessing to other young people about the Lord, and on Sunday morning it is the usual, rather than the unusual, at the close of the Sunday School class to see boys and girls accept the Lord as their Saviour.

We were so pleased when a few months past we received a letter from a lady in Akron, Ohio who said, "It is such a thrill to hear young people sing so in the Spirit, and seem so consecrated unto the Lord." She was speaking of our teen-age choir who had been to Akron for a week-end service. What is more beautiful than young boy or girl living a clean, wholesome life for the Lord? My heart yearns to find boys and girls in the prime of life, full of energy and talent, and teach them the way of salvation. What can God do with a life yielded unto Him, or a piece of clay that can be molded into a vessel of honor and service?

Are you concerned about the youth of this metropolitian city? Have you stopped to think that the destiny of our city, our nation our world will rest in their hands in a few short years? If the church does not reap a harvest of souls for the kingdom of God among our youth in the very near future, our nation will reap a catastrophe. It is not the missiles, rockets, and man-power alone that will save our nation but God — fearing and God — serving men and women whom God will remember.

We must reach out a hand to the Youth. We must let them know we love and want to help them find the Way. When they find the Way, the delinquency problems will be solved. We are so grateful that we now have a large Youth Center for our boys and girls to meet in. The first few months of 1962 have been wonderful and we are now making plans for many youth revivals. By the close of this year we believe we will not only have doubled, but tripled in boys and girls who have a desire to be an ambassador for Christ. This is a challenge to Evangel Temple! Pray for our young people and tell other young people about the Youth Center. Let us go forth as a mighty army to win the boys and girls of Washington, D.C. to Christ.

Oral Roberts University The Collegians

The Collegians, a 36 member student musical ensemble, will represent Oral Roberts University of Tulsa, Oklahoma this summer on an extended European tour which will include appearances in Israel, Scandinavia, Scotland, England, Greece, Italy, Switzerland, France. Holland and Bulgaria. Just before leaving for overseas they will give a concert on June 2, 8 o'clock p. m. at Evangel Temple, 3641 Georgia Avenue, N. W., Washington, D. C. You are invited to come hear this combined choir and instrumental ensemble. Bring a friend with you.

YOU HAVE A SPECIAL INVITATION

JUNE 2 8 o'clock P.M.

EVANGEL TEMPLE
3641 Georgia Ave.
Washington, D.C.

PASTOR   JOHN L. MEARES

A Spiritually Matured Christian
—John L. Meares

St. Mark 4:26-28. "And he said, So is the kingdom of God, as if a man should cast seed into the ground; And should sleep, and rise night and day, and the seed should spring and grow up, he knoweth not how. For the earth bringeth forth fruit of herself; first the blade, then the ear, after that the full corn in the ear." Jesus said, "So is the kingdom of God." It was a custom of Jesus to speak of the ways of nature and then compare them to the ways of God in dealing with us. The above verses of scripture are such.

The kingdom of God certainly comes without observation, and certainly without our complete understanding of it. In fact, most of the wondrous things we experience today, we take for granted, never understanding them at all. Here the Lord brings this out by pointing out that a man sows a good seed in the ground and then goes about his affairs and miraculously the seed springs up and grows. But as Jesus said, "he knoweth not how." The mystery that is in the little kernel of the seed is far beyond human understanding. Somehow within the kernel, it contains the miracle of life. And so it is as to the Spirit. It is impossible to understand how one may be "born again." Life—life from God imparted into the heart of mortal man. So great is this life that Jesus described it by calling it a new birth.

Jesus said when a man sows the seed that he then rests; he sleeps and rises. There is no power that man can have over the control of this miraculous life, for the earth bringeth forth of herself. Man only has the small participation in this glorious miracle of sowing the seed. So it is with this wondrous life that the Lord Jesus Christ gives to us through the Spirit. It is from God, with very little on our part but merely coming to Him and committing our lives into His hands. The Apostle Paul declared, "Being confident of this very thing, that He which hath begun a good work in you will perform it until the day of Jesus Christ." God's grace does not burst forth in our hearts because of our good works, but as mysteriously as a grain that is sown in the ground bursts forth and springs up, so it is that as soon as we place ourselves in the hands of God, His spirit will miraculously burst forth into a new life.

God still regulates things and there are no short-cuts. Jesus explained the miracle of the seed that is sown in the ground. He said, "First the blade, then the ear, and after that the full corn in the ear." This order cannot be reversed, nor can it be bypassed. There are no short cuts. The pulsating life manifests itself quite unnoticed as it first breaks the ground, and then with such a small blade it begins to appear. But in due course, with the sun and the rain, it grows up to a stalk and at the proper time, the full ear is matured on the stalk. But the farmer must be patient for his crop. There cannot be a harvest before the full season has come for the matured ear of corn.

When a child is born, he quickly begins to imitate the adults about him. The little girl will try to walk in her mother's shoes, and play with her doll as though it were her child. Young boys have growing pains to become a man and if it were possible they would completely bypass their childhood to become an adult. However, the childhood is extremely necessary for a person. When one is denied their childhood, serious reactions may appear in later life, not properly ever maturing. It is a great tragedy to give a child authority and power for himself or those about him. For a child can become an adult to early and cause great disaster. On the other hand, it is certainly pathetic for one to remain a child and never mature. A little babe is a symbol of innocence and purity and joy and delight. But over the years if it should remain a babe, it would be the heartbrake of its family.

When a child is growing, it may seem that they will never become grown. But let someone see the child who has not seen him in a long time, and their usual remark is, "my, how they have grown." We have to stop and look back before we notice they have grown very much. The same is true in our christian experience. It may seem to you that you are not growing in the Lord. Stop and look back to when you were first born—just a babe in Christ. See how far God has brought you—how you have learned to walk instead of crawl. Even though our spiritual birth is such a wondrous miracle of God, yet it is ordered by God to grow and mature on the same principle as God has ordained in all of nature. There are times that we have such yearnings in our heart and we wait upon the Lord and cry out that He will give us power; that He will exercise the gifts of the Spirit in our lives. I cannot help but believe that God blesses us with all of His richness that we are able to contain. Indeed, He gives us all of His power that He can possibly trust us with. But if we will keep our life submissive before Him, the Spirit will continue to work in us and bring us into a place of greater responsibility in His kingdom and of greater power. We should not despise that it is first the blade, and then the stalk before the full ear of corn can be matured. So then in every disappointment and every test and every trial, we should look up and rejoice and be thankful to God, for by letting patience have her perfect work, we are being made perfect and entire. And as Peter said, "the trial of our faith is much more precious than gold." God is ever striving to bring us into a place that more of His glory might be manifest through us, and that His power might be felt through our lives. Thus, the road to spiritual maturity is committing our lives into the hands of God, knowing that "All things work together for good to them that love the Lord and are called according to His purpose."

Himself He Could Not Save
—Mrs. John L. Meares

When someone says to you, "show me" in a manner that means if you could you would, it is a temptation, to say the least, not to show them.

Jesus was human the same as He was divine. And I believe if He had not already obtained the victory in the garden, He would not have been able to withstand the temptation of showing those that were mocking and making fun, that He had the power to come down off the cross, thus proving to his enemies standing around that He was the Son of God.

Early in His ministry He was tempted to prove Himself the Son of God. Satan had said to Him, "if you're the Son of God. turn these stones to bread. If you're the Son of God, cast yourself off this mountain, it won't hurt you." But Jesus had again already overcome the temptation. He had just fasted for forty days and was full of the Spirit. Throughout His ministry He was tempted even as you and I are.

Never did the Son of God manifest His power of the divine just to show people. He only manifested power to glorify His heavenly Father. Perhaps, you some time or other, have had someone to do evil to you and the human within you said, "I'll show you." but the divine said, "that would not be Christ-like, and I cannot afford to do it." Any power that is manifested through our lives should be for one reason and that is to glorify God, never ourselves.

Jesus knew, "I cannot save myself, for if I did, then I could not save others." He was thinking of you and me. The principle of the salvation of the world is a divine law that still lives. Jesus said, "he that would save his life would certainly lose it, but he that will be courageous to lose his life for my sake and the gospel shall certainly find it." Christ could not afford to show His power and come down from the cross. It was not the nails that held him there, but His love for you and me. No doubt, some that were standing by said, "Is not that the man that has healed so many sick people?" Another said, "He is the one that spoke and made our hearts burn within us. Why does He not show these people. Anyone that can can raise the dead can come off that cross." But as surely as Christ would not save Himself, neither can we afford to save ourselves. We must give ourselves—lose ourselves in Christ, that others might know that He gave His life that they might live. I am glad that I have a life to give to Him.

"A Well Within" —John L. Meares

St. John 4:14. "But whosoever drinketh of the water that I shall give him shall never thirst; but the water that I shall give him shall be in him a well of water springing up *into* everlasting life." When Jesus came to this earth there were many religious people that sought with great effort to please God in their rituals, and in many religious actions, However, to their dismay, Jesus did not commend them for all of their extreme efforts. In fact, He gave the example of the Pharisee who prayed his long prayer, declaring all of the good and honorable things that he did, and the publican's prayer who cried out for God to have mercy upon him a sinner. He stated that the sinner's prayer was heard rather than the Pharisee's. Christ did not come to keep the religious rituals and practices that were imposed upon the people. He said God does not want sacrifice, but mercy. He came to minister. "The Spirit of the Lord is upon me, because He hath anointed me to preach the gospel to the poor; he hath sent me to heal the broken-hearted, to preach deliverance to the captives, and recovering of sight to the blind, to set at liberty them that are bruised. To preach the acceptable year of the Lord." He declared that this scripture was fulfilled in himself. Not only did He come to minister, but he came to give of Himself a ransom. The end of his ministry climaxes in the shameful crucifixion, with mockings and railings. Indeed, it was the religious people that observed the traditions and ceremonies, and who demanded his shameful death.

To the religious people this was the finish of the man from Nazareth who claimed to be the Son of God, who healed the sick, and raised the dead—the man Jesus, who forgave the sinful and commanded them to go their way and sin no more.

The proof, however, of all these claims was not only verified by his works and ministry, but by the glorious event of his resurrection. All of our faith is anchored in this magnificent feat over death, hell and the grave. This resurrection power was not manifested only after the crucifixion of Jesus, but during his ministry. He said to the sisters of Lazarus that their dead brother would live again, for said He, "I am the resurrection and the life." It was this power of the resurrection that Jesus manifested in his ministry that broke the bonds of the captives, that caused the blind to see, the lame to walk, and the sinful to be turned from their evil ways. Something happened within all of those in whose life this resurrection power began to flow.

In describing this marvelous power, Jesus said it would be in you "a well of water springing up *into* everlasting life." This still remains the glorious miracle of salvation. It cannot be experienced in religious practices and dogmas, but only can be experienced as one shares in the resurrection which brings eternal life.

Every born-again Christian shares in this resurrection power. The scriptures declare, "He that is in Christ is a new creature." Jesus was manifested so that anyone who thirsts may "come unto Him and drink... and out of his belly shall flow rivers of living water. But this spake He of the Spirit." The scriptures are very plain concerning everyone who has truly experienced the saving grace that salvation gives—bringing one into an experience with everlasting life. It is an experience that is from within. Any trial or disappointment from without cannot destroy this lifegiving well of water that is springing up within. This is the glorious sharing in the resurrection that is an experience now for all that will have faith toward God through Jesus Christ. Thus, the resurrection is a present reality, a present victory, a present joy, as well as the complete triumphant over death in the ages to come, world without end.

The apostle Paul emphasizes this present participation that we have in His resurrection when he says, "But if the Spirit of him that raised up Jesus from the dead dwell in you, he that raised up Christ from the dead shall also quicken your mortal bodies by his Spirit that dwelleth in you." Rom. 8:11. It is no longer necessary to seek inspiration from without or try to prove by works your relation with God, but salvation is a glorious well of water within, springing up into everlasting life. This is our participation and sharing in the resurrection of Christ every day of our life.

Letters to the Pastor

Dear Pastor Meares:

I was healed while being baptized a few months ago at Evangel Temple. I had suffered numerous attacks of gastrins and had a mild case of it the night I was baptized. Also, my nose had been bleeding frequently for almost two weeks.

While sitting in service I listened as you told the congregation to obey Christ's command by following Him in water baptism. I had been baptized years ago but I was not saved at the time. Now that I was truly saved I wanted to be baptized again. While standing in the water the Spirit moved upon me and I was completely healed of both ailments and have not suffered since. God is so good.

John Borum

* * *

Dear Reverend Meares:

Thank you so much for mailing the Fellowship News to me every month. It seemed as though the message this month was meant just for me, for I needed healing in my body.

I pray that I will be able to visit Washington again this year and attend the wonderful services conducted at Evangel Temple. Reverend Meares, you have such patience and kindness with people. I miss so very much attending the services there and the rich, spiritual food that is offered. I wish you could come here to Atlanta and conduct a revival. I am sure the people would be greatly blessed. I am praying for you.

Callie Webster
Atlanta, Georgia

* * *

In the year of 1957 I was soldier stationed at Walter Reed Hospital. One night I visited the Temple and you prayed God's blessings upon my life. Today, thank God, I am in a full time ministry. I gave up a job as a registered pharmacist to go "teach all nations" God bless you.

Evangelist Eddie Southerland
Philadelphia, Pa.

Editorial   —Mary Lee Meares

This will be my last opportunity in 1964 to come into your home by way of the Fellowship News. We are now sending 4400 copies out each month—almost a thousand more than this time a year ago. We have been blessed by the letters received and it is our sincere desire that the printed page might be a greater blessing to you in 1965.

Christmas, no doubt, is the most beloved season of the year. I think there are several reasons why this is so. For one thing, it is a time of *remembering* others—usually family and friends. There have been Christmases past that Brother Meares and I have received greeting cards from people we had known years before and I had supposed they had forgotten us, but a card let us know they remembered. The thought came to me this year to send greetings to some people that might least expect it. Send a card to someone that might have the feeling that no one cares for them. There are those we  can cheer and bless by remembering in such a small way. Christ said that in as much as ye have done it unto the least, ye have done it unto me. Remember Christ by remembering others. It could be that there is someone that you have even had a little ill feeling in your heart toward and they felt it. A card could bring peace, one of the symbols of Christmas.

Christmas is a time of *giving*, and real giving is when you give from the heart. It is the spirit in which you give. There have been Christmases I have received some small gift, which actually was not of much value, and yet it meant a lot to me, for I felt the spirit in which it was given. The person gave of themselves, and most of the time it was a sacrifice. Is not this true giving? Let others feel the spirit in which you give this year.

Christmas is a time of *joy*. Why? Because the Lord has come and we have received Him as our Saviour. We have found room for Him in heart and He is with us in our every day affairs. He is our joy, and this joy is for *all* who will receive. Just as the angels sang "Joy to the World", there will be a song of joy in our heart.

Christmas is a special time of *worship*. We do not come with gold, frankincense, and myrrh, but with a sincere love welling up in our heart for our Lord. He is our life, our all, a gift of love to us, and we shall always worship Him as such. May the real joy of Christmas be felt in your heart because of the birth of our Lord and Saviour.

Chapter 7 – 1965

Will You Forget God In 1965?

—John L. Meares

II Timothy 4:10. "For Demas hath forsaken me, having loved this present world ---" This, I think is one of the most forlorn and tragic scriptures in the Word of God. Lately I have come in contact with a numebr of people who at one time really loved God, but now they have strayed away from God and gone back upon their first love and upon their promise unto the Lord. They have lost the touch of His glory and grace in their life, To me, this is one of the most tragic things that can possibly happen. It isn't a great tragedy for a person to die, if they know the Lord. If I have lived for God, have kept the faith, and there is a crown laid up for me, it is no tragedy for me to pass from this world into the presence of God. But for a person who has once known God and then let the devil come in and deceive them and turn their desire from the things of God, this is a tragedy.

I have learned you cannot force people to live for God. To always be telling one how wrong they are only builds a wall between you. You can't drive people to God. God doesn't make people serve Him. You serve God because you choose to serve Him. I am glad it is that way. So, it is the devil's business to dim the eyes and vision of people and cause them to walk in dark paths. Perhaps, you have no intention to backslide, and without really realizing it though, you will begin to drift. A person doesn't have to go out and kill someone, or begin to curse and swear—but you start with the little things. You lose your interest and joy in the Lord, and then way down the road Satan pulls the blind off your eyes and he has you in a miserable trap.

Here was Demas, a fellow laborer with the great Apostle Paul. He had lived with him; had ministered with him; had suffered with him; had been faithful and upright. He had gone with him to Ephesus where the city was turned upside down, and Paul was abused and beaten. He was with Paul when he was thrown into the den of wild animals and suffered many tortuous things. However, it wasn't hardships or persecutions that caused Demas to turn back and forsake the ways of the Lord. He had stood bravely and never flinched or complained. It is not always the persecutions that cause one to turn from God. You say, "What happened?" After all these years of being a faithful follower of the Lord, and now at the time the Apostle Paul was being put in prison and would soon be beheaded, Demas was forsaking him.

Yes, it is an old spirit that causes you to mind the temporary and passing things and get your eyes off the eternal things of God. And most always it starts out with little things that you can't classify as right or wrong. What is wrong is that it begins to come in and steal your devotion from God. Once you get your love and affection in the right place, you will not be too concerned about what's wrong and what's right. There is a missile so perfected, that has some kind of a guided system in it, until the thing can be set and that old iron bird just flies. It goes where it is supposed to. Neighbor, when you get your love flowing in the right direction toward God and the things of God, there is an invisible Being that is within you that guides you in the paths of righteousness for His name sake. It will guide you right. The way you judge your spirituality is not the things you do or don't do, but by the hungering and thirsting that you have in your heart for the things that are of God. This determines our stand with God. I thank God for the times when I feel that compulsion and urgency in my spirit crying out for God, that compulsion to pray more, and listen to God. If you love your children, there are some things you do because love compels you to do them. Otherwise they would be hardships. And when we serve God and live for Him, there will be those times we do things to bring this body under subjection. But oh, those wonderful times when my spirit cries out for God.

This is the only way we go from glory to glory. I couldn't live like I lived a year ago and be pleasing in the sight of God. Not that I indulged in sinful pleasures last year, but as I grow in the Lord, I must manifest more of the Lord. Our spirit must reach out to the Spirit of God, and as our spirit is drawn closer to God, more fruit will bear in our lives.

EVANGEL TEMPLE'S

10th

ANNIVERSARY

JULY 18, 1965

COME AND ENJOY THE
BLESSINGS OF GOD

Pastor Meares stacked it up

DINNER IN ROCK CREEK PARK
(Bring a Big Basket of Food)
(No Afternoon Service)

EVANGELIST PAULA JACKSON
Will be Sunday evening Speaker

REV. G. B. McDOWELL
Begins Revival July 20th

Ken, Virgil, Pete and Don

EVERYONE WELCOME

Where is your love? Where is your devotion? You may have clean hands, but do you have a clean heart? If you let your spirit be tuned into the Spirit of God, you won't go wrong. You won't go into the

city of Thessalonica and forsake all that is good and wonderful. May
you have implanted within your heart in the year of '65 a new love
and glory and hunger for the things of God. God forbid that you
should ever forsake them for the things of this world.

> Turn your eyes upon Jesus, look on His wonderful face
> Then the things of this life will grow strangely dim
> In the light of His glory and grace.

When the Holy Ghost comes!
—John L. Meares

"And when he is come he will reproye the world of sin, and of
righteousness, and of judgment: Of *sin*, because they believe not on
me; Of *righteousness*, because I go to my Father, and ye see me no
more; Of *judgment*, because the prince of this world is judged." St.
John 16: 8-11.

The Bible says of Jesus, "I will go to my Father and He will
send another comforter." In other words the Holy Ghost will come
and he will reprove the world of sin, righteousness and judgment.

Back under the law the priest would take a lamb and offer the
blood on the altar for the sins of the people, and it was not until the
priest came out of the holy of holies that the people knew whether
or not their sacrifice had been accepted and their sins forgiven. If
the priest did not come out of the holy of holies, they knew God
had struck him dead.

SIN

Jesus died and became the sacrificial Lamb. He rose again and knew
death no longer for mortality put on immortality and corruption
put on incorruption. No longer does a priest have to go into the
holy of holies for us, but we can go into the presence of God for
ourselves. Jesus ascended into the heavens and took the sacrifice

(His blood) and offered it on the mercy seat of heaven. Then He sat down on the right hand of the Father and became our High Priest. Every time I want to utter a prayer I can come boldly into the throne-room of prayer because my High Priest is there interceding for me. You ask, "how do you know?" Before Jesus left this earth He said, "that ye might know that I am with my Father, I will send the Holy Ghost and He will witness to you that I am with the Father." I will send you a comforter, and you will know that I have entered into the holy of holies. The assurance of Jesus as my High Priest is mine because the Holy Ghost witnesses within me. My conscience condemns me if I do wrong and I am aware of *sin*. I reach out for justification.

RIGHTEOUSNESS

The people tried to live right under the law but they could not. Thank God, when the Holy Ghost came it convicted me of my sin and He justified me and made me to know all is well. He has given me His own *righteousness*. Before Jesus came it was impossible to obtain this righteousness. All one could do was offer a dove, or a lamb, but now the Holy Ghost has taken the offering that Jesus placed on the mercy seat of heaven and sprinkled the blood on my heart. The Holy Ghost will reprove the world of righteousness and we can shout, "I am redeemed" and it will bear witness to your heart and you will know you have become a child of God.

The moon shines so brightly but it is said that the moon has no light at all. The moon is up in the sky and when the sun goes down and we can no longer see the sun, the sun shines on the moon and the moon just reflects the light the sun gives. So it is with the Son of God--He is before the throne, seated at the right hand of the Father and He reflects upon us and then we reflect our Father to the, world. As does the moon reflect the glow of the sun, so will our lives reflect the glory of God and shine in a world of darkness and let the world know Jesus lives.

JUDGMENT

"The prince of this world is judged." Jesus said the devil comes like a thief to kill and destroy. Everywhere Jesus went He was faced with the devil. When He would see a person bound He would not speak against that person but against the devil in that person. "Ought not this woman be loosed whom Satan hath bound?" He recognized the devil. The devil thought he had won when he met Him on Golgotha, but know this, the devil did not kill Him. Jesus gave up His life. Then He went into the bowels of the earth and took away the power of satan and became the victor. When the devil begins to beat on his tom-tom, the Spirit will come and say, "John Meares, he is not a lion, but only roars like one. Jesus is the Lion of the tribe of Judah. People in India and Africa worship the devil because they are afraid. If you will let the Holy Ghost speak to your heart you will not have to fear. "Greater is He that is within me than he that is within the world." When you bowed before the cross of Calvary and gave your heart to Jesus you were forgiven and you will never have to stand, before the judgment seat again. The devil no longer has power over you. The blood of Jesus has freed me of all my sins. This is part of the ministry of the Holy Ghost. Yes, the Holy Ghost reproves the world of *judgment*.

The Holy Ghost is *faithful*. Every day it will remind you of your devotion to God. Everyday it will cause a longing your heart to stay near the side of God and to keep the praises rolling from your heart.

LAW Grace & Truth —a sermon by John L. Meares

"For the law was given by Moses, but Grace and Truth came by Jesus Christ."

In this verse of scripture there is a contrast between Moses and the Lord Jesus Christ, and also between the law which Moses gave and the truth and grace which came through Christ. We say grace is the unmerited favor of the Lord, or it is the manifestation of the blessings of God which we are not worthy of. So to define it in a simplier word, I suppose it is love. For when you love someone you will share with them, not because they deserve, not because they have earned, but because you love them. That is what the Bible means when it says, "For God so loved the world that he gave his only begotten son." Certainly the world did not deserve the Son of God.

Moses and Christ are greatly contrasted. Moses was a servant, and Christ is the King of Kings. Moses was just a man, but Jesus was the God man. He was clothed in human flesh, but He was more than a man, He was the God man. Moses was the one who smote the rock, but Jesus Christ was the smitten rock. Moses came to show the way, but Jesus Christ came to be the Way.

The works of Moses and the works of Jesus Christ are tremendously contrasted. Moses performed ten most unusual miracles. They were different from the other miracles in the Bible. We have 32 recorded miracles that the Lord Jesus Christ performed.

The law that was given by Moses was upright; it was a good law; it was a just law; but it was a law that was bigger than everyone it made demands upon. You cannot name a person in the Old Testament that fulfilled the law. Even such a great man as David, a man after God's own heart, transgressed. Moses, the giver of the law himself, was disobedient and was not permitted to go into the land of Canaan. He could only stand on a mountain and look over into the promised land. Human flesh or human will is not big enough — not great enough — not powerful enough. There are only two things that will do the work for fallen humanity. They are *grace* and *truth*.

I don't know how you define truth. I do know that truth is always verified. By that I mean if you have a recipe and follow the directions carefully, whatever you are cooking comes out just like it is supposed to. It is a true recipe. But if you follow the recipe and it does not come out as it should, then it is a false recipe. Scientists tell us if we put certain components together, certain things will always happen, and they have verified that and it comprises truth.

Truth is related with Faith. Jesus said that "if you have the faith of a grain of a mustard seed, you can speak and what you speak will be locked up in the power of truth. So glorious will be this faith locked up in the sight of God that what you speak will not be a lie but just as you speak it. Jesus was the Truth. He did not tell people just what happened. He spoke and it happened. That is Truth. When He stood up in the raging storm of Galilee, He did not say, "This is the worst storm I have ever seen," but He raised His hand and said, "Peace be still," and Truth had so much power in it until all the elements became calm. Truth is the living, vital power that is in this universe. In the beginning the Word of God stood up and said, "Let there be…" He was Truth and the elements had to do what He spoke. The Bible declares that the whole world, the whole universe, is held in fashion by the Word of His power. That is how powerful Truth is.

Truth is not as one philosopher said, "A great relative matter", but Truth is the power of God Himself. It was more than someone clothed in human flesh and walking among men. When the Truth of God spake, things that were not began to be. The blind began to see and the lame began to walk.

The Gospel Mission

—5th and H Streets, N.W. (Chapel)
Washington, D.C. 20001

Dear Reverend Meares:

We wish to thank you in behalf of The Gospel Mission for the use of your camp for children, and to give you a little report of our summer's activities. We conducted week-end camps for five weeks during the summer and also a one week program, as a pilot project for the use of the camp. It was very successful and we were thoroughly satisfied with the results. Many of the children had an opportunity to be out of doors, to be in touch with and ministered to by sincere Christian workers and to enjoy the lake as well as the program that was planned for them.

There were souls saved; a little group) of junior counselors came along in a knowledge of Christ. We did minimum maintenance and are planning for some fall week-end use of the camp. I don't believe I would be presumptious in assuming that The Gospel Mission is very interested in working out an arrangement whereby we could have the camp for our own.

We would like to use the camp for one or two years and, if all goes well, obtain the camp as a permanent effort for our youth and keep it really Christ-centered for the salvation of souls and the deepening and furthering of the work of the Holy Spirit in the hearts of the believers.

You have been very kind and thoughtful and guileless and have displayed great generosity to us without requiring payment, and this is an example for us to follow.

Sincerely in Christ,
Harvey V. Prentice, Jr.
Superintendent

(Note) The Gospel Mission is doing a wonderful work here in the city. They sleep around 350 men each night — the down and outers. They have service each evening for these men, and approximately two to three hundred attend the services each night. Also there are Bible classes taught in the afternoon. They are reaching the young and the old for the Lord Jesus Christ. Editor

The Miracle of Rome — Mary Lee Meares

According to Webster, a miracle is a wonder, marvel or wonderful thing. So I can say when I saw the Evangelica Church International last November in Rome, Italy, I saw nothing less than a miracle. I know that in this nation of ours it is nothing unusual to see large beautiful church edifices and even in foreign countries there are some of the most beautiful Moslem mosques, Japanese Temples and Catholic Cathedrals you would ever want to see, one of them being St. Peter's Basilica in Rome. But, when you see a big, beautiful Protestant church in a 95 percent Catholic nation, you are witnessing a miracle. It was Brother Meares' and my privilege to be at the dedication of the Evangelica Church International last November 28th, and my soul was thrilled and my faith seemed to double and even triple as I listened to the story of how this church came into being. I want to share it with you, for I believe it will strengthen your faith in God, and you will rejoice with me because of the moving of God's Spirit in Rome, the city where Paul said, "So, as much as in me is, I am ready to preach the gospel to you that are at Rome also. For I am not ashamed of the gospel of Christ: for *it is the power of God unto salvation* to every one that believeth; Rom. 1:15-16.

Several years ago there was a very successful business man, John McTernan, who lived in California. He had a winning personality, was making extremely good money, and in the natural had everything his heart desired. Only one thing became a stumbling block—alcohol. In fact, he became an alcoholic and the black sheep of his family. He had a lovely wife, but she was unable to stop him from drinking. Then one day he was gloriously saved and filled with the Holy Ghost and he became a new creature in Christ Jesus. He no longer was bound with drink; he no longer needed two packs of cigarettes a day, but now his desire above all else was to serve Christ and love Him. He began to feel the call of God upon his heart so he enrolled in a Bible School in Los Angeles, California, where he studied for three years. During this time he felt that God would have him and his wife go to Italy as missionaries. He presented himself to the mission board of the Full Gospel denomination to which he belonged, but they thought him unqualified to go and rejected the offer. However, his spirit continued to burn within him more as the days passed by. So he finally decided to sell all he had, and without the backing of any mission board, but a faith and trust in God who called him, left American soil for the nation of Italy. This was ten years ago.

In the early part of November Brother Meares' telephone rang and it was Brother McTernan on the other end at Rome. He said, "Brother Meares, I have purchased a new building and plan to move in November 28th, and while I was praying about someone to preach the Dedication sermon, the Lord spoke to me and said, 'Get Brother Meares.' He also confirmed this to my wife. Will you come?" Brother Meares said, "Well, if God told you to get me, how can I say no? I will be there." He hung up the phone a little dazed at it all, but rejoicing in his heart of what God had wrought in the city of Rome. However, it was not until he actually beheld the beauty of the church and saw it first hand, that this miracle really dawned upon him. Brother David DuPlessis, who has visited practically every Evangelical Protestant church on the continent of Europe, and was at the dedicatorial service, says, "It is the largest and most beautiful evangelical church on the continent of Europe."

Since my children are all away in school, I was thrilled to be able to accompany Brother Meares to Italy. I had been to Rome before, but certainly I had never seen any Protestant church that sounded like the one Brother McTernan described. I wanted to see it for myself. He had also asked Brother Meares to remain for at least a week and preach for him. As I sat on the large stage looking over the vast congregation of people that had assembled for the dedicatorial service, and saw the beautifully robed church choir, and the many, many preachers and friends that had come from Canada, Germany, Holland, France, Switzerland, South Africa and other countries, sitting on the stage, my soul thrilled within me, and I knew I was witnessing a miracle. Of the four hundred and fifty people that had flown from the United States to London to attend The Full Gospel Business Men's convention, thirty flew on over to Rome to be in the services there. I remarked to my husband, "I don't think I ever saw any one man and his wife that have so many friends." This winning personality that had put Pastor McTernan ahead in the business world was now being used to win people to God. He and his wife had been faithful and believed God for big things. He has a monthly paper, a Bible School where he teaches and trains young men and women and then they go out and pastor and preach the gospel. He feeds them and keeps them entirely free during their three year Bible tiaining course. He has three fine associate pastors who work with him, and it is marvelous to see the zeal with which his people witness for the Lord.

Editorial
—Mary Lee Meares

Robert Morrison went to China in 1807. When asked if he really expected to make an impression upon the idolatry of the great Chinese empire, he replied, "No, but I expect that God will." How true a statement. None of us can do anything without God. "Not by might, nor power, but by my Spirit—." When one is on foreign soil, more than ever they realize it takes the Spirit of God to win a soul for the kingdom of God or to turn a nation to God.

It was a great privilege Bro. Meares and I had recently to spend a few weeks in South America. I never return from any foreign soil the same person. I am always more grateful to be an American and live in such a prosperous country. I am always impressed so deeply how good God has been to me to bless me so abundantly. Why? I will never know, for I am sure God loves all peoples just the same, but still the fact remains that I and my family enjoy so very much more than most of the peoples of the world.

It was such a joy to visit the work Bro. and Sis. McAlister are doing in Rio de Janeiro, Brazil. We have pictures in this issue showing the construction of the church, etc. What a wonderful and sincere group of people he pastors. As building has always been a love of Bro- Meares, he was at home in giving suggestions and changing plans and designing of their church. Then when he learned that he had been able to save them a couple thousand dollars by the changes made, he felt extremely pleased. For any couple to go to another country, learn the language, the customs, etc. of another people takes courage and a great faith in God. This why I so esteem Bro. and Sis. McAlister in the Lord. It takes much less courage and less of God to give of our means for missions than it takes to give ourselves.

Then in Sao Paulo, Brazil, our hearts were thrilled as we visited with Bro. Harold Williams and Bro. De Melo. Bro. Williams, some of you will remember, was with us in a revival last summer. He has labored in Brazil for eighteen years and ordained some 300 ministers there. Bro. De Melo was one of the ministers he ordained, and certainly this man has a great faith in God. About three years ago Bro. De Melo purchased over an acre of ground to build a church on, at the fantastic price of $750,000.00. I just don't think of ground in other countries costing such. But the most amazing part is that in these three short years they have paid all but $15,000.00 on it. When finished the building will seat twenty thousand people. As far as I know this is the largest Pentecostal church anywhere. We were with him in service on a Saturday night (one of his lesser nights) and yet the building was packed and people standing around the walls. They were worshipping in a basement type building until their new church is completed. It would perhaps seat twelve hundred people. As we entered the building, I could feel the presence of the Lord, and as I listened to them sing (even though I knew not the words they were saying) I just sat there and cried the whole time. Here was a large group of people that had come out on a bad, rainy night, to worship God with all their heart. When I stood to greet them, I was too full to do anything but cry. We felt a kindred spirit of the Lord.

A couple of years ago Bro. Meares had been in services with Bro. & Sis. Taranger in Porto Allegre, Brazil, and he wanted to again visit with them. So on Sunday night we had the pleasure of being in service in Porto Alegre. Bro- Meares preached with the aid of an interpreter to a large crowd of people and many people responded to the altar service in closing. They are doing a great work for the Lord which includes an orphanage for homeless children.

Space will not permit relating in detail our visit, but certainly I know we cannot forget we in America have a responsibility for peoples of other lands. Once Bro. Meares and I were sitting out in one of the parks and here comes two little shoe-shine boys wanting to shine our shoes. Bro. Meares said, "all right," but I said, "No." However, the little boy kept insisting and the look in his eyes made me give in. Bro. Meares did not have the correct change so he told the little boy to get the bill changed for him. When he came back, it still was large bills and when he hand- the two little boys one of them, they hurriedly picked up their kit, with a grin from ear to ear and ran to one side and just stood there and looked at us until we left. They were so overjoyed, they couldn't believe what had happened. I many times said to myself, "what if this were my boy or girl begging on the street?"

May the Lord help us to share our blessings with all humanity everywhere.

The Spirit of the Resurrection
—John L. Meares

But if the Spirit of him that raised up Jesus from the dead dwell in you, he that raised up Christ from the dead shall also quicken your mortal bodies by his Spirit that dwelleth in you.—

Romans 8:11

Loneliness, suffering, tradgedy, heartbreak and death must preceed resurrection. The vibrant story of Easter could not have been a reality were it not for the tradgedy of the cross. How that God could turn such a defeat into mighty victory is beyond human comprehension, but this is the very basis of the Easter account. He arose from the *dead.*

Easter would have to be a very special incident to be related from generation to generation, year after year, had it only effected the Son of God. But its influence is not limited only to the person of Jesus Christ, for just as surely as death came to all humanity through Adam, life comes to all through the second Adam, Jesus Christ. The power with which Jesus broke the bonds of death is an everpresent Spirit that is available to all believers. It so permeates this age of grace until this gift of eternal life reaches into the hospital and sick rooms of the believer and brings about complete healing. This is only an initial evidence from God to the believer that eternal life is a jubilant reality.

In the above scripture it emphasizes the Spirit of the Resurrection. I rejoice to know that this Spirit is an ever present reality of the grace of God. It is not a spirit of fear nor death, nor weakness, it is a Spirit of joy and peace and life forever more. And of this Spirit we are partakers here and now. There is a tendency to relate this scripture to the hereafter only, but it is a present tense reality. The writer declares, "if the resurrection spirit dwell within your mortal bodies"—this is our present bodies of flesh and blood. Thus, the life of Christ or the living resurrecting Spirit dwells in the heart of every believer. So strong is this Spirit that the believer may accept and receive divine healing and divine health here and now. For it is this resurrection. Spirit that quickens—makes alive—makes anew these mortal bodies.

Each time I hear the victorious testimonies of the child of God, I must relate it to the resurrection. Each time I hear of the healing power, I am aware that eternal life dwells in every believer now. For the Spirit of the resurrection quickens our mortal beings, thus when I sing the resurrection hymns and read the resurrection story, I shout hallelujah and because He lives I live also.

Do YOU love children?   —Mary Lee Meares

Jesus loved people. He loved the sick, the crippled, the blind, and those whose bodies were infirmed and twisted. He loved people who were all alone, people that were sinful, and even criminals. Yes, Jesus loved people.

Knowing this then, it is very easy to understand that Jesus would love the children. Who can resist the radiant, smiling face of a child? One day as Jesus was ministering, some mothers came through the crowds with their children in their arms, bringing them into the presence of Jesus. The disciples felt that the Lord should not be bothered with mere children, so they were told to leave as the Lord did not have time to minister unto therm When Jesus heard this, He was much displeased and said, "let the little children come unto me; do not forbid them, for of such is the kingdom of heaven." And He laid hands on them, and bless them." He had time for them.

Because we want children today to know of His love, we have spent thousands of dollars and multiplied hours with great effort to reach them. Multitudes of children are not aware of His love, for the love of Christ can only be manifested to a child through a human being. Therefore one of our greatest burdens and responsibilities is to let all children, everywhere, know that Jesus loves them,

Down at Camp Adventure Land, a place dedicated to children and to the presence of Jesus Christ, many hundreds of boys and girls came this summer from homes with various backgrounds. Some had never heard of the love of Jesus, or His saving grace. But as soon as they found themselves surrounded with the beauty of nature, the open spaces, the big blue sky, the woodland, etc., they lost themselves in an estacy known only to a child enthralled in the handy work of God. Add to this, swimming, riding horses, and a multitude of other activities that children dream about. In such an atmosphere they realize that they are loved. In sharing our love with the children, we can get them to understand that Jesus loves them, and when they realize this, their hearts are warmed and blest by the Spirit of God. It changes their lives, and they will never be the same again. Almost one hundred percent of the children that attended camp this summer came back home with a warm experience of Jesus Christ in their heart. They only needed to learn that Jesus loved them, which is the most important discovery in the life of any human being. This was our endeavor at camp. When we can get them to know this while their hearts are yet young and tender, how much more blessed it is. Our efforts, our toils, and finances are well spent for what has been accomplished at Camp Adventure Land this year.

We at Evangelistic Center must dedicate ourselves anew to reach every child possible for Jesus Christ, and get them to understand the love of God. In this way their lives will be blessed and made profitable for the Kingdom of God. Do not despise the time you spend ministering to them. It is most important' I pray that the love of Christ in your heart will reach out to those of whom Jesus said, "of such is the kingdom of heaven."

Chapter 8–1966

Editorial

—Mary Lee Meares

Recently when reading the office mail I picked up a letter which began, "If everyone were as happy as I am—". The next letter I read began, "I am a very unhappy person—". There was such a contrast in the two letters until I read them both again comparing the two. Both people that had written were Christians, but there was certainly a difference in their attitude toward life and the things of God. If every Christian had the joyous praise that the first letter resounded, many more people would become followers of the Lord Jesus Christ.

I think the most important lesson I have learned since coming to Washington ten years ago is that God inhabits the praise of His children. I have often remarked to others, "I have never seen people worship God in praise like they do at Evangel Temple." It is not a strange or embarrassing thing to lift our hands and voice in adoration to God. Why? Because there is a "well springing up within." Have you ever been asked to raise your hands and praise the Lord, and you did, but your "praise the Lord" had an empty sound, and your arm didn't stay raised long? Unless there is a real thanksgiving in your heart, you have a hard time worshiping God. The reason the visitor to Evangel Temple enjoys the services so, according to their own words, is the spirit of praise that is always prevalent in the services. I think that is what attracts people to pentecostal services. However, just because there is a lot of noise and shouting, doesn't mean that it is a spirit of praise. There is a difference.

I can sincerely say I can't think of one thing that has ever happened to me in life that I should complain or grumble about. But on the other hand, I could never think of all the good things and the blessings of God that have been showered upon me. I would never be able to praise God enough for His goodness and mercy toward me. On this our tenth anniversary, it is with a joyful heart that I write. How could I ever praise God enough for having spoken to Bro. Meares' heart to come to Washington? Where could I ever go to find such a lovable group of people who worship God in "Spirit and in Truth"? As I listen to the victorious testimonies of the saints, my heart is made to praise God with them. As I look over the congregation and see the different ones that are rejoicing in the Lord, and then think of how those same people came at one time to the services, sick, burdened, unsaved, troubled, financially depressed, and every other conceivable trouble, tears of joy cannot be held back. My inner well begins to overflow. I see both men and women that have been in the penitentiary, men that couldn't hold a job because of alcohol, families that hardly had enough to keep them going from one week to the next. Now, they sing and praise God with a smile that is contagious. Christ has come into their life and they are a new creature in Him.

It is not a praise that comes only when one is in the house of the Lord, but it is an abiding praise, on the job, on the bus, wherever we are and in whatever we are doing. No matter how different a path our life might lead, we can all have the abiding presence of Christ, and this is the source of our happiness, our joy and our peace. I can think of no better verse to quote than Ps 103: "Bless the Lord O my soul, And *all* that is within me, bless His holy name."

Letters to the Pastor

Pastor Meares, the services are so wonderful. I enjoy your messages so much, and it seems as you are preaching as never before. The Lord bless you is my daily prayer.

Georgia Hall
Washington, D.C.

* * *

About six months ago I visited Evangel Temple for my first time and it was there I found Jesus Christ and He changed my whole life. I know I have a lot to learn, but I am learning more at each service. I was a terrible sinner and lived a life of uncleanness, but Jesus lifted me up and helped me in my time of need and desperation. I called on the Lord to have mercy on my soul and I remember it as though it were yesterday. God changed my life and has been changing it ever since. I can't write it all down, but there have just been showers of blessings.

Geraldine Tolson
Washington, D.C.

* * *

I had cancer and had only one week to live, but you all prayed for me and I am still living. This was in 1963. I can never forget it.

Anna Mae Glenn
Cumberland, Maryland

* * *

Praise the Lord, God is so good, even to a sinner like me.

On June 9, 1966, my four year old son, John, was burned and had first, second and third degree burns on his right leg. After plastic surgery he was still unable to walk.

I receive the Fellowship News and have also attended your church and know what God can do. After crying and praying and thinking about my baby perhaps never walking again, I decided to call the Temple. A Brother William Harrison from your church came to the hospital on Sunday, June 12, and prayed for my baby and he started to walk that same evening. He was discharged from the hospital on June 14, walking, and is still walking.

I know God must be a real and true God because my husband and I both have seen a real miracle performed on our child.

Enclosed please find a small donation for the church. I am thanking God again for a miracle and for such wonderful people as those at Evangel Temple. May God bless you all.

Mrs. E. M. Evans
1421 57th Pl. N.E.
Washington, D.C.

Where there is no missionary vision, the people perish

Confession...   —John Meares

Text: Rom. 10: 8-11. "...The word is nigh thee, even in thy mouth, and in thy heart: that is, the word of faith, which we preach; That if thou shalt confess with thy mouth Jesus as the Lord and shalt believe in thine heart that God hath raised him from the dead, thou shalt be saved. For with the heart man believeth unto righteousness; and with the mouth confession is made unto salvation. For the scripture saith, Whosoever believeth on him shall not be put to shame." R. V.

This subject is one that we have oft times been instructed along and necessarily so, for it is a must in our christian birth and life. This is the route of true repentance that will cause the sinner or saint alike to strike the rock with a flame of spiritual fire bursting out in one's soul fresh from the altar of heaven. Such is John's exhortation: That "If we confess our sins, he is faithful and just to forgive us our sins, and to cleanse us from all unrighteousness."

Then, there is the daily confession of Christ before men that we may in turn be confessed by Him before our heavenly Father. (Matt. 10:34)

But there is still another step in our confession that is as essential to our spiritual growth as three square meals daily are to our physical development and must be practiced just as regularly. In the text the Apostle Paul speaks very plainly of this confession for said he: "The word is near you, even in your mouth, and in your heart that if you confess with your mouth, and believe in your heart (mind) you shall be saved. Then he explains further in the simplest of terms, that with the heart (mind) man believes and thereby finds favor in the sight of God. But he quickly adds that God does not make delivery until we have declared ourself as having accepted the promise of His Word:... "For with the mouth confession is made unto salvation."

In so many cases we read the promises of the scripture and wish that they might come true in our case. But they seem to be vague and unapprehensive as we reach out in prayer seeking, begging and pleading that God should come to us. And many times because of these vain experiences to receive of God we are prone to take many of the promises that are for the here and now and place them in the distant future. Because of this tendency Paul, like the old testament prophet, let us understand that "today is the day... now is the accepted time." Paul emphasized that, "the Word is nigh thee." To make it more eminent he declares, "even in thy mouth." Because of this simplicity of receiving the promises of God's Word we oft-times stumble. However this is essentially the same simplicity that Christ stressed when he declared, Whatsoever things you desire when ye pray, believe that you receive them and ye shall have them." Paul says, if you shall declare with your mouth the promises of God and believe in your heart, that you then shall obtain the promise. But regardless of your believing, without a positive confession of that promise, we shall never receive its benefits. For "confession is made unto salvation."

The Hand of The Lord Was Upon Me
—Ed Lawson

First I would like to thank God for saving me a few months ago here at Evangel Temple, and then second for bringing me safely through an incident that happened on a fourth of July weekend.

My family and I had taken a few car loads of neighbor youth to our farm for a picnic. As we were returning home on a lonely stretch of highway, something moved me to pull to the shoulder of the road and wait for the others cars which had fallen behind. I did not know that this something was the Hand of God. I glanced into my rear view mirror but did not see anything behind me. I pulled to the side of the road and before the car had come to a complete stop, a car traveling down the middle of the road at a very high speed passed me, being chased by a policeman. It was a car I had not seen, and which further down the road caused an accident in which two cars were ruined. This car could have sent me and those in the car with me to eternity, had it not been for the hand of God, and for the fact that the call of the Lord was upon me.

The Lord came to me one night in my room 5 years ago. I was sixteen years of age at the time. I had just returned from a gang fight at which I could have been killed, but my heavenly Father had other plans for me. That night God called me to preach His gospel. He told me to minister unto His young and that He would make the way for me, however, I did not heed the call.

Through the grace of God, I got a job in a well-known church downtown Washington. And in three years I rose from a $10.00 a week job to the assistant to the social minister of the church. I held the position of director of the community program for the Council of Churches. In these years I had achieved many things and had been instrumental in shaping many young lives. I became known as a young man with a great future in the social work-field, and even received many honors. But the more I was blessed, the less of the glory I gave to God. Yet the call of the Lord was still upon me. The more I was around ministers who smoked and drank and could find a way to get around (by scriptures) what they wanted to do—after being around these kind of men, I became disillusioned with the things of God.

Time passed, and within a half year's time, I had fallen from a responsible position to the gates of a living hell. Yet the call of God was still upon me. There is not space to write all the sins I committed just in that one half year. The sins were so terrible that even now I shudder when I think about the past and the times God could have claimed my soul and I would have gone to an eternal hell. I was sent to the hospital for psychiatric treatment as an alcoholic and acute neurotic. God brought me out even from this, and yet I would not heed His call. I became agnostic. I took every opportunity to belittle anyone who professed a belief in Christ. I could not prove that there was no God, but at least I did not believe in Him.

Then one Sunday I was invited to attend church. I told the one who invited me that I did not want to go. But that evening as I sat in my living room, God spoke to me. He said with finality, "this is your last chance, Ed." I don't know how I felt at the moment. I seemed to be in a daze, but I called my cousin and told him to pick me up on his way to church. I called him three times within the next hour to make sure he was coming. When at church I did not hesitate to go to the altar when the evangelist, Rev.

Holder, called for sinners. God set me free that night and He has been with me ever since. I now know no other way than that of the cross, and my whole life's desire is to become perfect in Christ. Again, I thank God that I came to the Temple. I feel filled with His love and His spirit. The call of the Lord is upon us.

(Note) Brother Lawson is constantly bringing the unsaved into the services here at the Temple, and he is responsible for many people having been saved in the last few months. We too can say, "The call of the Lord is upon him."

* * *

Letters to the Pastor

Rev. Meares:

I was an invalid for three years. I had pneumonia, heart trouble, high blood pressure and had lost the use of my left side completely. I had no life in my feet or ankles, and even had to be fed at times. The doctors had given me up on two different occasions. Thursday night, the 12th of this month, I dreamed I would be healed if I would attend the service on Friday night. So in pain and with the aid of a cane I came to Evangel Temple expecting to be delivered. When you laid hands on me the pain left and without the use of a cane I began walking around the church praising God for healing me. I was able to be in the Sunday morning service and am feeling fine.

Bertha Burns
Wash., D.C.

* * *

I just had to write you and tell you how much I enjoyed the last two issues of Fellowship News. I had just come from the closet praying and went to the mail box and your Easter issue was in it. I came back and read it through. I never had anything to just come in so at the right time and be such a blessing. Then the next one I got—well, it is hard to tell which one of you are the best teacher, you or your wife. I could never say in words how much I have been blessed by receiving the "News."

Juanita Williams
Athens, Tennessee

* * *

Greeting you again in the name of our Lord Jesus Christ, who would have all men everywhere to be saved. Well, it won't be long before I will be coming home for good, the first part of March. Things don't look too good here, but there is still a God in heaven who has all power, and my faith and trust is in Him. I know He is able to keep that which I have committed unto Him. Pastor Meares, I have been hearing some good reports of the services and I understand you have really been preaching the Word. I can hardly wait to get back and be in spirit-filled services again and enjoy the blessings of the Lord. I want to thank you and the church for your prayers and continue to pray for me. Enclosed are my tithes.

Willie Perrin
Vietnam

≈ ≈ ≈

Editorial...
Is Your God Too Small   —Mary Lee Meares

Ninety-five per cent of the people today say, "God is a big God," but do they really believe that? Do their actions speak such? Too many people have never given God a chance to grow big in their lives. God is only as big to us as we will make Him. Even though we believe God created the world, and every living creature therein, and even though He holds the world in His hand, we are afraid to believe that He is interested in our personal needs, and will do anything for us. You must think big, believe big, and expect big things from God. Then He will become big in your life. God will do as much for you as you will believe Him to do.

God is all powerful, the very source of power. He is big, enough to save the entire universe, and loves every person upon the face of the earth. He gave His Son that not a single human being would be lost, if they would only accept Him. Even though a person spurns the Saviour and goes into the depths of sin, He still yearns to come into your heart and show you the way of eternal life. He wants to live and abide in your heart daily and be a friend that is closer than a brother. He wants to help you solve all your difficulties and problems; He wants to prosper you in your job and supply all your needs; He wants you to have abundant health and enjoy life.

So many people read about God in the Bible, and think of Him as a God of the past, and they hardly know God as a *present* Spirit. They can only vision Him in their mind in days gone by. They think He is beyond reach of us today. We let all our problems and obstacles dim the presence of the Almighty out of our life. God is too small to most people. Nothing pleases a parent more, than for their children to have great faith in them and what they can do for them. This is such a vague comparison to our heavenly Father. Nothing pleases Him more than for us to ask largely of Him; knowing that He is not only able, but *will* do what we ask.

There has never been a day in the history of mankind that people needed to know more of the greatness of God. Sin and disease, sorrow and heartache are everywhere. Will you, as a Christian, think big, believe big and receive big? Don't be satisfied with just a prayer answered now and then and just enough joy to exist on spiritually, but have an abundance of God in your life and let Him be the biggest thing in the whole world to you. Our big job is to let the world *know* how *big* our God is.

"Jesus Wept"   —John L. Meares

"And when he was come near, he beheld the city, and wept over it, Saying, if thou hadst known, even thou, at least in this thy day, the things which belong unto thy peace! but now they are hid from thine eyes." St. Luke 19:41-42.

There are only two places in the Bible that we have record of Jesus Christ weeping or crying. We have record of His praying in the garden of Gethsemane until His sweat became as great drops of blood, but as to his crying we only have two recorded instances. The first one was as He was walking to the tomb of Lazarus. He was touched by the heartbreak of the two sisters of Lazarus, because of the loss of their brother. But he didn't weep for long, for he brushed aside the tears and said, "Lazarus, come forth." All the people that were standing by wiped away their tears and their hearts were filled with gladness.

The next time we have a record of Jesus weeping was when He was ridng a colt into the city of Jerusalem to be crowned King. The people were waving palm leaves; they were rejoicing, and even taking their cloaks and coats off their backs and throwing them in the path of Jesus, so the colt could walk across their own clothes. They were shouting, "Hosanna in the highest. Blessed be the name of the King who cometh in the Name of the Lord." It was a holiness service of praise that day. But mind you, in the midst of this great rejoicing, Jesus stopped. And there on the Mount of Olives, just before He was to descend the mountain and ride through the gate of the King of kings, He stopped. The Bible says He looked over the city of Jerusalem and wept. He said, "how oft would I have gathered thee together as a hen doth her brood, but you would not." You wouldn't hear me—you wouldn't come—you would not receive me. He said, "if you had only known the things that belong to you." How many times He would have liked to gathered them under His arms, but they would not heed His call. And because the people of this great city knew not that the King of glory was in their midst, He wept.

I wonder if He has ever looked down upon us and wept because of our lack of understanding—of recognizing. How many times have we come into Evangel Temple and He was seeking our attention, but we got our eyes on a man and failed to see Jesus. How many times has He walked the streets of Washington unrecognized. How many times has He been present to cleanse the sinner from his sin, to heal the sick and diseased bodies, and has stood with outstretched hands of compassion, waiting for us to come, but we went away with empty hands and empty hearts. Many times He has waited to bless us, but because of the deafness of our ears, and our dullness of heart, and scaled eyes, He could not. No doubt, He has wept many times because we would not take what belongs to us.

Jesus knew in His heart that even though this crowd was rejoicing and was ready to crown Him as their King, they would soon be shouting, "Give us Barabbas, crucify Jesus." Yes, this very same crowd of worshippers would soon be crowning Him with a crown of thorns. How can you explain this. How can you explain that Peter with all of his enthusiasm and courage denied the Lord? He had pulled a sword out of his sheath and was ready to battle with a whole troop of soldiers that had come after his Lord. But only a few hours later he began to cuss and swear and say he never knew the man. How can you explain that the disciples who walked with Christ for three years and saw Him turn water into wine, saw Him still the raging sea, saw Him feed the five thousand, saw Him open the eyes of the blind, saw Him raise the dead, flee from Him because of fear for their lives? How can you explain that Judas broke bread with Him in the Upper Room and then slipped away and betrayed Him for 30 pieces of silver? There is no way to explain.

How can you explain it when we take our glorious salvation so nonchalant—when we forget all that God does for us and fail to witness and bring His name honor and glory? Do you suppose He ever weeps over us? He didn't weep when the cross was on His back and He was dragging it up Golgotha's hill. He never wept when everyone forsook Him at Pilate's judgment hall. He never wept when they lashed His back with stripes or crowned His head with thorns. Then what made such a courageous man as this weep over the city of Jerusalem? If a man would not cry over himself, why would he cry over others? It was because Jesus knew that this same crowd that was praising Him and trying to crown Him king would soon be crowning Him with thorns. And as He looked over the city He said, "if thou hadst known—the things which belong unto thy peace." Because they would not accept what belonged to them, He was grieved to tears.

Editorial   —Mary Lee Meares

In this issue of the Fellowship News we want to bring you reports from just a few of the harvest fields where a reaping is in progress. There is a time of sowing and there is a time of reaping. No missionary goes to a land and over night has a great harvest of souls. Just as it takes time to plant seed and that seed stay in the cold, dark ground, and inch by inch push its way to the top of the soil and finally mature and bear fruit, so it is with the workers and missionaries or any one called to work in the vineyard of the Lord. Usually, there is great opposition that accompanies the planting of God's Word in any new field. Even though good seed is sown, the enemy comes along and sows tares with the good seed. And the Lord has to teach us patience and love and to wait upon Him, knowing that in due season we shall reap if we faint not. I believe the time to thrust in the sickle is at hand. In these last days the sickle of truth will go forth in power and it it the Word of God. I believe it will go forth in power and authority through vessels that have especially been prepared for this day in which we live. God is not only going to move in one land, but all lands and among all people. The more the spirit of iniquity abounds and we see rebellion on every hand, the more the power of the Lord at the same time will be manifested.

Our nation is fighting a war, we say, to combat communism and keep the communists from taking control of the world. The symbol of Russia is the hammer and sickle, and communism has its seat in Russia. They have thrust in the sickle of iniquity throughout the world to destroy and kill. But God also has a sickle and it has also been thrust forth to bring forth a harvest at the same time. The Bible says, "Lift up your eyes unto the fields which are white to harvest." We cannot afford to be blinded by the cares of this life and the material gains and fail to see that a field lies just ahead and will be wasted if we don't do our part in the vineyard. If we refuse to give financial support to our missionaries that are laboring in the heat of the day, we are saying, "I don't care what happens—if the grain is wasted." There is no adventure, as some might think, in being a missionary. The many times I have been overseas and have seen the conditions of the land, I always breathed a prayer of thanksgiving that the Lord had only ask of me my support and prayers, rather than my going and living among the people.

I heard a minister not long ago say, besides his being saved, the greatest revelation he ever had was the vision or revelation God gave him of the Body of Christ. When you see that this Body is made up of every nation, kindred and tongue, and that we are one in the Spirit, then it will change your thinking, your attitude toward your brother and sister, and your giving and sharing the knowledge you have of your Lord. We are members one of the other—joined together. We have begun to see this at Evangel Temple as never before. We know that we must function as a body and not separately, each doing what is good in his own eyes. But we must submit ourselves to the Head which is Christ. We must go beyond the four walls of our church. Our vision must reach out to other lands and to other people whom Christ died for. Here in the city of Washington we must awake and go into the bars, saloons, the parks and the dens of iniquity where the sickle has been thrust by Satan, and be a witness to this generation of the power of God. Plans are now being laid to do just this, and on Saturday and Sunday afternoons a group from the church are going out to sow seed among the thorns and thistles. God is stirring our nest, and we are not going to wait for the sinner to come to the house of God, but we are going out where the sinners are. We are awakening out of our sleep, and our robes of self-righteousness are being shed and we are going on Satan's territory to conquer the enemy. There will be those that will remain at church and pray for those that go out. And we believe that as the Bible says, "He that goeth forth weeping, shall doubtless come again rejoicing bringing in the sheaves." Thank God for the vision to win the lost and show them the way of salvation.

This little girl is able to walk after prayer.

～ ～ ～

Chapter 9 – 1967

From South Africa
— Mary Lee Meares

This year as the clock struck twelve and the New Year of '67 was being ushered in, I was on my knees in one of the pioneer churches of Pentecost in Johannesburg, South Africa. As I knelt there I thanked God for His goodness and mercy that had followed me throughout the year of 1986, and I entered the beginning of another year with a praise in my heart. More every day, I am made to know that the answer or secret to a successful and happy Christian life is one where the child of God has a constant praise in his heart.

When Brother Meares and I landed on the 28th of December in Johannesburg and had cleared customs, we found that my suitcase had somehow been lost. The authorities told me it would take several days to try to locate it (which I did). My first reaction next morning was, "What am I going to do?" I was to be at the convention the next morning and I had no change of clothes. When I left Washington, D.C., there was snow on the ground and I had a warm suit on. Now I was in a country where it was hot. That night before retiring, I opened my Bible to the 34th Psalm and read these words: "I will bless the Lord at all times: his praise shall continually be in my mouth." So I said, "Lord, suitcase or not, I'm going to praise you, and I believe it will be found."

We left early the next morning for East London where Bro. Bhengu's annual convention had now been going on for five days. Some of the African brethren were at the airport to meet us and took us directly to Duncan Village where the convention was being held. As Bro. Meares and I entered the large tabernacle seating around 3,000 people, they began to sing, "Jesus Is The Light" under the direction of Bro. Petrucelli. He had been in the convention from the very beginning. I had felt tired in body, but as I listened to those people sing, all tiredness left me and the Spirit of God refreshed both soul and body. As I listened to this vast audience sing I thought, "This must be a sample of what the singing in heaven will sound like." There was no piano, no organ, no clapping of hands, but such harmony. I shall never forget the sound of one song that they closed every service with.

It only had two words, Amen and Hallelujah, but what a melody it made as they sang it.

Bro. Bhengu introduced us to the people and then I sang. I did not know that Bro. Petrucelli could play the guitar, but he accompanied me and did a good job. It was a joy to sing to them and I was blessed as we all worshipped together. There were all classes of people present — some well dressed, and others barefooted, but it made no difference. Many had come by foot and bus from hundreds of miles away. They had come to worship God and be blessed and they were not disappointed. As we would go to our room at night after service, I would see the old and young alike, by the hundreds, walking home. I could not help but think of the people in America who have cars and transportation to church and yet do not go very often.

Seventeen cows had been slaughtered for the people to be fed during the convention. They stood patiently in long lines in the hot sun, waiting their turn. No wonder God blessed them so.

On the closing night of the convention, Bro. Meares was preaching on, "Christ In You, The Hope of Glory." The anointing of God was so great until his interpreter became so thrilled and overjoyed, he had to stop interpreting. He could not contain himself. Another brother came up and interpreted for a few minutes in his place. The Word of God blesses in all lands. It is the power of God.

Our heart was warmed as we worshipped with those precious Africans and we left the convention feeling we had been blessed more than we were able to bless. Now, I understand why Bro. Meares and Bro. Petrucelli were anxious to be in another one of their conventions.

Sister Meares
singing a solo.

Bro. Bhengu had made arrangements for Bro. Meares to have meetings in Bloemfontein, Kroonstad, Aliwal North, Zastion, Queenstown and Port Elizabeth. I am sure we will not have time to go to all these locations, but we are looking forward to being in several campaigns with the people here in South Africa. Today we were in service in a newly erected church here in Johannesburg. God greatly blessed,

After Rev. Bhengu's convention in East London, where God so mightily blessed, we went to Bloemfontein to hold a week's meeting. This was a nice, large brick church. It had just recently been built and as yet had only a dirt floor and no electric lights, only gas lanterns. But before the meeting ended we told the people that Evangel Temple would match every dollar that they gave and help them get a concrete floor poured. They have a fine pastor, Rev. Mookopilo, and we left his church in a spiritual high tide. The last Sunday night the place was packed, children sitting all around the front and how they did sing! No one can equal the Zulas in singing. Later Brother Bhengu told me that before our meeting in Bloemfontein, Bro. Mookopilo had written him that he would like to resign his church, but since the meeting he received a letter saying, "I want to stay." I shall never forget on the last Sunday afternoon of the meeting, a man was brought to the services that had heard there was a white man preaching for the sick, and he came to the church to see if it was true. He had been an invalid for 14 years with a heart ailment and was in pain most of the time. We preached a simple sermon of Peter's faith to walk on the waves that were about to drown him, and how we too could walk on top of our problems through faith. Before the service ended, his expression of pain had turned to a smile of joy and he was running with joy exclaiming, "I'm Peter—I'm healed." "I can walk on my sickness."

We then went to Johannesburg where we ministered to the Indian and colored people on Coronation location. We rented a large hall in which to conduct the services. Again we saw God save and heal. The policeman who tended to the building (picture on page 11) was saved and healed. Bro. Jacobs, sponsor of the meeting, has a wonderful church and was greatly encouraged in his faith to work for God.

A Missionary Reports The Convention

Dear Friends and Fellow Workers:

In this letter we will take you with us on a visit to East London, to the great African convention, held there for the 20th time. East London has the biggest Pentecostal church in all of Africa, 5000 members with seating capacity for 7,000 or 10,000 crowded in. This has been the center of Rev. Bhengu's work for years. God has used him in many ways and has given him leader ability and spiritual gifts in great measure so he has been able to found hundreds of self-supporting assemblies. It was great to see him at work in the midst of his own people—all glory to God

Christmas morning we met this great congregation, and oh how they could sing. They sang the choruses over and over 20-30 times. There is no singing anywhere as when the Africans give themselves to sing and worship the Lord. It is just like heaven on earth. There were many choirs of all sizes. The East London choir had 100 members sing the Hallelujah chorus. WONDERFUL!

The main speakers were Rev. John Meares and Rev. John Petrucelli from Evangel Temple, Washington, D.C. The Lord used them in a mighty way. Their anointed messages touched our hearts. Several missionaries and African pastors spoke from time to time under great anointing. It was a spiritual feast. The meetings lasted 9 days, with

4 three hour meetings a day. So we were well fed on the Word. Bro. Bhengu led the 6 A.M. prayer meeting. Many miracles took place through the mighty Name of Jesus.

The feeding of this great crowd was a sight to see. Seven thousand were fed in 1½ hours. They used two oxen, several thousand loaves of bread and loads of other stuff a day. The Africans themselves gave offerings to cover the expenses of the convention. God moved on the hearts of the people and they gave till it hurt, but they received an abundance of blessings for it all.

EVANGEL TEMPLE'S

12th
ANNIVERSARY

JULY 9, 1967

COME AND ENJOY THE
BLESSINGS OF GOD

MORNING SERVICE 11:00 A.M.   PASTOR MEARES

DINNER IN ROCK CREEK PARK
Grove 23
(Bring a Big Basket of Food)
(No Afternoon Service)

EVANGELIST ROBERT GREEN
BEGINS YOUTH REVIVAL
SUNDAY EVENING, JULY 9
8:00 P. M.

EVERYONE WELCOME

≈ ≈ ≈

Editorial

—Mary Lee Meares

Something is wrong with any Christian who is not enjoying their walk with the Lord. As I heard one preacher say, "If your life in Christ is hard, then you have your neck in the wrong yoke." For Jesus said, "My yoke is easy, and my burden is light."

Quite a number of years ago when Brother Meares and I were pioneering churches from scratch, he would hear different ones say, "O isn't it wonderful the sacrifice that John and Mary Lee are making for the Lord." We didn't think of ourselves as making any sacrifice for God. We were happy as could be. We thought God was being better to us than anyone else. And I still think that! Something happened just this last April that makes me think as I do, and I want to share with you just one testimony of God's goodness to me.

The first two months of this year were spent in Africa and Europe. It had been good to be away and to feel that you were helping people who did not have the opportuities to hear the Word of the Lord as we do here. But as is always the case, on our return we found a lot of work that had piled up in the office and at home. It also was right before Easter, and as is our custom here at the Temple, we always give a sunrise Easter play, and for three weeks prior to Easter I was busy with Easter practice on top of the office work.

Don, Pastor, Mary Lee and Virgil Meares

Ever since a little girl I have loved church, loved working in the church and then after marrying a preacher, it seemed that practically all of my time and interest centered around the church. But for the last two or three years I had tried to get a release in my spirit to quit working in the church office and spend more time at home and do some of those things that all of us say, "one day when I have time I want to do this or that." I had for some time desired to edit some of Brother Meares Sunday morning sermons and put them in print. I felt that they could be a blessing to many people by building their faith in the Word of God. Many nights I went to bed wishing that there were more hours in the day so I could get all the things done that I felt needed doing. I kept making excuses of why I could not quit the office. But then the week following Easter, just as I was getting ready to retire on Saturday night, the Lord spoke so very clear to me. This was not in an audible voice but in my spirit. Very clearly He said, "quit work." And for some reason I did not give any excuses why I couldn't. I just felt real happy inside, and as soon as Brother Meares came to bed I said, "guess what, I am quitting work." He laughed because he had heard me talk about it before but always kept working. But I assured him I meant it and related what God had just spoken to me. He was gracious and said, "Well, I have depended upon you for a lot of things, but I am glad you are quitting and will be home more."

So I went about trying to get my work in shape for another person to take over. Then a few days later some minister friends, Brother and Sister Petrucelli, my husband and I were at a restaurant having a bite to eat after the church service. We were through eating, just sitting there talking when all at once I became very sick. I handed the bill and some money to Sister Petrucelli and said, "here, I must go, I am sick." Bro. Meares helped me to the car, and no longer had I reached the car until I could hardly breathe. He drove home as quickly as possible and immediately put me to bed. The pain was excruciating and I could not turn over on my side. I continued to have a hard time getting my breath. I did not know I was having a heart attack, but Brother Meares thought I was and he asked me did I want him to call a doctor. I said, "No, if what I have been telling others all the time is real, then it is real for me right now." I had often wondered what I would do myself if a real test would come to me. Would I believe God would do for me what I told others He would do for them? Bro. Meares walked out of the room and I sensed he might be going to call the doctor anyway, and I called out and said, "don't, I will be alright." I was not afraid, even though I was in great pain, and I had a real assurance that I was going to be healed so I did not need a doctor. I finally went off to sleep and woke up the next morning weak but well. I even kept an 11 o'clock appointment that I had previously made, I went for a complete check-up a few days later, and the doctor said I was normal in every way, heart and all. Just last week my husband and I started getting up early and running a mile or more each morning, and he remarked to me, "The Lord certainly healed you or you could not do this." So I just wanted to share this testimony of God's healing power in my life. It is a wonderful thing to put your trust and faith in One who never fails.

Blessings Never Stop When You Are Thankful — Mary Lee Meares

Have you ever given someone a gift and you never received any kind of reply or thank you from them? If so, you were not as enthusiastic about giving them the next time were you? It is just natural, if we have a thankful heart, to express our thanks. And yet, how many, many times God blesses us and we fail to say, "thank you." We take for granted that God knows we thank Him. But just as much as you enjoy doing for people that show you they are thankful for what you do for them, so it is with God. He enjoys showering blessings up on us. It delights His heart to give His children good things, just as much as it delights your heart to give your children good gifts. And just as much as it delights our heart to hear our child say, thank you, so it delights the heart of God to hear our "thank you, God."

If you have ever taken notice of some Christians that seemingly are always having it hard, you will notice that they rarely have a praise upon their lips. They may say God is good, but to hear them talk, His mercy and goodness are following someone else, not them. Then there are others you look at and they seem so happy you think they never have any heartaches or trials. They are always talking of God's goodness and how good He is to them. Yes, they have their trials, but God is so real to them in these times, until they can only talk of God's power and how great He is. God does not run out of blessings if we are thankful. We our selves cut off His blessings at times because of our own selfishness and attitude of heart. Thankfulness activate a continuous flow of blessings. If it seems that there is a slacking of blessings from God in your life, it might be that your tendency to be thankful has become weak and lacking.

Do not wait until some tragedy almost befalls you and then thank God for staying it, but when things are going well and you foresee no harm, be thankful. Let this attitude become a part of you, the biggest part. It has been said that a person does not know how to be thankful for his health until it is gone, or until the Lord has healed them. Perhaps this is true in a sense, however, I believe we should be more thankful in that we have our health and can give thanks in our well-being. We should *not wait* until a need in our lives is met and then thank the Lord, but have an attitude of praise and thanksgiving continually in our hearts.

You have heard the illustration of the man that complained about having no shoes until he met a man that had no feet, and then he realized he had so much to be thankful for. All of us this Thanksgiving could name numerous blessings that our forefathers did not enjoy. Most of our tables will be laden with good things to eat. They had meager crops, yet they were thankful for what they had. I have found that if I will praise God for the little things He does for me, He even surprises me then with some big thing—something I don't expect and the least deserve.

When it seems that it is hard for you to really have a praise in your heart because of your surrounding and circumstances, just pick up your Bible and begin to read Psalms. Read Ps. 103 "Bless the Lord O my soul, And all that is within me, bless His holy name. Begin by faith to praise the Lord with all that is within you. That is your whole being, everything inside you—all of you. Part of your body cannot praise the Lord without some other part reacting accordingly. When your heart is glad and happy, your mouth will speak joyfully. "From the abundance of the heart the mouth speaketh." When one begins to praise God with their lips, they can feel something begin to stir within side them. Have you ever raised your hands to praise God, and it seemed that no praise came out, or your hands got tired and you soon dropped them by your side? That is because there was not a praise within. But let all that is within you praise God, and it isn't hard to lift your hands or clap them for joy, or even dance a dance of praise.

The person who praises God continually with all that is within them will never backslide. It just isn't possible, for God inhabiteth the praises of His children. Who can backslide when God's presence is abiding within them? If you will build Him a temple of praise, He will never fail to live in it. Too many Christians know only to beg and plead and seek after God's blessings. If they could only learn to change that prayer to one of praise, then they would soon know the joy and reality of God's blessings. Blessings never stop when you are thankful. Your lips can bear fruit for the Master. You can have a praise in your heart that will last and live throughout eternity.

November 15, 1967

To All Of Our Fellowship News Family:

It is my joy to come into your home through our magazine during this Thanksgiving season. There are so many blessings that we share, and I am most grateful for the Christian love that binds our hearts together in Him.

I trust as you think of the blessings that God has bestowed upon you in 1967, you will also take inventory and ask yourself, "Have I been a blessing? Have I sown seeds of happiness along the way? Have I told the Good News to others?" I cannot answer this for you, but I do know you have been a blessing to me. Without your prayers and financial support I could have accomplished nothing, but through your faithfulness we have been blessed together. My prayers are daily with you.

May there continually be a praise in each of our hearts to the One "who daily loadeth us with benefits."

Christian love,
John L. Meares, pastor

Bernice Morris, John's Oldest Sister's Miracle

It was on Christmas day that Mrs. Morris or Bernice began to feel so very weak and lay down to rest. She just assumed that the busy activities of the Christmas season had caused her to be extra tired and after a little rest she would be O. K. She had a slight fever, and instead of the fever leaving and strength returning, the fever began to rise and she became weaker in body. She would sweat so until the bed would be soaked. This continued a day or so and then the family doctor was called. He could not give any reason for the continued fever, so it was decided that she should go to the hospital where she could be checked more thoroughly. In all of her previous

53 years she had known hardly any sickness, certainly nothing of a serious nature.

So New Year's eve, Mrs. Morris was taken to St. Joseph Hospital in Tampa and on Wednesday tests and check-ups began. During this time there was no pain, just a high temperature and extreme weakness. Thursday x rays were taken and then on Friday Dr. Hardy, the family doctor, called Mrs. Morris' husband and daughter, who was there visiting during the holidays, into his office and told them. "Your wife and mother is consumed with cancer in both lungs which has originated in the pelvic region." He advised the daughter to not leave Tampa as it could be only a short time for her mother. He ended by saying, "It will have to be a miracle."

Mrs. Morris was not told her condition, but she told us later that on Friday several times when she would close her eyes she would see this long corridor in a dense forest and at the end was a bright light. There was her mother and father and the Lord waiting for her. She knew she was near death, but there was no fear. She said, "I knew if I would just say, Lord open the gate, He would, and this was really my desire, but then I thought of my nine year old, Gary, and I knew it would be selfish of me to want to go to heaven and leave him when he needs me so. So I said, no, Lord, don't open the gate now," and turned and walked back.

Then on Saturday around 11:30 in the morning, a pastor and his wife, Rev. and Mrs. Pitts came to see her and have prayer. Mrs. Morris's husband, who is also a minister of the gospel, and Rev. Pitts moved up to her bedside and began to pray, when all of a sudden, Mrs. Pitts, who is a modest, retiring sort of person, came up to the bedside and in the spirit pushed both ministers aside and began to pray for Sister Morris. "It was during her prayer that I knew I was healed," said Bernice. God used this humble vessel as a point of contact for this miracle. Still no one told her of the real cause of her sickness, but all present did rejoice because they knew the victory had been won.

More x rays were taken and this time nothing showed up, no sign of cancer anywhere. Baffled by these reports, Doctor Hardy asked permission to call in a cancer specialist, which he did. So the x rays continued even though Bernice was feeling fine and her temperature was normal. The cancer specialist had no explanation of all the x rays. He would just say, "somehow it has gotten away from us, even though nothing shows up."

Then on Wednesday the family decided to tell Bernice just what she had been healed of. Having no pain, she never once suspected cancer, but she did know she was at death's door. So all the family gathered in her room and listened as her husband related to her the whole story. Tears trickled down our cheeks as she said, "I'm unworthy." Haven't we all felt our unworthiness so many, many times, but God is rich in mercy. While we were all rejoicing in God's goodness, Dr. Hardy walks in. Rev. Morris said, "Dr. Hardy we have just told my wife about all the x rays and that now there is no trace of cancer to be found." He bowed his head and Rev. Morris put his arms around him and prayed another prayer. Dr. Hardy said, "Yes, it is a miracle." The nurses were at a loss for words, but one nurse said, "We need more miracles." Othes just could not believe it to be true.

Thursday Sis. Morris began to make plans to come home on the following Friday. Brother Meares and I left to come back to Washington. But to show you how one's faith will always be tried after a great victory is won, the cancer specialist came into Mrs. Morris's room and these were his first remarks— "Mrs. Morris, I want you to know you are not healed and you still have cancer, no matter what the x rays show." His theory was if you once had cancer, it was still there unless removed by surgery. Mrs. Morris said she felt an anointing and boldness come over her and she answered by saying, "Doctor, I don't care what you or anyone else says, or what any x rays show or don't show, I know I was healed at 11:30 last Saturday morning." The doctor left her room and immediately here came a friend, her husband and daughter and another friend. She related to them the previous conversation between her and the doctor. At this time tongues and prophecy came forth through her daughter confirming her healing and again everyone in the room was rejoicing in the spirit.

Friday found Mrs. Morris at home and Saturday she was at the beauty parlor getting her hair fixed so she could go to the house of God on Sunday morning and give her own testimony of God's miracle working power in her life.

Thanksgiving   —John L. Meares

You remember the healing of the ten lepers. All of them were healed on their way to the priest. But only one of them, after finding himself cured, returned to Jesus and threw himself down at his feet and thanked him. Jesus asked the question, "Were not all ten cleansed? The other nine, where are they?" We all are guilty at times of failing to return and give thanks for what He has done for us. How ungrateful are we?

Thanksgiving Day should have a real significance to us. Our pilgrim fathers should not be forgotten. It is because of their faith and courage and desire to live in a country where they could worship God, that they endured the hardships and even death. It took a strong faith in God to set sail in that little Mayflower boat to a New World. What if someone told you that America would soon be a land where there would no longer be freedom of speech, or freedom to worship God to the dictates of your conscience. But they said, we know a land that has only wild animals, and a few Indians (savage) on it and we can all go there and start life anew. They told you there might not be much food and you might have to sleep in the cold, but we could build a nation that would be free and you could worship God the way you wanted to. Would you have enough faith and courage to go? I wonder how many would retain their faith? I believe the day is fast approaching that we will know the meaning of really standing up for our faith.

God has abundantly blessed our nation as no other nation in the world, and yet how many recognize Him as the Giver. Let us have courage to stand in this day of ridicule and proclaim the greatness and the goodness of God. May this be a Thanksgiving Day in which you numerate your blessings and sing praises to your God. God is the Giver and Source of them all. The more I praise God, the more blessings I receive. It will work the same for you, so try it not only on Thanksgiving Day, but 365 days of the year.

He is Come

—Mary Lee Meares

Several years ago I stood in the old city of Jerusalem and watched people kneeling at the wailing wall, praying for their Messiah to come. Would that I could have gone up to them, tapped them on the shoulder and said, "dry your tears, He has come." If only they would have believed it—the Messiah or the Promised One has been born.

Jesus was born at a time of vice and brutality, a time of slavery and oppression, a time when Israel was anxiously and hopefully awaiting for the promise of Isaiah to be fulfilled, for the Promised One to come and deliver them out of their bondage. The prophet Isaiah said, "For unto us a child is born, unto us a son is given: and his name shall be called Wonderful, Counsellor, The Mighty God, The everlasting Father, The Prince of Peace." This was a promise, and no promise of God has ever or will ever fail to be fulfilled. How happy is the man or woman that can believe God fulfills His promises. Many of us believe the promises of God for the future, but not for the present.

The people in the day of Christ's birth had said within their heart, "One day our Messiah will come—it is a promise." Then is it not strange that when He did come only a few would accept and believe that He was that promise? Because He was not born as they thought their King would be born, they refused to believe He was their Saviour, the Hope of the world. He did not receive the honor and esteem a King should get. He did not exert any power over the Romans, but rather let the Romans exert power over Him. He was not called Wonderful, but rather He was cursed, and called a blasphemer when He said He was the Son of God. Because He told them He was their King they finally hung Him on a cross. They failed to believe, and are still looking for their Messiah. How sad when we fail to believe God's promises.

However, there were a few that believed and rejoiced. Believing will always bring rejoicing. Mary believed, even though she did not understand, and asked God how it could be. We will never understand the promises of God. We just accept them by faith because it is a promise of God. Mary rejoiced in her heart and what the angel proclaimed to her came to pass. She could have doubted and had fears of what others would say about her as a young virgin girl, but instead she rejoiced that God would choose and so honor her to be the mother of the Saviour of the world.

The lowly shepherds heard the good news and rejoiced. The wise men believed it so much they were willing to make a long, hazardous journey to find the Messiah that had been promised. When we believe in our heart the promises of God, nothing is too hard for us. We will rejoice, even as they did when they found Him. If we will dare to believe, we will never be disappointed.

There was the man of God, Simeon, who had asked God not to let him die until his eyes could behold the Promised One. He believed he would live to see Him, and his faith did not fail him. When Jesus was carried into the Temple by his mother and father and Simeon beheld Him, the Holy Spirit quickened Simeon's heart and he immediately knew God had answered his prayers. He knew that the Messiah had come! He was so overjoyed until he was now ready to depart from this life. He felt a peace within him that he had never before experienced.

This Promise was for *all* people, not just a few. Even so God's promises today are for *all*, yet only a few will believe them. Many people believe Jesus was born 2000 years ago and also believe (so they say but don't always act as though) that He is coming again. But this is not enough. We cannot accept the birth of Christ as just an historical event. It is not enough to believe that he lived thirty-three years and was hung on a cross and will one day come again. To really believe "He is Come" will not be something of the past or something that will happen in the future, but that right now He is a present reality and a present promise. When this becomes a truth within our hearts, there will be great rejoicing. We will see the promise fulfilled. He will be *our* mighty God, *our* everlasting Father, *our* peace, the one who governs *our* life, and the one who counsels us. The Promised One will fulfill all His promises. We do not have to weep at our wailing walls, but we can rejoice, "He is Come." He is the gift of God. He has become our Hope. He has come into our heart to abide. We rejoice in that what God promised He fulfilled. And our God is still fulfilling His promises today to those who will believe. The Promised One Is Come!

Christ was born and born for one purpose — to manifest His love toward us. He was born that we might in a small way understand this love. And now we who have been born again can only express our love toward God as we express it toward our fellowman. May this Christmas season be one of joy and happiness for you and one that the love of God is expressed in everything you do.

Chapter 10–1968

A New Year
—Mary Lee Meares

New Years are soon old years; cherished years are soon forgotten years. At the beginning of every new year, all of us have a zeal and determined attitude to really make it a year of service unto God. But sometimes as the months pass by some of us lose that zeal and vision and our desire that burned within us at the beginning of the year dwindles and burns at a low ebb. This shouldn't be. It isn't Gods fault, for we know He is the same the last day of the year as He is the first. God has not left man to his own efforts. He who is the Author of the inborn craving within the heart of man to be better and to live a holier life, has also made a way for man to attain these heights. When we were born again there was a new life begun. Old things are passed away. And all of the struggling and striving to live a better life becomes simple when by faith we day by day put our trust in the Lord and let Him live in us.

This year we should enter into a fuller and richer life than we did in 1967. No matter what has been accomplished with our lives in the past, God can still do more with them in the future. Or we could say, all that God has done for us in the past, He can do more for us in the future or in this year. The Bible says, "Give, and it shall be given unto you; good measure, pressed down, shaken together, and running over."

So many times this verse is interpreted only in terms of money: But I believe it means also to give of our time to Christ; give of our love to others; share our blessings with others, speak words of kindness to those we work with, etc. Any time we give of ourselves, we receive in return either through God or man, or both. God does not always give back to us in the same form as we give Him. Health, happiness, peace, and prosperity are just a few of the many ways God gives back to us for giving of ourselves. He sees our deeds and they do not go unheeded or unrewarded.

For some people it is relatively easy for them to give of their finances to God's work, and yet they find it hard to take time out to spend alone with Him in prayer, or to sit down and to meditate upon the Word of God. When you love someone you don't want what their money will buy you, but you want to spend time with them and talk with them. So it is with God—we are His children, and He loves us and desires to be alone with us. He wants more than just our money to spread the gospel. When we take time to commune with Him, we will receive blessings in measure that cannot be obtained in any other way.

The revival that began New Year's eve here at the Temple seems to be one where people are learning how to worship God. It is a revival that is stressing the need for each other in the body of Christ. We are learning that each of us have something to bless someone else with. Just as the little boy gave his lunch and Christ blessed it and then gave it back to be given out to bless and feed the multitudes, so we are offering our songs, our psalms, our testimonies, tongues, or whatever God speaks to our heart, and are blessing one another with it. We are becoming one in Him. Love is flowing from one heart to the other. We are being brought into an increased understanding of His love and His blessings and His desire for us to live a fuller life. To live a full life in Him, we must freely give. "With what measure we give, it shall be given—." If there comes the time in 1968 that you feel others are receiving more from God than you are, then stop and see if you are giving all you have to Him. Are you really in love with Jesus?

Then if you want to be a victorious christian during 1968 be sure you understand one thing—God loves you! Too many people have never become sure of this. And because of this they are not sure God understands their problems, their heartaches; they are not aware that His presence is constantly with them; they are not positive that His promises included them. But once you know of a surety that God will always love you, then most of your battle is already won. For when you are sure of one's love, you have a complete trust, and when your trust is in the Lord it will have to be a victorious year.

I shall never forget as a young girl traveling with a girl's quartet an experience I had. We were singing in Naples, Florida, and at the close of the service an elderly lady came by and handed each of us four girls a quarter apiece because she said our singing was such a blessing to her. She said she only had a quarter left but she was happy and said the Lord impressed upon her to give it to us. This really touched my heart and I slipped a dollar into her hand before I left the service. I have never been more blessed by any offering given me than I was that quarter that Sunday morning. It is the spirit in which we give that God honors. I was once asked why a certain faithful Christian never prospered even though he paid tithes, and my answer was. "In my opinion, he pays out of duty and not out of love." All of us know the difference. All of us have served others at times only because of duty and not of love. Some people pay tithes dutifully—because they are afraid of being cursed if they fail to. You might as well not pay, for God knows your heart.

EDITORIAL   —Mary Lee Meares

It was a pleasant surprise to have Reverend John McTernan of Rome, Italy phone us and say he would be with us on our 13th anniversary here at the Temple. Less than three years ago Brother McTernan had phoned Brother Meares and ask him if he would come and dedicate a lovely new church for them in Rome. We shall never forget the time we spent with him and the wonderful Italian people. Some of you will remember "The Rome Story" that was printed in the January issue of The Fellowship News in 1966. We received many letters telling of the blessing and inspiration it was to them. In turn, Brother McTernan blessed our congregation as he ministered to us on our church anniversary.

As yet we do not have a large church building and the needed facilities that we would like to have and feel that we must have in order to do the work that God has given us to do in our nation's capital. More and more I am beginning to have a clearer understanding of why God called us to this city. More and more I am realizing the great opportunity that God has placed before us in this metropolitan area. I feel that Evangel Temple has a place to fill even as Esther had in the days of old. "And who knoweth whether thou art come to the kingdom for such a time as this," was the question asked her, and it is the question we feel God is asking us as His people here at Evangel Temple.

It has been a joy to follow the Lord in the past, and it will be a joy to listen to His voice and to be led by His Spirit in the days ahead. No man can take credit for what has been accomplished in the few short years we have been here. To God be all the praise. God found a hungry people with open hearts, and He has blessed us beyond measure. We have grown together in the understanding of God's Word, and we have become One in Him. Our eyes have been opened to God's truths. We have found that we need each other in the Body of Christ, no matter how small or insignificant a member might be. Our love is increasing for our brothers and sisters in the Lord, and God is preparing our hearts and giving us this oneness in order that we might go forth as a mighty army to harvest a great ingathering of souls right here in Washington.

Because of the great task, and not only task but opportunity, that lies ahead we knew that we must take a step of faith and purchase property on which to build the needed facilities. So through the leading of the Spirit, ground was purchased and now plans are being drawn by an architect for a church that will seat 2000 people and with Sunday School accomodations for 2000. The estimated cost will be $800,000. We again know even as Esther had to have faith and courage in her hour, so will we as a church have to have faith and courage. But we know as we labor together with God, it will be accomplished through faith in Him who never fails. Never have I seen Brother Meares so excited about the things of God as he is now. Never have I seen him so sure of his direction from God and how His work is to be done. One *can* be sure of these things.

Our hearts are filled and overflowing with praise as we meditate on the goodness of God and the assurance that He is with us. We are marching forth to conquer the territory of Satan and by God's help this city is going to know in a greater measure that there is a living God who is the answer to the needs of this troubled generation of people. With a determined faith we are claiming the lost sinners of Washington, D.C. for our inheritance. We have victory through faith, and faith is our victory.

In the early years of Brother Meares ministry, I remember our going to a small country church in North Carolina for a revival. A lady had seen him at a convention and said to him, "I do not know you, but the Lord said for me to come and ask you to come to our church for a revival." In those days we were just glad to get revivals so he told her we would be there. When we arrived we found out that the church was "split" and that sisters in the flesh would not even speak to each other. I had never seen such division and certainly they needed a revival of the saints. The first Sunday we were there, the clerk of the church resigned. The preaching of the Word began to stir hearts and before the week was over different ones were going to each other asking their forgiveness. And when this began to happen, the church was restored. The clerk came back the last night of the meeting and was saved. When the Christians will honestly look into the mirror and search their heart and see where the weakness or fault is, then the sinner's life will be affected.

Letters to the Pastor

As you and all present Easter Sunday night a year ago can witness, I was gloriously healed of a leaking heart. I also had broken my hip December of 1962 and could only walk on a crutch. When I gave you the crutch I knew God was going to heal me. I even knew it in my heart before, while I was listening to your radio program. I know it was to me His Spirit was speaking. I also had the smoking habit taken from me. I began smoking when I was 25 years of age, but one night at church I got the victory over it and haven't smoked since. I now am 68 years old. I can now say, "I am born again." My healing and deliverance have meant so much to me and I have made Evangel Temple my church. Through your messages, Pastor Meares, you have led me firmly, yet gently, and I have grown in grace. I had never heard of the Baptism of the Holy Ghost until I started attending there. I became interested and read everything I could find about it. Finally, I decided this experience was for me, so I prayed and asked the Lord for it, and He answered my prayer. It was so easy. I was continuously praising the Lord when suddenly my tongue clung to the roof of my mouth and I was unable to speak a word in English. After I reached home, this speaking in other tongues continued for hours. Now I wonder how one can keep from speaking in tongues? My feelings cannot be told by mere words — the joy is so complete. The best way I know to say it is, "I feel all new as though I was another person." The joy and release is indescribable. May these words warm your faithful heart, and may God bless you as you bring His joy to lost souls.

Gretchen Romine
Washington, D. C.

* * *

Dear Brother Meares:

    Greetings in our blessed Saviour's name from Japan!

My what a joy it was to receive your most encouraging letter today. Thank you so very much for it, and for sending the check in the amount of $50.00. It will truly be used to reach the unreached for Him.

    It is wonderful to read the reports in your paper of the things that are being done for the Lord. I receive many magazines from the states, but yours is the only one I read from cover to cover. Your messages, as well as those of your wife, are so inspiring. Several times when things looked rather dark and uncertain for me here on the field, I found just the words of encouragement in your messages that have inspired me to carry on with even more zeal than ever before. I really means this from my heart. I have wanted to write to you for a long time and tell you this, and now I have done so. Praise the Lord. I also was so inspired by the message I heard you preach on Sunday morning when I visited with you in Washington.

    I want to extend an invitation to you to visit Japan some day. I pray not too long from now. I am sure you would have glorious meetings here, maybe not as large in attendance as those you had in Africa, but great in concrete results. I know you would love to visit our people in the Islands and to preach to those who have never heard the gospel before. We would love to have Sister Meares come along too.

    God is so gracious to us here. We praise Him for those who are being saved in every phase of our ministry. To Him goes the glory and praise.

Yours in His love,
Ray T. Pedigo

* * *

I am writing to let you know that God answered your prayers for my daughter. She was very sick in bed, but after you prayed for her the Lord answered prayer and she is up out of bed and walking around.

Estelle White
Washington, D.C.

* * *

I am seventeen years old and have been attending Evangel Temple ever since I was a little girl. When your sister was here and gave her testimony it inspired my faith for healing of a terrible cold I had and could not get rid of. I came down to the front for you to minister to me and when you laid hands on me the Lord healed me instantly. I am glad I have found the Lord and that you are my pastor.

Flora Johnson
Washington, D.C.

≈ ≈ ≈

Faithfulness   —John L. Meares

In many instances Jesus spoke of talents or money being given to servants to use in trading and at a later time the master coming to take an account of what the servants had accomplished with the money that was left in their care. On one other occasion the Lord spoke of a vineyard being given to a servant to manage and care for with the owner returning at various times to receive his portion of the profits. In each case Jesus would explain that if the servant had been faithful and profitably used that that had been left in his care, he was highly commended and rewarded abundantly. But if the servant had been careless and the vineyard had not been well taken care of, and a harvest reaped, or if the money left in his care had not been properly used so that a profit was shown, then the servant was severely punished. These examples were used to illustrate the kingdom of heaven. Jesus would then further explain that he that is faithful in a few things would be made a ruler over many things. But to him that was unfaithful, Jesus said that the little he has shall be taken away from him. Our faithfulness in the kingdom of heaven does not have to do with our eternal life, but it does have to do with our blessings and rewards now and in the life to come. Many times I have wondered about these illustrations that the Lord gave, and how they applied to our life today. When one has asked forgiveness of sins, and believes upon the Lord Jesus Christ, God in His mercy accepts us as His own and gives us life that is everlasting. Then an account is kept in heaven of our faithfulness to the Master for which we shall be rewarded. In 1 Cor. 3:10-15 the Apostle Paul spoke of the judgment of rewards when he said, "If any man's work shall be burned, he shall suffer loss, but he himself shall be saved". So it is plain to see that our rewards in heaven, as well as numerous blessings here and now, are based entirely upon our faithfulness with that which the Lord has entrusted us. Many times we are prone to use the excuse as the servant that was given the one talent—that we are afraid and we just hide it; or what we have is so small and insignificant until we excuse ourselves for our unfaithfulness.

Each day of our life I believe that we are judged in heaven for our faithfulness to the cause of Christ—our opportunities to witness for Him and lift up Jesus. In fact, the Bible declares we shall give an account of every idle word.

Letters to the Pastor

Dear Pastor Meares:

Greetings from the love of our Lord. I have received your letter and also your Fellowship News, and they both have been so inspiring to me. I have attended your services a couple of times, and how much my soul has been filled with a new faith. I am a foreigner, and I didn't know that when I came to live in Washington I could find a church like the one I grew up—one where you could praise the Lord with all your heart and soul and sing to Him the way your heart desired.

My husband is stationed at Andrews Air Force Base, and no doubt
we will be going overseas soon again. I will appreciate receiving the
paper until then, as I feel as if I am one of you already. May the
Lord continue blessing you every hour of the day.

Teatesta Coward
Washington, D.C.

* * *

Dear Reverend Meares:

Your Fellowship News is a blessing to me. It even saved my life
one time, as I was at the point of no return in a weak point in my
life. I looked up to God for help, and there, no more than 3 feet
from me was a Fellowship News. I read it, was encouraged, and the
next day I sold my gun. I now believe in God again.

Name withheld by request

* * *

Dear Pastor Meares:

I am very sorry for the long delay in writing to you. I had a
wonderful trip over the Atlantic Ocean to Morocco. I like it here and
also my assignment at the Embassy. All the people are nice to me.

I received my first bulletin a few days ago. It was very much
appreciated. I have found a Protestant church here and enjoy it.
However, I miss the "Inspiring Voices" and the choir director, Bro.
Anderson. I have done a lot of gospel singing here. The Moroccans,
Arabians and French like the gospel singing very much. I had a
packed theater when I sang in Rabat and I am singing in Tangier,
Morocco, tomorrow night. I also have another concert scheduled in
Kenitra, Morocco, and one in Fez, Morocco. God is good to me and
blessing me, and I will ever praise His name.

Thank you for the prayer the Sunday before I departed from
Washington. It was kind of you to take the time with me. I have
always enjoyed the services at Evangel Temple and also singing
with the choir. Continue to pray for me, as there is no distance in

prayer. Give my regards to all. Enclosed find a small donation for the church.

Miss Lois Gene Gore
Secretary to Agriculture Attache
American Embassy
Rabat, Morocco

* * *

Brother Meares:

"O give thanks unto the Lord, for he is good and his mercy endureth forever."

I know God is good, for He has been so good to me. I thank Him from the depth of my heart for giving me a good pastor — one who feeds my soul with the living Word of God. For the almost eleven years I have known you, my faith in you as a man of God has never wavered. One of my desires of the Lord is that He will let you be my pastor as long as I shall live.

Rosalie Johnson
Washington, D.C.

* * *

Dear Rev. Meares:

I don't belong to your church, but enjoy coming very much. We understand your preaching and teaching more than anyone we have heard in our 61 years. You preach from the Bible, and your sermons are uplifting to my soul.

Mr. J. Wilbert
Washington, D.C.

* * *

Dear Bro. Meares:

Perhaps time has erased from your memory the name that appears on this card. If you can go back in time 20 years ago and remember a little cottonheaded boy at John Sevier Church of God, a boy whom your wife tried to teach to play the piano, a boy who I am sure tried your patience many times, a boy who loves you very much and who has never forgotten the kindness of you and your wife, that boy is me.

I wandered away from God, as far too many young people do, but on Easter of 1963 I publicly confessed Jesus Christ as my Saviour. Since then I have devoted my life to serving Him and trying to win others to Him.

It has taken me this long to get your address. It seemed the most important thing in the world to me to tell you of my reunion with God and that the labor you spent on me was not in vain. I trust you rejoice with me and that you will pray that God in some way will use me for His glory. I was licensed to preach April 1, 1965, and have the privilege to teach the Men's Bible Class at John Sevier.

Alvin Webb
Knoxville, TN

From the TV mail bag

Dear Bro. Meares:

Was so very glad to see and hear you on television on Sunday. I have heard you a long time on radio and enjoyed it so much, but it is wonderful to see you on TV. Thank God you will then be able to win more souls for God. I felt better after you prayed for those who were sick in body.

Please send me your book, "Faith Cometh by the Word." Enclosed is a small offering for your program.

Mrs. Luther Payne
Warrenton, VA

* * *

Since I was eight years old, it has seemed that something was pressing against my ears.

I have been to doctors, who didn't seem to know the cause of this condition which has been steadily growing worse.

Half of the time I couldn't hear at school, and had planned before school opened this year, to go back to the doctor.

Friday night when Bro. Meares prayed for those suffering from deafness, it seemed that someone had their hands over my ears. Then something popped and suddenly I could hear.

I am very happy and I thank God for my healing.

I thank God for saving me when I was only six years old and then filling me with the Holy Ghost. These are the greatest miracles that have ever been performed in my life. I thank God He helped me realize that sin is transgression against His will, and one cannot enter the kingdom of heaven who wilfully sins. In Him I have found love, peace, wisdom, and understanding of His Word. About five years ago I started attending Evangel Temple, and I am very grateful for the truths of God that have been revealed by the Spirit to me since coming here.

Rosaline Hunter
Washington, D.C.

* * *

I was an alcoholic on the street before you prayed for me. Now thank God I am saved and delivered from the demon of drink, and swearing and all the unclean things. I want the Holy Ghost now. Reverend Meares, pray for God to strengthen me and make a real man out of me. I want others to know how God answered your prayers for me. The Lord bless and keep you.

Clarence Turner
Washington, D.C.

When to Remember Your Creator

—Mary Lee Meares

"Remember now thy Creator (the Lord) in the days of thy youth." This is the best advice that could possibly be given any child. Our character is formed in our youth; our goals are often set in our youth; and our ambitions and desires are created within us while we are young. Youth is something we cherish, and as we grow old we find ourselves many times talking about what we did as a child. For some it is a happy time to remember and for others it is a time of unhappiness because of a broken home, or a drunkard father or for many other reasons. But if it were a home where Christ was honored, then it was a home of love, and the child felt that love.

True, times have changed to what they were twenty years or even ten years ago. Children have many more material advanges today; they do not have as much work to do and many things are different now than a generation ago. However, I believe that rearing children is still the same method. To instill within every child the love of God and give them a faith they can grow and live by is still the important factor in bringing up any child. We all know this is the parent's responsibility, but what if the parents have no knowledge of this faith or of the love of God, or what if they just don't care? Can we let our youth be wasted and their lives ruined and destroyed without having tried to help them?

I did not wait until I became a young lady to start going to church, but I remember going to church as a tiny tot and many times lying on the bench and going to sleep. My little sister and I played church as children. I can remember my mother calling me in from playing outside and saying, "it is time for family prayer." As a child there was something created within my heart for the things of God. Those desires have not left me, but are with me at this present time. I accepted the Lord as my personal Saviour at the tender age of eleven, and how often I have thought of the Lord's goodness to me to keep me from my early youth from the many pitfalls that Satan has for every boy and girl born into this world.

Not long ago I received a card from a grown man saying he was saved as a child when we pastored our first church at John Sevier, Tennessee. The second church we built consisted mostly of young people (teen-age and children) to begin with. But today that church consists of these same people and their children. I am afraid too many of us are guilty in that we neglect the younger ones, thinking, "Oh, they are just children." God forgive us. How many mothers write in asking for prayer for their children that are unsaved and are causing heartaches that seem beyond bearing. If they had only been guided in the ways of the Lord when a child, then they would be spared of many heartaches and troubles. If the parents do not know the Lord, does this relieve the church of its responsibility to teach them of God? Are we as a church failing? We must find these jewels in the prime of life, full of energy and talent, and teach them the way of salvation. What God can do with a life yielded unto Him—a piece of clay that can be molded into a vessel of honor and service.

There is something wrong with any church that does not attract young people and children. The destiny of our city, our nation, and our world will rest in their hands in a few short years. We must take time now to make them the person that God wants them to be. They must remember God in their youth, but how can they remember something they are not taught? Maybe we are a little late in reaching the majority of the beatniks, so classified, in this generation. Thank God for the Teen-Challenge Centers that have sprung up in our large cities, but we would not need these Centers to such a great extent if we only took time to reach the children first. Their lives would already be to a great extent molded before they became a grown young man or lady. As a mother, my greatest joy is to see my three children, all teen-agers, going to the House of God and worshiping God. It is not my greatest concern what occupation they choose in life, or even what church they might join, but it is my concern that they put God and acknowledge Him in all their ways. I am asking God to give me a compassion and concern about other children whose parents "just don't care." May I show the love of God in such a way that in some measure it will influence them to give God their heart while a child and in doing so reap a life of joy and happiness for which God intended when creating us.

In Appreciation   —John L. Meares

Have you ever looked at a person and his face shone so until you thought, "My, that person must really love the Lord"? And you were exactly right. They were in love with God and it caused their countenance to glow with the glory of God. Jesus could be seen in them. This is the case with our Associate Pastor, Reverend Petrucelli, or Brother Johnnie as so many like to call him.

It has been nearly fourteen years now since I first met Brother Petrucelli and I can say that I have never met a man that I have greater respect and love for than I do him. We have worked side by side in the work of the Lord. He first came to be my associate or minister of music while I was pastoring in Memphis, Tennessee. Then when I felt the Lord leading me to come to Washington, I told him he could come also if he cared to, but I had nothing to offer him for I knew no one in Washington, or had no guarantee of anything. I just knew I was to come. He did not hesitate, but said, "I'm ready."

Both he and his wife, Ethel, have been a great blessing to the many, many people that have come to Evangel Temple. She has been faithful in playing the organ and also working in the church office. They have four daughters, and they are wonderful examples of children any minister or mother and father can be proud of.

To me, Brother Petrucelli was just a part of Evangel Temple, and I never gave it a thought that one day perhaps he would feel that his work was finished here in Washington. However, for sometime now he has been feeling that he should make a move. After much prayer and fasting he came to me and told me his feelings. I have enough faith in his dedication to God, that I must not question God's will for his life. I am sure this is not an easy move on his part to make, and it takes a real consecration to leave a people and a church that he so dearly loves.

Brother Petrucelli had the God-given ability to make a service come alive with his songs. His messages stirred our hearts, and there is just no way to put in words what his ministry has meant to Evangel Temple and to the city of Washington. The Petrucelli family leaves a multitude of friends and brothers and sisters in Christ. They have endeared themselves to all of our hearts and we will greatly miss them. We know, however, that where-ever and whatever they do, that God will be with them. And our prayers are ever with them that God's best be theirs throughout their life.

Pastor's Desk

A MISSIONARY VISION

Mary L. Meares

A lot of people have visions, but very few have missionary visions. But I am grateful that even in the beginning or the birth of Evangel Temple, we have had a missionary minded pastor and a missionary minded people. Space in this issue will not permit our going into detail of the times we have reached out to share our Lord with others. One of our first missionary offerings was for a great campaign in poverty stricken Haiti. Later when Senator Bonhomme of Haiti visited us, the people gladly gave for the purchasing of radio equipment for a religious station there.

Also E.T. had a part in the birth of New Life Temple in Hong Kong in 1959. It was my privilege to be with Bro. Meares on this mission endeavor and my heart was warmed as I saw the desire in the heart of those Chinese people to know and serve a living God. I visited temples there and watched them offer pigs on the altars and then bow down in worship, but such a contrast as I watched them worship God in spirit and truth. Recently, I received a letter from Bro. Sung of New Life Temple saying the church was prospering and the Lord blessing them.

Then in 1961, the building we had used for a bus garage was turned into a mission in Glenarden, Maryland, and Rev. Kearse became the pastor. To help get Bro. Kearse started he was given a salary for the first year and also E.T. has regularly made the monthly payments on the building there. There is a great need in this section for the glorious gospel of our Lord.

When Brother Coe started his meeting in Washington, I never missed a one. I felt he was a man of God that the Spirit used to bring miracle after miracle. Before he left Washington, he introduced Brother John Meares to the congregation and said Reverend Meares will open a church here. He told us he was a great preacher of the Word. So Brother Meares did start services at Turner's Arena and God continued to pour out His Spirit upon us with signs following. We have been blessed with the best of speakers with the gifts of the Holy Spirit being manifest in our meetings. I want to say from the bottom of my heart that this is really God's church. Our pastors, Reverend Meares and Petrucelli have grown so deep in God's Word and our church today is full of God's Spirit. Our people have learned how to worship in the Spirit. Why not come and of blessed of God and see for yourself what God is doing?

Ina Gladden

I received your Fellowship News and enjoyed reading it very much. No matter what I am doing, when I receive it, I stop right then and read it. It helps me so much to go through the day. Enclosed is an offering from the depth of my heart. May the good Lord give you strength to carry the Gospel on for many years. Your radio broadcast is also a blessing to me.

Rosa Cooper
Bethesda, Maryland

≈ ≈ ≈

Tithing is Love in Action — Mary Lee Meares

One of the greatest ways the devil cheats us in receiving blessings from the Lord is to make us imagine and not only imagine but convince us, as good christians, that it is all right if we do not pay our tithes. He will say to us, "God knows your circumstances and you need your money more than your church, so He will understand your keeping the ten percent or the tithe." Yes, many sincere christians have convinced themselves that they are not doing wrong by keeping the ten percent that God said is *holy* and belongs to Him. You say, "I give in offerings and the Lord knows that is all I can afford."

If you owed a friend a debt and you decided you were not able to pay it, but you would give him a gift, do you think he would consider the debt paid? No! Then why do we try to make ourself believe God will accept and bless our offering until we have first paid the tenth that He says we owe Him.

We believe literally the other commands the promises in God's Word, but for tithing, that is just one command that within our heart we say, "The Lord didn't mean that." It is though we just cut it out of the Bible. It could be no less wrong to say that God did not mean it when He said, "Ye must be born again." Who of us would believe that we could get to heaven without being born again? We don't dare try to deceive ourself. We don't dare take the risk of waiting and seeing when we die if He meant that we must be born again in order to get to heaven. And yet, we take the chance of coming before Him and being pronounced a robber or a thief. No, you would not think of taking anything that belonged to your friend or your neighbor, but God? Oh, well, He understands! He does not understand, but this God knows — if you really had faith in His promise to bless you if you gave Him the tenth that He said belongs to Him, you would pay your tithe. You would not hold back His part if you believed He really meant He would bless the nine-tenths that you keep and make it go farther than if you kept it all.

Who of us would not give to someone if they told us that in turn they would give us something much better or much more than we had given them? Then why will we not believe God? Why do we make excuses for not paying our tithes? It is only because we do not believe God. How can we love Him if we do not believe Him? When one loves I someone, it is not hard to give to them, even though it may seem to be a sacrifice.

We have heard testimonies again and again of God's blessings after one began to tithe, but the devil whispers in your ears, "that wouldn't happen to you." And you believed the devil and consequently are still struggling on the 100 percent. God will not force you to pay Him the tenth, just as He will not force you to live for Him, but you are the loser. You will never be a victorious christian; you will never be the example to others that you could be; you will never have overflowing joy; or you will never be blessed as God would like to bless you because of your disobedience to His command, until you once and for all say, "Lord, here is the tenth that belongs to you. Whether or not I have money left for my needs, I am first going to bring my tithe into the storehouse." Do you believe that God in all His goodness and love would let your needs go unmet if you came to Him in this attitude of faith? Never! There has never been a testimony as such and there never shall be. God's Word is true and the devil is a liar.

Praying and fasting alone will not make us a victorious and happy child of God. Giving of our tithes and offerings is a vital part of our christian life. "The Lord *loveth* a cheerful giver." I want God to love me, and I know I have not given an offering until I have first paid a tenth or that which belongs to Him. If you are having a battle in the paying of your tithes, be determined to win the victory. Tell the devil you need God's blessings and cannot afford *not* to pay your tithes. Tell the devil you are not paying to a man, but unto God. Tell the devil you love God and with joy you are going to trust Him for all your personal needs. Tell the devil he has cheated you from God's abundant goodness too long and from this time forth you have won the battle of tithing. If you will, your life will be changed and you will have a testimony of victory and no one will be able to tell you God will not bless those that will have faith enough to give Him the tenth that belongs to Him.

Stop Thief! — Mary Lee Meares

"Stop Thief!" shouted the policeman as he chased the robber who had just held up a shop on the corner. A bystander, observing the incident, remarked to a friend, "how terrible to take something that doesn't belong to you". His wise friend replied, "tis true, but the greater sin lies in taking that which belongs to someone else".

This reminds me of a question in the Bible (and you know a question can be pretty searching) "Will a man rob God?"

Are You A Robber?

There are many folk who would never think of robbing a bank, store or another individual, but never give a second thought to the fact that they are robbing the God of the universe! People will pay their debts regularly and rigorously and at the same time forget that which belongs to God Another question comes, this time into the mind of man. "But you say, Wherein have we robbed thee (God)?" The answer: "In tithes and offerings."

It Belongs To God!

He Goodness to Us

I really should have given this testimony some time ago, but just failed to do so. The Lord impressed upon my heart a few days ago to take practical nursing. I went to school and took the examination but was so long hearing from it until I was sure I wouldn't be accepted. However, a week before school was to start I received a card to come for an interview. I was accepted and began evening classes. In the day time I did domestic work. I completed my two semesters of pre-clinical training at night, and then I had to train in the hospital for eight hours per day, five days per week for eight months. This was going to be difficult because I am a divorcee and have myself and two children to care for. During this time I was working for a high government official. For some reason they had always been very kind to me. I had told them I was going to school and would have to stop work and train in the hospital. Every time I would work for them, the wife would ask me how I was going to manage. I told her I didn't know, and she would answer, "something will work out." I just smiled and continued to work. Then the day finally came and I told her that this would be my last day. Then she said, "I will ask my husband about your doing some office work in your home." I was hoping this would work out, but it didn't.

I gave up all my work and started training as if I knew how I was going to manage. I had trained one and a half weeks with no finances in sight. I was sitting on the bus one afternoon and I said, "Lord, if nothing happens by Friday I will have to give this up and go back to work." That afternoon when I arrived home there was a letter for me from my former employer. In it was a check and a note which said, "I have talked this over with my husband and we have decided to donate $160 per month until you graduate." This they did every month. I praise God for this and these precious people. I contribute this to regularly paying my tithes. These people had only known me a few years, so I give God all the praise.

Member of Evangel Temple
Annie Richardson
Washington, D. C.

* * *

I was in your office recently and you prayed for me. Someone had taken my purse with twenty-four dollars in it and also all of my permit cards, etc. I needed the Lord to help me get my bills straight. You told me God would perform a miracle for me. Monday the foreman called me in his office and told me that my purse had been found.

Everything was in it, money and all. It had been gone for over a month. I thank God for answering your prayers.

Martha Smallwood
Washington, D.C.

Our Abundant Blessings — Mary Lee Meares

I often thank God for the strength He has given me to do my work. I enjoy it. I believe we can learn to give thanks continually for all things.

One day I was in the grocery store buying the weekly groceries. It so happens that grocery shopping is one chore I don't particularly like. But all at once it dawned on me that I should be very grateful that I was financially able to go to the grocery store and buy food for my family. There are so many people, especially in other parts of the world, that have no money to go grocery shopping with. God has blessed us in America abundantly, much more than we deserve.

It is so easy to take our blessings for granted, and sometimes it takes misfortune or disaster to come our way to make us realize how well off we are. I am reminded of the man I saw walking down a busy street recently. On his back was a sign which read, "Have you thanked God today for your eyes?" Looking closer, I noticed the man was blind. I said, "Thank you Lord for my eyes." It could have been me instead of this man who was without sight.

On and on we could name our blessings. No, it isn't just the last Thursday of every November that we pause to give thanks, but it is a daily giving thanks for all things. Especially, do we thank God for the faith in an Almighty God that has been handed down to us by our forefathers hundreds of years ago. I am sure we do not appreciate as we should the privilege of meeting together in the house of God to worship Him as we please. Not only is this a privilege, but to worship the true and only God. So many people are worshipping a god, but not the true God. To be able to pray to a God that you know loves you and watches over you is a wonderful thing. Just as a child I can remember my mother would call me in from my playing in the yard and say, "it is time for morning prayer." I wonder what kind of a world we would have today if mothers and fathers would take the time to teach the children to pray. I have often heard Brother Meares tell how his mother and father would gather the children around the table before retiring and would read the Bible and have family prayer. With Bible reading being taken out of the schools, certainly that much more should we stress the reading of it in the home and taking time to pray and thank God for His blessings.

The Bible says God inhabits the praises of His people. You can bless God by praising Him. All of us like to have someone say "thank you." It makes us want to do something else for them. And so it is with our heavenly Father. The more we thank Him, the more He showers us with "good and perfect gifts." So during this Thanksgiving season let us not make it a mere time to entertain friends with a lovely meal, or a day we don't have to get up early to go to work, but let us make it a time of sincere worship to God. And the most sincere form of worship to God is the simple worship of PRAISE.

Editorial

In the eight years since the birth of Evangel Temple there has been those times that we have had to wait upon God. If we had made our own paths we would perhaps taken some roads that would have offered less resistance and been a short cut to where we have come today. But God's way is inch by inch, foot by foot, yard by yard, and mile by mile. We have not been able to see all the way—only step by step, and as we dare to look back we must stand in awe for what God has done, and where He hath brought us. There has been those times that we were in the dark and had to walk entirely by faith. In fact it has been a "walking by faith" from the very beginning, eight years ago, up until now. And I am sure this will be the pattern for the future. There has been those times had we not known our trust was God and He would not fail us, we would have become faint hearted, but an inner faith kept us *joyfully pressing*.

I am reminded of the story I read recently of the little boy who was afraid of the dark. He lived on the farm, way out in the country. One night his dad asked him to go to the barn and get him some tools. He said, "I don't want to go." When asked why, he answered, "I'm afraid." His dad got a lantern, lit it and gave it to son and said, "Come on." The boy followed his dad to the back steps of the house and then they stopped and he said, "Son, how far can you see with this lantern you are holding?"

"I can see to the back-yard gate."

"Walk to the gate," he said.

The father stayed on the back steps and when his boy reached the gate, he called, "Now, how far can you see?"

"I can see to the gate into the barn lot."

"Walk to it."

When he reached the barn lot, the father said, "Now, how far can you see?"

"I can see the barn door."

"Walk to the door."

The boy opened the barn door and went inside where the lantern made plenty of light.

At first the lad could only see the back-yard gate and after walking to it he could then see the gate to the barn lot, and after that the barn door.

You can't always see all the way at one time, but if you carry the "light" Jesus Christ, He will always give enough light to show the next step. This keeps one trusting in *Him* and not in self.

No new convert attains the full stature of Christ at birth. No church becomes a mother church over night — it is step by step. We rejoice that this is God's way!

God has over and over again stretched forth His hand in the past eight years to set the enemy at nought. He has shown forth His power to save and to heal and to bind up the broken hearted and pour in the oil of Gilead.

Since our last anniversary we have had the beginning of several mission churches. Several men from Evangel Temple have gone out full time in the ministry. Then as we listened to the numerous testimonies of God's goodness week after week, our heart could only whisper, "thank God, thank God." We cannot forget those weeks that financially a miracle had to be wrought, and God did not fail us.

We must mention the remodeling that has taken place the past year and is still going on. After remodeling the outside of the church and replacing the old ticket booth with a beautiful glass front, we began redecorating the inside. Now as one walks inside they see a beautiful altar which has become a very worshipful part of our service, each Sunday morning in particular. There is now a much better baptistery and also a new seating arrangement for the choir. The gold and white color scheme that has started on the stage will be carried out to the back of the auditorium. The radio room, back stage, is being panelled in a beautiful wood and will serve as a small church office. However, one of the most needful additions to Evangel Temple is the prayer room that will soon be completed. For so long we have wanted a place where the penitent could come and remain as long as they wished, and where the saints could get alone with God. At the time of completion of the prayer room, it will be dedicated by the saints coming together and spending a week of fasting and prayer.

We are most thankful for the increase we have enjoyed year after year. We now have a little over 1500 fellowship members. Never have we been privileged to work with such a lovable people. These eight years have been the most rewarding years of our lives. For the many, many times that each member and friend has prayed and given of their time and means, we thank you. Some day we will rejoice together in the harvest of souls that the Lord Jesus has allowed us to work together to win.

It seems that in recent months there has been a worship and praise in the hearts of the people at Evangel Temple that has surpassed anything hitherto known. We recognize an abiding Presence. He isn't someone that meets us only when we come to church, but He is someone that is with us from sun-up to sun-down. We thrill as we think of what God has done for us since coming to Washington, but we get a greater thrill when we begin to think what God is going to do in the coming days, months and years if the Lord tarries.

We are contending for an un-movable faith in Jesus Christ and that we as one great family of believers will share this faith with all whom we daily meet.

Testimonies

I praise God for His goodness to me. God spoke to me in March, 1967 to go out on the mission field. I did not know where I was to go so I went before the Lord in fasting and prayer to get an answer. He said for me to go to Nassau, so I went at His command and worked in the mission field there for three months. Then the Lord opened the door for me to come to America. Now, miraculously I am in the home of Pastor Meares and also worship with the people at Evangel Temple. It is a place where God meets His people in a wonderful way.

I speak from my heart that it pays to serve Jesus. My God is a Big God and a God of miracles. I am happy, happy, right here. Pastor and Sister Meares are taking good care of me. They are a humble family and real children of God. May God continue to bless them and their ministry.

Muriel Avis
Jamaica, W. Indies

* * *

The more I read the Fellowship News, the deeper my appreciation for such a fine publication becomes. It is such an inspirational and enlightening magazine that I look forward eagerly to reading the next edition.

I find myself telling others about the articles that appear therein, in my Sunday School Class, at work and wherever I may be. There seems to be always something fitting to meet our daily needs and to broaden our understanding.

Enclosed is a donation of $14.00 to help you in the furtherance of this fine work.

Johnsie Mickey
Washington, D. C.

BRAKPAN, TRANSVAAL, AFRICA

Dear Brother Meares,

I thank God for the support I received for the month of July. It is a great help to me and the work of God. It is my transportation, food and clothes.

This month God is using me in the mines in my ministry. Many souls are being saved. One elderly lady was brought on a stretcher to be prayed for. For 25 years she could not walk, but God touched her and she now attends our meetings without being carried around.

Brother Meares, I am trying to get a tape recorder, and praying that God will give me one. Then I can always send you the tapes of all the testimonies and of the singing.

I look forward to winning lost souls for the Lord. Had I wings, I would just fly and drop myself in Evangel Temple May the Lord bless you.

S. Thos. Miva

HEALED IN FRIDAY MORNING SERVICE

In January I fell and slipped a disk in my right knee cap. Since then I have not been able to walk without a cane or get in and out of a car. Neither could I raise my leg. Every two weeks I had to see the doctor. I was told about the Friday morning healing service at the Evangelistic Center and got a friend to bring me for prayer. After you prayed for me I was healed and no longer need a cane. It seems so good to be able to walk normal again.

Tannie Bell
109 35th St., NE

Ye Shall Be Witnesses Unto Me
—John L. Meares

The most important aspect of happiness and | fulfillment is to have a place in life, to belong — to be sincerely loved and appreciated. And just as important, is to have a place in life where you can contribute, bless and be helpful.

Many individual's lives decay and fall apart because of the lack of belonging and finding a place of service. God having implanted in us these desires, then shared with us the most important business of the universe — the business of the kingdom. God could have entrusted His kingdom to immortal beings, but He chose to leave it in the hands of us mortals — to witness for Christ!

There is always a hesitancy and fear when one endeavors to do something they do not understand or are not equipped to do. But when one knows how to do something, they not only have courage and boldness to do it, but it becomes a joy. A musician enjoys playing before an audience. A singer thrills to sing to others, and so it is when we are equipped to witness, it is no longer a burden or duty. There is no greater thrill for a human heart that is annointed with the Spirit of God, than to witness for the Master and to see the gospel of Jesus Christ take effect in the life of another.

The Lord did not command us to witness for Him without making the proper provisions so that we would be thoroughly equipped to perform the business of the kingdom. Thus, He commands, *"After that the Holy Ghost comes upon you, ye shall be witnesses unto me."*

Perhaps Peter showed more courage than all of the other disciples at the trial and crucifiction of the Master, for the others had fled completely. However, he miserably denied the Lord. Only a few weeks later this same Peter, who became annointed with the Spirit of God after waiting for the promise of the Father, stands before the same crowd that accused and condemned Jesus Christ, and with boldness and courage beyond the ability of the human heart, declared the gospel of the kingdom.

Witnesses Unto Me   —Acts 1:8

Not only upon the preacher, it was at work in the hearts of the congregation.

The work of the Holy Ghost is to "testify of Christ". Peter was annointed to preach "Christ" to the multitude. "Ye men of Israel... Jesus of Nazareth... ye have taken and by wicked hands have crucified and slain: Whom God hath raised up..." This message borne by the Spirit pricked the hearts of the hearers. It was not a common oratory. It was a message that gripped the hearts of the hearers. Conviction seized them until they cried out, "What must we do to be saved?"

One of the greatest works of the Holy Spirit was the transformation He made in the lives of men when He came to abide with and in them. The 120 people who were in the upper room were changed in an instant into men and women full of zeal, aggressive witnesses for Jesus Christ! The difference is probably more noticeable in Peter, but is no less remarkable in the others. This experience of receiving the Holy Ghost into their lives made the difference between a group of people who were sympathizers of the crucified Nazarene and a militant army of witnesses for the resurrected Saviour. The advent of the Holy Ghost on the day of Pentecost was the risen Christ's 'telegram' to His disciples that He had arrived back at the right hand of the Father and had commissioned them to carry on His work of saving the world. They could not do it alone. It was a supernatural task. But they could be vessels of His Spirit and through His empowerment the plan could be carried out. The Holy Ghost came; endued them with the power; and they became fearless witnesses of the resurrection and of righteousness. The very same day He decended and took up His abode in the hearts of the disciples, three thousand souls were saved! The working of the Holy Spirit in their lives made the difference!

John said, "I indeed baptize you with water unto repentance; but he that cometh after me is mightier than I, whose shoes I am not worthy to bear: he shall baptize you with the Holy Ghost, and with fire". Fire is energy. Those who received the mighty Holy Ghost baptism on the day of Pentecost were "bursting" with spiritual energy. After receiving the Holy Ghost we never see the disciples again except that they were witnessing, preaching, praying, exhorting or carrying on the work of the risen Christ in some manner. There was something about this mighty baptism they had received that would not let them be still. Not even the threat of death itself could quench the desire burning within their hearts to tell the world that "God hath made this same Jesus, whom ye have crucified, both Lord and Christ." These people who had received the Holy Spirit were in an instant transformed by the mighty enduement of the Spirit. They began to grow into a force of spiritual power that has shaken the kingdoms of men and devils. They were referred to as "the ones who had turned the world upside down"; or would it be more proper to say "right side up"?

This same enduement of power is yours, my friend, and will bring the same results in every life it rests upon. You cannot help but to speak the things you have seen and heard concerning the kingdom. As you witness for Christ, the same annointing will touch the heart of the hearers. You can expect the same thrill that Peter knew, as you engage in God's business… "witnesses unto me."

~ ~ ~

Forgiveness   —Mary Lee Meares

Forgiveness is something that is seldom preached from the pulpit, and yet the Bible has an awful lot to say regarding forgiving. It is strange how we take certain parts of the scriptures to live by and leave other parts unheeded, as though they were not important. We would not think of doing certain things that the Bible teaches against, for our conscience would bother us too much. It would be a sin, and yet how many Christians hold misgivings in their heart toward their brother or sister, neighbor, husband or wife? We somehow skip over the teachings of Jesus on forgiveness and think we are alright in the sight of God.

For the last couple of months there has been a lot said at Evangel Temple on forgiveness and as a result things are happening. It has been preached from the pulpit and it has stirred, not the sinners, but the Christians into searching their own life to see if there has been any misgivings buried within their heart. Different ones in the church have gone to each other and to their pastor and said, "forgive me. Have we as a church been guilty of calling in evangelists to hold a revival to get the sinner saved, while all the time what first needed to be done was get the Christian on the right foundation? Could it be that the reason we don't see more results from our praying is that there is ought against our brother? Mark 11:25-26 reads, "And when ye stand praying, forgive, if ye have ought against any, that your Father also who is in heaven, may forgive you your trespasses. But if ye do not forgive, neither will your Father, who is in heaven, forgive your trespasses." I have been amazed at some of the testimonies lately of answered prayers and they are the result of people asking forgiveness. There have been husbands and wives that have felt hard toward each other for different reasons—both Christians, both justifying themselves in the way they felt, not conscious of the fact that this was keeping them from having their desires and pettions granted from God. Are we not all guilty of having said or done things that we earnestly have to come before God and ask His forgiveness? Yet we harbor unforgiveness in our own heart? Can we expect God to forgive us if we don't forgive? Does the Bible really mean what it says? Are we sincere when we pray the Lord's prayer, "forgive us our debts *as we forgive* our debtors? Perhaps we are not being honest with ourselves.

"Therefore, if thou bring my gift to the altar, and there rememberest that thy brother hath anything against thee, Leave there thy gift before the altar, and go thy way; first be reconciled to thy brother, and then come and offer thy gift." So even if you don't have misgiving in your heart but know someone has feeling toward you, the Bible says don't pray until you have gone to that person. How many of us do this? We just soothe our conscious by knowing that we haven't done anything to them. I remember a few years back I heard that a person felt hard toward me. I did not feel that I had wronged them in any way, but I could not feel right until I went to that person's house and asked their forgiveness. We both hugged each other and I left that house crying tears of joy and feeling all clean inside. It does something for you spiritually that fasting and praying will not do.

Editorial

There have been hundreds of books written on prayer and the power of prayer and what it will do for you. The most of us have experienced some time or other an outstanding answer to prayer personally or in our own lives. We all know the value of it and yet, knowing it, by far the majority of us spend very little time praying. The week of the dedication of the prayer room is one to be remembered. As I would enter the prayer room my flesh would literally break out in goose pimples, the presence of the Lord was so mighty. You could see forty or more people kneeling, worshipping God. Everyone brought their Bibles, and after praying for a while would then read and let God's Word be written upon their hearts in a fresh and revealing manner. Numbers stayed the entire week, while others came for a day or two, and yet others for some time each day. It was a time of meeting God. Healings took place by just being in the presence of the Lord. One lady who had been stabbed by a drunken husband last November and had not been able to breathe all the way down in her lungs since, cried out, "I'm healed, I can breathe all the way down." Another lady who had low blood said she felt blood coming into her body, and the tired and sleepy feeling she always had left her. People received the Baptism of the Holy Spirit, and others were gloriously saved. Early one morning, an alcoholic lady dropped in for prayer and soon after (around 1 o'clock) a man passing by the church and seeing so many people on their knees praying, began repeating over and over, "It's amazing, it's amazing." He was visibly touched. It is amazing in this day to see people on their knees before God and wait upon Him. Over and over we sang:

"They that wait upon the Lord shall renew their strength,
They shall mount up on wings as an eagle
They shall run and not be weary, They shall walk and not faint
Teach me Lord, teach me Lord to wait."

I believe Evangel Temple is entering into a deeper depth with the Lord and that we have received the power we need to be "witnesses" right here in the nation's capital. I believe others will be drawn into the fold, for they will take note that "we have been with Jesus."

≈ ≈ ≈

Why Honor Mother?   — Mary Lee Meares

Card shops, flower shops, candy shops—and many other shops remind us at this time of the year to remember our mothers. The florist shops with their red and white roses remind us of our duty. Why should mother be honored by having a day of her own? Why should we shower her with gifts? Back in 1914 the first Mother's day was observed in the United States. But the rendering of honor to Mother is simply obedience to God's command given at Mt. Sinai nearly four thousand years ago! "Honour thy... mother." God did not require the setting aside of one day a year on which we should render special honor to Mother. He required and still requires us to honor her every day.

In Old Testament times, barreness was the saddest plight of womankind. Today many marriages are childless and steps are taken to prevent the rearing of a family. But God said, "Be fruitful, and multiply, and replenish the earth." I do not think a marriage can be a happy one unless, there are children born into the home. The trials that a mother is called upon to endure, the service she is called upon to render should only cause her to be drawn more closely unto the Lord for strength and courage.

Motherhood bespeaks God's love. When a woman bears a child, she has received of God the most precious gift she could receive outside the gift of salvation and eternal life. The psalmist David expressed it in these words: "Lo, children are an heritage of the Lord..." And even though a mother only has perhaps a tiny inconvenient apartment in which to bring up her child, she can know joy in the children which God has given to her.

Then there are those women who have no children of their own, but have taken into their homes some unwanted child or orphan. They certainly are to be honored also. These children are not bound to them by ties of blood, or by suffering. Theirs is a bond purely of a woman's devotion to a child, and her compassion and desire to help some child in need.

Hannah wanted a child. She wept and refused to eat, so great was her sorrow at her barrenness. Then she went to the Temple of God and prayed and wept. She made a vow, "O Lord of hosts, if thou wilt indeed look on the affliction of thine handmaid, and remember me, and not forget thine handmaid, but wilt give unto thine handmaid a man child, then I will give him unto the Lord all the days of his life." God answered Hannah's prayer. Hannah remembered her vow and gave to Israel the great leader Samuel.

Some of us have made solemn vows before God to instruct our children in God's Word, to pray for them and with them, to live godly lives before them, and to endeavor to bring them up in the nurture and admonition of the Lord. These vows are written in heaven. They should be written in our hearts. The children whom God has given are to be His children. Let us not forget our vows.

Much could be said about the mothers or women who have children but are far from being a mother at heart. But we are speaking of the mother who bespeaks a life of unselfishness and self-sacrifice. The woman who loses herself in her love and service for her children finds herself rewarded above anything imaginable.

God wants mothers honored. This is the duty of the child to fulfill. But He wants mothers to be worthy of honor. This is the duty of the mother. She should provide them with love and the physical necessities of life, but then above this, there is a great responsibility of training that child. Our children have immortal souls—souls that will never die. You and I must constantly, diligently instruct them in God's way. Behind it all, our lives should be examples to them of what life can be when lived in the influence of prayer and God's Word. If you will instill within your child a living faith in the Lord, Jesus Christ, you have given them the greatest treasure that could possibly be. Yes, you can live the life that will be due the honor of a mother; you can live a life before your children so that in later years they will like to sit down and just think of the times and events that took place around "mother." May God help all women to realize the great responsibility, as well as joy, that goes along with the word, "mother."

EVANGEL   TEMPLE'S

13 th

ANNIVERSARY

JULY 14, 1968

COME AND ENJOY THE

BLESSINGS OF GOD

Morning Worship 11:00 A.M.   Pastor Meares

DINNER IN ROCK CREEK PARK

Grove 23

(Bring a Big Basket of Food)

(No Afternoon Service)

EVENING SERVICE   8 o'clock
EVERYONE WELCOME!
SPECIAL MUSICAL PROGRAM

∾ ∾ ∾

Positive Faith Brings Positive Blessings
—Mary Lee Meares

Positive believing and power go hand in hand. Where the positive Word of God is being preached, you find the power of God moving to meet the needs of the people. Where you see the power of God manifested, you can know that the positive message has been declared.

The power of God works in an atmosphere of faith. Faith comes when the positive Word of God is received. As Paul related the miracles wrought in the Name of the resurrected Christ to the people at Lystra, it caused a man who had been crippled all his life to believe that he could be healed. It caused him to believe it so strongly that when Paul commanded him to 'stand upright' on his feet, he leaped up and began to walk!

Many good, honest, and sincere Christians are in constant need and are living oppressed lives because they are not being taught the precepts of 'right believing' that would help them receive the blessings that God is so desirous for them to have that would enrich their lives and glorify His name.

On the other hand there are multitudes who are receiving Divine help to satisfy the needs of their lives.

These are the people who have learned how to claim the promises of God's Word. They know how to receive from the hand of the Lord those things they have need of.

These are the folk who are doing something to promote the gospel of our Lord, for they have found Him to be the answer to their every need and they are declaring His goodnness to others.

They are living happier and more prosperous lives because they have found that God is desirous to bless them and perform His Word in *their* lives. These are the people who have learned to think and believe in positive terms. They know that they don't have to depend on their pastor's prayers but that the Word will work for them if only they believe. We continually get letters from people here at the Temple telling how God has answered their prayers, and thanking Pastor Meares for having taught them how to believe God and trust Him for their every need. To me this is the greatest compliment that could be paid any pastor.

I shall never forget when faith became such a vital part of my every day living. We were pastoring in a small southern town in Tennessee. Rev. T. L. Osborn came and held us one of the very first revivals he conducted in the states some eighteen years ago. We saw miracles of salvation and healing as we had never seen before. Even though we had been reared in a pentecostal church and taught "Jesus Christ the same yesterday, today and forever," we had seen very few healings, and knew very little how to really trust God in meeting our everyday needs. But after this crusade our faith began to grow until it was an easy thing to believe God for the impossible, naturally speaking.

Our daughter was only a small baby at this time and she had a tear duct that was stopped up, and one eye had to be cleaned daily. I started thanking God for her healing. Some friends told me that I should take her to the doctor for it was serious and could cause blindness, but I kept believing and one day, not long afterwards, I just happened to think, "I haven't cleaned Cynthia's eye out today. From then on it never ran again. That was the beginning of our believing God for whatever need was in our home. From then to now, it has been a life of simple trust and thanking God. I have found that thanking God rather than asking God brings victory for my needs.

When one will dare to declare God's promises and stand upon them, He will confirm His Word. Faith alone will cause the power of God to be manifested in the lives of men and women.

After Brother Meares had this revival with Brother Osborn, he was a different preacher. One day I said to him, "honey, all you preach any more is a sermon on faith." He said, "What else is there to preach?" Meaning that the only way to receive anything from God is through faith, therefore the most important thing to learn.

Positive faith will bring the impossible to pass.

If you believe that you can live a good Christan life above sin, and in the Name of the Lord will endeavor to do so, all the angels of heaven and the power of God will be behind you to make you the child of God you ought to be.

If you believe that God has power to heal the sickness in your body, even though it may have gripped you for so very long, the power of God is there and ready to bring it to pass, even as you believe!

If you believe that by the help of God you can win souls to the Lord Jesus Christ, then the anointing of God will rest upon you to win souls for the kingdom of God.

The power of God will begin to work for you when you believe God's promises are meant for you personally. God wants to meet your needs more than you want them to be met. Without faith it is impossible to please Him, just as it would be for us to be displeased if our children lacked faith in us as a parent.

May God help you to live a victorious Christian life by just simply believing and accepting His Word. It can only fail when you or I fail to believe it.

Chapter 11 – 1969

God's Tenth

—Mary Lee Meares

Tithing is a doctrine that I have been taught ever since childhood. It has come as natural for me to give a tenth of whatever I have had as it was to go to church. Whereas "tithing" has been a battle to some Christians, it has never been a burden to me. I have always firmly believed that those who joyfully honor God with their tenth will be blessed not only materially, but physically and spiritually as well. I do not believe that God's people have to go in want or need.

My three children have had this taught to them. Whether it be a small weekly allowance or money that has been given them, they bring the tenth of it to the house of God. I have told them if they will honor God in tithing and giving cheerfully, they will always be blessed. To me this is a big part of worshipping the Lord. There is such a blessedness in giving to God's house.

Now, the dime or the quarter one of my children might give is certainly not much to give God. If they were to go and offer it to a rich man, he would either feel insulted or feel that he would be robbing the child and not treating them fair in accepting it. But, think of God who owns the universe, and certainly does not have to have what a child would give Him, accepting the smallest mite and blessing the small amount the same as a large amount, for a tenth whether small or large has God's blessings.

Letters to the Pastor

I was a visitor at your church Sunday at the morning service and also on Tuesday night. I caught a cab to go to another church and by mistake the driver took be to your church. I did not realize I was in the wrong building until I received a visitor's pamphlet and saw the address on it. By then, the service was practically over. I enjoyed the sermon so very much. I learned exactly what I wanted to know all these long 34 years. My soul feasted at your table. I had a broken heart and was full of fear, but now my heart aches no more, for I have laid my burden down. I will be visiting with you again this Sunday.

Helen Harris
Washington, D.C.

* * *

Reverend Meares:
It is with a grateful heart that God has made it possible for me to send my widow's mite to help you carry on your inspiring ministry another year. He is truly a great God. I pray He will bless you abundantly.

Verlena Anderson
Washington, D.C.

* * *

Pastor Meares:
I have been a Fellowship member of your church for about three Sundays. I was saved there on July 14, 1963. It seemed that a still small voice said, "open your heart's door and let me come in." Then on September 8. I went to the prayer room and received the baptism of the Holy Spirit. I enjoyed your sermon so very much this Sunday morning on Isaac and Ishmael.

Paulette Duncan
Washington, D.C.

* * *

My brother, William, attended Evangel Temple before I did, and because of the great change in his life, I knew something had happened to him. I started to attend the Temple and on May 28, 1961 I was saved and filled with the Holy Spirit. I am enjoying serving God with a group of young people who are sincere. I enjoy crusading each week, and my desire is to be what the Lord would have me be.

Herbert Addision

Notes of Praise

Greetings in the lovely name of our Lord! It is a privilege to write to you. Two summers ago I was visiting one of my older brothers, Robert Patton, and his wife and family in Washington. While there I was able to attend one of your Friday night services. Truly, the Lord was in that service. As I entered the doors I felt the presence of God in a very real way, and since returning to Nassau, I have been telling everyone about that service and the feeling of oneness and the love that exists among your saints. I was very much impressed.

The Fellowship News has been coming to me monthly and I enjoy every letter of testimony and your sermons have been a real boost to me. I can truly say they give me a lift spiritually. I pass the Fellowship paper on to my mother and some of my friends to share the blessings of God with me.

Yours for Christ's service,
Sybil Patton Deveaux
Nassau, Bahamas

* * *

I am writing to thank you for the great blessing you have been to me and thousands of others. I enjoy the 11:15 radio programs each morning. They are a source of encouragement.

I thank the Lord for your being here in Washington these four years, and I hope you will be here many, many more. Only the Lord knows what it has meant to this city.

Mrs. Annie Clore

* * *

Now, as is often the case, when I try to express myself, words seem inadequate. So please just try to see my sincerity in what I shall try to say. I am grateful and deeply appreciate your humility, unselfishness, and genuine interest in both the members and visitors of Evangel Temple.

I can see why Brother Petrucelli enjoys his work as co-pastor and why he never shows he is tired. Sometimes I think of you and

Brother Petrucelli as father and son; again, you remind me of Elijah and Elisha. Finally, I see you as two Spirit-filled men whom God called to work together to minister to people who desire so much to grow in grace that little else matters. I am sure God is pleased with your labors.

In studying any subject, the more we learn about it, the more we realize how little we know. So it is in our spiritual lives, as you preach and teach and unselfishly permit other men who are Spirit-filled evangelists to preach and minister to us at Evangel Temple, we hunger and realize the more our great need of God. As we seek to know Him in a greater way, we remember He has said, "Blessed are they which do hunger and thirst after righteousness: for they shall be filled." Pastor Meares, I pray daily for you and Brother Petrucelli and pray God to richly bless you both.

A fellowship member

* * *

I do enjoy your weekly broadcast so very much. I know your ministry has the anointing of God upon it, for I can feel it. I will be 82 years old in December. I love God and feel so close to Him each day. Am sending you a little donation to be used for God's glory.

A servant of God
John Hutchins, Prince

It Takes the Cross To Remove The Veil
—Mary Lee Meares

Are you one of those people that thirst for more of God and long to be in His very presence? I trust you are.

In the Old Testament there was a veil that separated the holy place from the Holy of Holies. The latter was where the very presence of God dwelt. No one but the priest could go into the Holy of Holies and this only once a year. But when Jesus hung on the cross, the veil in the Temple was rent from top to bottom and now every child of God could enter, not just once a year, but each and every day into the Holy of Holies where Jesus himself dwells. It is His will that we as His very own redeemed should live in His presence. It is a life to be enjoyed every moment of every day.

Then why don't we enjoy this Presence more? Why do we stay outside in the holy place when we can enter the Holy of Holies? If Jesus removed the veil by His death on the cross, what hinders us from enjoying His very presence, Could it be there is a veil in our hearts that is keeping the light of God from us? Could it be this veil of flesh is hiding God's face because we have never been crucified with Christ? Perhaps, if we will take a close look into our own hearts we will see this veil hanging there. It is not a pretty thing to look on, for it is not woven of the fine threads that the veil in the Temple was woven of. But it is just as effective in keeping us from entering into the presence of God. The threads are woven of self sins—not a lot of things we go out and do which we term as right or wrong, but self-right-eousness, self confidence, self- love, self-sufficiency, etc. Self has never gone to the cross. It isn't an easy task or a pleasant one, so we have shunned it. Any thing that touches our life or makes our flesh suffer we shun. None of us enjoy pain. If the cross were not tears and blood, then we would not call it a cross. But when we are willing to put self on the cross, no matter the suffering, and let self be crucified, we will be set free. This fleshly veil in our hearts that has kept us from enjoying the very presence of God will be rent in two. We may have heretofore enjoyed the holy place, but now we can go into the very Holy of Holies and oh! what a difference.

There is grace for the cross, if one will only yield their life to God. We will not hang on the cross always, but as soon as the work is finished in our lives, and we die out to self, we will be raised with Him in a new glory and a new power that we have not before known. We will find a new and living way. Oh, the joy that comes when the fleshly veil of our hearts is rent from top to bottom and we enter into and live in the very Presence of our God!

"I Am Alive Forevermore"

There was a sign over a door recently which read, "My God is not dead, sorry to hear about yours." Even though some people are saying God is dead, we that have the indwelling of His Spirit know differently. Something that is dead does not move, nor does something dead speak. And I hear Him speak to me and I feel His Spirit within me. So this Easter season I can say with all assursurance, He lives!

The words of Christ, "I am alive forevermore" have been quoted again and again. These words have brought comfort many many times to our hearts. But what really makes me happy is the fact that I, Mary Lee Meares, am alive forevermore. This body, 'tis true, is always dying in a process of decay, but I am an immortal being. Jesus Christ was as immortal when He walked the dusty roads of Galilee or hung helplessly upon the cross as He was when He burst out of the tomb and shouted, "I am alive forevermore." The real Jesus was not slain. Christ is immortal.

Because I am a child of God I have immortality within me. "He that believeth in me hath eternal life already… he that liveth and believeth on me shall never die." My body may be put in a tomb, but the Christian tomb is always empty. Perhaps I cannot prove this, and shall not try, but this I truly know. Eternal life is a gift given to us at the time we accept Christ, not something to be received somewhere out in the future. A few years ago I stood inside the empty tomb in Jerusalem. I had not gone to seek the living among the dead. My faith is in a resurrected Christ, and because of this faith, my life is a resurrected one from a life of sin to a life of peace and joy. How can I ever find words to praise Him this glorious Easter for having resurrected me and given me eternal life?

If Jesus did not resurrect from the dead, then in the tomb of Joseph there is a pile of bones. In that tomb there is a dead Christ and a dead religion. There are many tombs that people visit in this world just because they want to see where people of fame have been burried. Thousands of people visit here in Washington the grave site of George Washington. Hundreds and even thousands of people have come to Arlington and looked upon the grave of the late president John Kennedy. Their bones and a little dust are in those graves. But their bodies never came forth from the tomb. Our hope and joy comes from an empty tomb. It gives us the assurance that this life does not end with the grave, but really it just begins. Then do we meet Jesus face to face. After the resurrection of Jesus, He recognized His friends and His friends recognized Him. So shall we know and be known after we are resurrected. His tomb is empty, and your tomb and my tomb will one day be empty. Because He lives, we too, shall live. Where do we get such hope? It comes from the empty tomb of the Son of God. Thank God for the promise, "I Am Alive Forevermore."

—Mary Lee Meares

All That Is Within Me   —Mary Lee Meares

Ps. 103 "Bless the Lord O my soul, And all that is within me, bless His holy name".

As I read this verse the other day, the words *all that is within me* seem to just stand out. I thought, "now just what is David saying, "*All that is within me*"? And then I said, "well everything I am made of; everything inside me; my whole being—just simply *all* of me." Part of my body cannot praise the Lord without some other part reacting accordingly. When my heart is glad and happy, my mouth speaks joyfully. The Bible says, "From the abundance of the heart the mouth speaketh." My lips speak forth praise; my hands clap for joy and thanksgiving. Some dance for joy all because of the praise *within* them.

It is true, most all of us are more or less created alike in the natural, but in the spiritual it is not so. Some christians live victoriously while others just seem to exist spiritually. There is a reason for the difference, and to me the reason is the attitude that comes from within that person. I have yet to see a person who praises God continually, with all that is within them, ever backslide. It just isn't possible, for God inhabiteth the praises of His children. Who can backslide when God's presence is abiding within them? If you will build Him a temple of praise, He will never fail to live in it. Too many christians know only to beg and plead and seek after God to do this or that for them. If they could only learn to change that attitude to one of praise (even in their trials) they would know the joy and peace and thanksgiving.

Perhaps, some have been in services at Evangel Temple and thought too much time was taken up in just praising God. But it has been said, and I agree, "You are never wasting time when you are praising Him." When you love someone, you don't have to be asked to tell them, you just can't refrain from it.

Some folk think, "Oh if I could just do this or that for the Lord." But I think you please God the most when you are merely offering Him the sacrifice of praise—praise from *all that is within you*. Your lips can baar fruit for the Master.

When I desire the Lord to do something for me, I just begin to repeat my thankfulness to Him for the past and present blessings and I soon have no trouble being in an attitude of faith for my needs. Yes, God dwells in the temples of those that praise Him. Praises have begun in my heart and within me that will last and live throughout eternity.

~ ~ ~

Editorial

—Mary Lee Meares

Christmas, perhaps, is the most loved day of the year to us. People are more expressive of their love for others at this time than any other. Joy is expressed in the Christmas carols, children get wide-eyed and excited, and even we older folk get younger in spirit during this season. To be remembered, if only by a card, is something we enjoy. Showing our love toward others is God-given. I think God is pleased with our giving, for did not He give us a Babe wrapped in swaddling clothes the first Christmas nearly 2000 years ago. Then did not the shepherds come and give of their worship to the Christ Child? They could not express their love by giving expensive gifts as did the wise men, but they gave thanks and adoration before Him as He lay there in the manger. And so today you and I may not have expensive gifts to give one to another to express our love, but we can have a kind word, a smile, a card signed, "God bless you" or in some little way show love in giving of ourselves. This is worshipping Christ for only when we manifest love can we worship Him. This same Babe who was born in a manger, later *gave* His all, His very life for the redemption of mankind. So when I think of Christmas, I think of giving. Many people will be giving only to get in return or from a thought of necessity, but let us as children of God give because of a deep rooted love, a Christ spirit within us.

Christmas should be a time of joy and gladness because of the glorious gift given to the world. Yet the majority of people have not this true joy and peace that the angels sang about. Many people will be lonely this Christmas, and it seems that one is lonelier on holidays than any other day. I can well remember about six years ago Brother Meares and I were in London, England on Christmas day. No one was on the streets but home with their families, and if they had been we would not have known them. We were in a hotel room, away from the children and our families. It was a lonely time. If only we could have been with friends and shared our giving, and ourselves, there would have been joy. Now, what about the mother's boy who will be in prison this Christmas? What about the person in the hospital who will eat Christmas dinner in bed? What about the boy in the Armed Forces who will be far away from home? What about the little child who will receive no gift, because of a drunken father who didn't care? I know it is easy to forget for we are so busy thinking of those who are dear to us — in our own circle, but I cannot help but think of the words of Christ, "For I was hungred, and ye gave me meat: I was thirsty, and ye gave me drink: I was a stranger, and ye took me in: Naked, and ye clothed me: I was sick, and ye visited me I was in prison, and ye came unto me." The Lord said, "When you do this for the least of my brethren, ye have done it unto me."

Let us breathe a prayer that we will have the opportunity to tell someone the true meaning of Christmas and show them by some act of love.

Let us express joy, deep joy, to all this year. It is contagious and can lift a sad heart and make him glad. May you have a rebirth of the Christ-Child within your heart and share with others this wonderful gift.

Letters to the Pastor

We were at church a few Saturday's ago for the Young People's meeting, and enjoyed it so very much. It was such a blessing to see young people taking a part in the Lord's work.

I just thank the Lord for giving Washington, D.C. a man of God like you to preach to the people there.

My dad believes greatly in your prayers. He was sick with gall stones, and you sent him a prayer cloth and God healed him.

Mrs. Raymond Smith

* * *

Greetings in the dear and precious name of our Lord and Saviour Jesus Christ!

Permit me to state that I enjoyed your message Sunday morning regarding "The Holy Spirit of God and the Anointing." Truly your messages have been a blessing and inspiration to me. It is my sincere and heartfelt desire that many more souls will be saved through your ministry.

Eric Rollocks

* * *

During the crusading campaign when Bro. Popoff was at the Evangelistic Center, two of the ladies from your church came to my home and prayed for me and my family. I was saved and have been attending your church ever since. I would like to become a Fellowship member. Since I have been saved I have been blessed in so many different ways.

Regina Hawkins, Washington, D.C.

* * *

I would like to tell you about the wonderful Easter I enjoyed at the Evangelistic Center. [was there Sunday morning, noon, and night. The services, play, singing, film, and everything was wonderful. It was the best Easter I have ever had—because I accepted Jesus Christ as my personal Saviour. I am born again through faith by the Word of God, which liveth and abideth forever. I believe Jesus bore my sins and I am now forgiven. I cannot be at the Center often because I work in Easton, Maryland, but will come when I can. I want to send you $10.00 a month to help in your mini stry.

A new-born babe in God's family, Viola Amos,

"A Very Blessed And Fruitful Visit"

Rev. & Mrs. Meares and
Rev. & Mrs. McAlister

The recent visit to Rio de Janeiro of Pastor and Mrs. Meares was a great blessing to both Gloria and myself, and a real time of inspiration for the people of the New Life Pentecostal Church.

It was a thrill for us to have them in service in our down-town auditorium to see the fruit of our daily radio ministry, in which they and the people of Evangel Temple have had such a large part. Brother Meares' message, interpreted into the Portugese language, was a great blessing to these new converts.

Although their visit with us was very short, we were able to show them our radio studio where we record the over 75 broadcasts each month, and also the new addressograph equipment which Evangel Temple has helped us to buy recently, and which makes possible the publication of our new national magazine, "The Word of New Life."

However, I must report that this was not merely a time of mutual blessing and fellowship. We had arrived at a critical stage in the building of our new church in Rio's north zone and had come up against a number of building problems. With our blueprints in hand, and standing together with our contractor on the actual building site, Pastor Meares, through his years of building experience was able to clear up these problems, and save us almost two thousand dollars in the over-all cost of construction. From the standpoint of our building program, this visit was Spirit-planned and we surely do appreciate this help.

I would just like to add a personal word. Both my wife, Gloria, and I were aware of a new touch of the Lord in the lives of our dear friends, Brother and Sister Meares. It is true that no one stands still in his Christian walk, and we were thrilled to notice the wonderful way in which God has been leading your pastors into new and blessed experiences with Himself. So we thank the Lord for what this visit has meant to us personally and to our people who formed a deep love for Brother and Sister Meares, even though their stay was brief. We pray God's continued blesings on you all.

Bob McAlister

Congregation in Porte Allegre, Brazil, where Rev.
Meares preached on Sunday night.

CPSIA information can be obtained
at www.ICGtesting.com
Printed in the USA
LVHW01s0155020518
575656LV00010B/265/P